BYE BYE BABY

BYE BYE BABY

My Tragic Love Affair with the Bay City Rollers

Caroline Sullivan

BLOOMSBURY

First published 1999
This paperback edition published 2000

Copyright © 1999 by Caroline Sullivan

The moral right of the author has been asserted
Bloomsbury Publishing Plc, 38 Soho Square, London W1V 5DF

A CIP catalogue record for this book
is available from the British Library

ISBN 0 7475 4703 3

10 9 8 7 6 5 4 3 2 1

With thanks to the following for permission to quote from song lyrics:

Complete Music: 'You're a Woman' (Faulkner/Wood); 'Rock'n'Roller'
(Faulkner/Wood); 'Sweet Virginia' (Bay City Rollers); 'Dance, Dance,
Dance' (Bay City Rollers); 'Don't Stop the Music' (Faulkner/Wood);
'Eagles Fly' (Faulkner/Wood); 'Strangers in the Wind' (Faulkner/Wood);
'If You were My Woman' (Faulkner/Wood).

EMI Music Publishing Ltd: 'Saturday Night' (Martin/Coulter).

Saturday Music/Four Seasons Music/Windswept Music: 'Bye Bye Baby'
(Gaudio/Crew).

Charisma Music Publishing Company Ltd: 'It's a Game' (Christopher
Adams).

J. Albert & Son (UK) Music Publishing Ltd: 'Yesterday's Hero' (Vanda/
Young).

Every effort has been made to trace all rights-holders. The publishers
will be glad to make good any omissions brought to their attention.

Typeset by Hewer Text Ltd, Edinburgh
Printed in Great Britain by Clays Limited, St Ives plc

To Paul Mann, Rosemary Davidson and TTTs

PROLOGUE

THE BAY CITY ROLLERS were sitting on the floor of my room.

Let me repeat that. The Bay City Rollers, the biggest teen idols of their day, possibly of all time, were sitting on the floor of my room, watching television and conversing in dark Scottish mutters.

Be still, my beating heart, I told myself as I gently chewed the collar of my cap-sleeved T-shirt (all the rage that summer, especially with a picture of Betty Boop on the front, as this one had). I'd like to think I appeared less stunned than I actually was, but their presence was so overwhelming that it took a genuine effort to keep my mouth from hanging open.

To be honest, only two of the Rollers were there – Leslie McKeown, the singer, and Woody, the bass player – along with their security guard, but the fact that any of them were there at all, in *my* room in a hotel in downtown Detroit, was the most thrilling thing that had ever happened to me. You could say that almost everything I'd done between 30 September 1975, the date of their first American visit, and tonight, 25 August 1977, had been with an eye toward this moment.

Those two years were flashing past me now, much as your life is supposed to when you're dying. Apt, as this was the closest I'd ever come to death by suppressed hysteria.

These were some of the things flashing past: the freezing afternoons – it always seemed to be winter – hanging around outside hotels for a ten-second glimpse as they dashed into waiting limousines. The hours poring over magazines, cutting out the smallest mentions to ceremonially glue into five brimming scrapbooks. The fake Scottish accent adopted to convince airline booking clerks I was a Roller employee, and could they please remind me what flight the band were on again? The absences from work to go to every gig, every TV show. The Saturday night strategy meetings with equally tragic friends.

And suddenly my quarry were right there, breathing the same smoky air as my friends Kim, Sue P, Barbarino and me. Amazingly, Leslie and Woody were unaware of the effect they were having as they sat there, staring at the TV, smoking a joint and mumbling impenetrably. It was getting on toward midnight of the day they'd played the third-from-last show of their current American tour, and they were tired and uncommunicative.

None the less, my sister Rollermaniacs and I were excited beyond words. On the pretext of getting a cigarette, I pawed through my bag till I found the tape recorder I'd used to record that afternoon's show, and switched it on. I knew that if I didn't somehow preserve this occasion, I'd have to kill myself.

Meanwhile, we tried to make conversation with our idols – now our sort-of friends – as they smoked, chugged Budweiser and talked in burbling Edinburgh dialect. But what do you say to someone you loved so much that you'd once stolen their cigarette from an ashtray and glued it into a scrapbook?

Still, we tried a little small-talk. 'So, did you enjoy the gig today?' I asked Leslie, who, excitingly, was wearing not his tartan Roller uniform but plain jeans and a Starsky & Hutch-style wraparound cardigan.

He slowly turned his head and looked at me directly for the first time in the half hour they'd been there. My vitals quivered.

'It was all right.' His thin lips barely moved as he spoke. With an air of great finality, he faced the television again.

We weren't doing very well here. It was clear that they didn't want to chat, and were only tolerating our company because we'd supplied the beer and pot. My friends and I exchanged glances of consternation, and Sue, who was a buxom girl, folded her arms underneath her bust to make it more prominent, as if the sight would bring the Rollers out of their shell. But beyond a slight widening of eyes, it produced no reaction.

The good hostess trying to save a dying party, I offered more brews and cigarettes, and Barbarino rolled another joint with an expertise that belied his middle-class Jewish origins. Leslie sucked at it for a while, finally commenting, 'It's a bit dry.' It wasn't much, but we hung on to his words hungrily. More precious fodder for my tape recorder, busily whirring inside my bag.

Sue and Kim were, I knew, barely restraining themselves from begging Leslie and Woody to phone up their favorite Roller, guitarist Eric Faulkner, and invite him to our little soirée. It was lucky they did restrain themselves, because with the way things were going, any fannish behaviour would have sent them right back to their own rooms, never to be seen at such close quarters again. And we didn't want that. God, no.

We'd achieved our incredible feat through the simple device of befriending the security guard, Big Bobby. It was Kim who did the befriending, and before you get any ideas, their relationship was platonic, though I suspect Bobby would have preferred otherwise. They'd struck up a conversation a week ago at another gig, Bobby taking a shine to Kim because she was older and sexier than the average BCR fan. At twenty-one, she was actually the oldest person in the room after Bobby, and had the kind of golden-skinned prettiness that men are such suckers for. Fortunately, she was also endowed with a honking Queens accent that kept her charms from being too overwhelming.

Anyway, at today's show, in Youngstown, Ohio, it was the

work of a moment to find Bobby and learn that they would be spending the night in Detroit, 125 miles north-west on the other side of Lake Erie.

After the gig, the four of us raced across the state, from Youngstown to Cleveland, to catch the last flight of the day to Detroit. Once we'd arrived at the Rollers' hotel and checked into two adjoining rooms on the fourth floor (Kim drew the short straw and had to share with Barbarino, a snorer and groper), we'd hooked up with Bobby, who had produced Leslie and Woody.

So there we were, the Rollers and us. And my, what a disappointment they were turning out to be. We eventually gave up trying to get through to them and simply watched them sink more Bud and finish Barbarino's marijuana. They slunk back to their own rooms after an hour or so, and the second they left, I nearly ripped my bag apart retrieving the tape recorder. Kim, Sue and Barbarino gathered round, barely breathing. I pressed play. 'Doosagreetmufflewump,' said Woody. 'Haggafnarswufflemump,' Leslie replied, greatly amused. It was the accents. We couldn't make out a word. Typical.

I TURNED A CORNER the day I threw out my Roller scrapbooks. There was a time when I would have happily walked naked down Broadway before I'd have abandoned those scrapbooks, no problem. But now it was October 1996, and their mysterious power over me had waned to the point where I no longer needed their leatherette links to the past. But before I dispatched them to the incinerator in my mother's Manhattan apartment building, I flapped through them for a last look at the detritus – newspaper cuttings, half-smoked cigarettes and whatnot – I'd accumulated between discovering them in 1975 and deciding I was too old for this sort of thing, around 1979.

I'm usually vague about the latter date because no one with even an iota of credibility admits to having been into the Rollers as late as '79. Elvis Costello, sure, or The Police or even the Bee Gees, but owning up to fancying the Rollers that late in the day is tantamount to announcing you were a friendless sociopath.

Even in their heyday, 1974 to 1976, they were hideously uncool among everyone but fourteen-year-old girls. It wasn't just their feeble teeny-pop music but their puritanical image, epitomised by their habit of drinking milk at press conferences. It later emerged that their manager forced them to, but the damage was done.

No, poor scrawny Leslie, Eric, Woody, Alan and Derek were never cool. Even the seventies revival that has made bands like Abba and Hot Chocolate kitschly hip again has overlooked them. To add insult to injury, my own best Roller buddies, Sue P, Sue J, Emma and Cathy, have gone revisionist, and now pretend they never liked them. When I called Emma to tell her I was writing a book about them, her response was swift: 'You'd better change my name.'

But some of us don't mind coming out of the closet about the Rollers. Not that I was ever really in it. I loved them desperately. For four years I lived for them. It's not a pretty story.

1974-ish

T O BE A TEENAGER in America in the mid-seventies meant many things, bad hair and worse musical taste among them. To be a teenager in New Jersey, which was just across the Hudson River from Manhattan yet blissfully oblivious to trends emanating from the big city, meant that every single day was a bad hair day, every night an excuse to listen to Eagles albums. And to be that teenager in Millburn, New Jersey, a small town twenty miles west of New York, meant something even worse.

Not that Millburn wasn't a good place to live. It was small in the best sense of the word, its old-fashioned center based around a railroad station, movie theater and Schnipper's Stationery, where generations of schoolkids bought ringbinder notebooks and pens. Heading down Millburn Avenue, away from the shops, you came to the town hall, where a plaque commemorated Millburn's finest hour – when, late in the Revolutionary War, Washington's troops stopped a British advance and kicked Redcoat butt all the way back to New York. 'The British never again penetrated so far into New Jersey', it concluded triumphantly.

Another half mile or so down the tree-lined street was Millburn High School, a tan brick fifties pile set in a couple of acres of playing fields. A parking lot was provided for kids who drove themselves to school, and a surprising number did, as a new car was the standard reward for having passed the driving test. There was money around – people's fathers were lawyers or doctors, or commuted to Manhattan to jobs on Wall Street – but it was offset by a communal atmosphere where people knew and actually liked their neighbors.

My mother and I lived across the street from the high school, in a two-bedroom apartment in a small development overlooking a pine-dotted lawn. My room, where I spent most of my time in fits of teenage pique, was dominated by a pink shag-pile carpet and what I proudly called my 'stereo', a record player so antiquated it had one of those devices that let you stack records on the spindle so you could play three or four in a row without getting up to change them. It also featured an eight-track cartridge player that had been broken in shipment, so I'd never been able to use it. Just as well that eight-tracks were then being phased out by cassettes, which I listened to on a separate machine measuring about twelve inches by eight.

A rebellious moment had seen me unscrewing the legs from my bed so it sat on the floor. The look was complemented by my posters, which took up the entire wall above the bed. Pride of place was given to a large Bad Company one, featuring the English rockers' hairy heads against a green background, and the legend, 'Does your mama know you've been keepin' Bad Company?' My other heroes were also represented: a picture of Mick Jagger clasping his hands like an angel, a sticker reading 'The Kinks: Ray Davies does it to me!', a ribbon from a ZZ Top souvenir cowboy hat, acquired at the Texas band's 1974 Madison Square Garden gig, and a small snapshot of The Who's Roger Daltrey onstage. That last was my own work – I'd had the idea of sticking a magazine photo of Daltrey on the wall, then taking a picture of it, so it would look as if I'd been near the stage and taken the photo myself. I hadn't counted on the glare from the glossy magazine page, so my shot was marred by a white streak that blotted out most of Daltrey's face.

But as pleasant as Millburn life was, it didn't bestow much in the way of credibility, not back then. Credibility was all about what music you liked, and our town wasn't like urban Newark or Jersey City, where kids listened to trendy disco music. Millburn's affluence took its toll in a surprising way. Kids could afford to buy as much dope as they could smoke, and with dope came the desire to listen not to hip disco but to Led Zeppelin, Pink Floyd and, pain me though it does to recall, Emerson, Lake & Palmer.

But it didn't stop at just listening. Once you were sunk into a beanbag chair in someone's wood-paneled basement rec room, Robert Plant's polecat howl piercing the marijuana fug, it was inevitable that someone would start analysing the music. We had hours of fun with stairways to heaven and bustles in hedgerows. What did it all *mean*?

Then someone else would start in on an album sleeve, often Led Zep's *Houses of the Holy*, which was considered pregnant with symbolism: 'What are these kids doing on the rocks? Are they trying to get to the top or the bottom? Does it represent futility or hope?' Then they'd pass the joint to the next person, and realise that the dope had given them an insatiable appetite, which they'd deal with by stuffing down a bag of Lay's potato chips, sputtering crumbs all over the album cover. It could go on like that for hours.

I wish I could say it all had nothing to do with me, but I was as guilty as anyone. I owned the entire Led Zeppelin catalogue, a bunch of Deep Purple albums, even a live album by Grand Funk Railroad, a prototype metal act so unloved that their name has practically been expunged from rock history.

That was Millburn all over. That was American suburbia all over. If you were white and middle-class, you got wasted every weekend and listened to bad music. It was the law. Especially the bad music. There was an eighties movie called *Dazed and Confused* (named after a Led Zep song, as every seventies child knows) that had a line that summed it all up: 'In the seventies, every kid in America owned a copy of *Frampton Comes Alive!* – you were practically issued with one.' How right they were.

Frampton Comes Alive! – and, yep, I had it – was the archetypal suburban seventies album. It was the biggest seller of '76, a two-disc orgy of endless guitar solos and complementary mewling by baby-faced English singer Peter Frampton. It was tuneless and went on for about three days, which made it perfect for its bleary-eyed time. Even Millburn's plushest rec rooms, up on White Oak Ridge Road, where kids could afford six-packs of Bud to wash down all the dope, reverberated to Frampton's tinny ululations. We'd nod our heads a beat out of time, awed by his sheer class.

And in the unlikely event that you weren't a Frampton or Zep fan? There was plenty of other heavyweight stuff to get your teeth into. Yes provided much food for thought with their keyboard-based progressive rock and famous swirling artwork. The sleeve from *Tales from Topographic Oceans* kept us going for weeks. Then there was earthier Deep Purple, whose Ian Gillan made me growl appreciatively. And if you preferred American rock, which I didn't, West Coasters like The Eagles provided 'mellow sounds' (their words) to smoke your weed to.

Just think – while we were getting high to Yes and the Zep (actually, it was my friends who got high – it never did anything for me, and I stopped after a few experiments) the disadvantaged kids in Newark, a scary big city ten miles away that we never went to, were listening to Marvin Gaye and The O'Jays. How we pitied their inability to appreciate real music.

As you can see, there was nothing in my musical background to suggest that the Bay City Rollers would come to dominate my life. Like every other adolescent I knew, I listened to the naffest music of a naff era. But it was normal-naff, not tragic-naff. Normal-naff was the bands I've just mentioned; tragic-naff was the Osmonds, David Cassidy and the other hairless chests that passed for teen idols in the early seventies.

Okay, I'd had a brief flirtation with Cassidy, buying a couple of Partridge Family singles, but his floppy cuteness left me unfulfilled. Then I experimented with a crush on Bobby Sherman, the shaggy-haired, porcine star of a TV show called 'Here Come the Brides'. He branched out into making records – making him the forerunner of all the misguided actors who do it today – and I quite enjoyed his commanding style on the hit 'Little Woman'. 'Hey, little woman, please make up your mind,' he ordered. 'You gotta come into my world and leave your world behind.' I liked a take-charge guy, but was disgusted when, sometime in 1971, he called a press conference to admit that he had been secretly married for two years and was about to become a father.

But I was motivated most of all by Pete Duel, the darkly handsome 'Alias Smith and Jones' actor who shot himself in the head on New Year's Eve 1971. The date sticks with me because I'd written him a fan letter the day before. It was perhaps the dozenth time I'd written to him, but I'd never had a reply. He probably never saw any of the letters, which I sent to the TV station in Los Angeles, but I simply assumed he was deliberately ignoring me. I'd gotten increasingly miffed at his rudeness, so when I heard about his death on the news that night, I wasn't as devastated as I'd have been a few months before. If anything, it made me decide I'd had my fill of teen idols.

Hence, I got my teenybopper phase out of my system early. By fourteen I was immersed in 'real' music – not just Led Zeppelin but The Kinks, Rod Stewart, Fleetwood Mac, even, daringly, David Bowie. I went to my first gig the summer I was fourteen, an outdoor show in Central Park starring the grizzled old English blues veterans Savoy Brown. Protracted negotiations with my mother resulted in her letting me go alone, though she insisted on waiting for me outside afterward, something on which no amount of pleading would sway her.

The gig was a turning point. Although Savoy Brown
turned out to be fabulously dull, with a partiality for beards
and tuneless jamming, I was intoxicated by the atmosphere.
Big guitars, big amplifiers, big men; it spoke to me. The buzz
of the crowd, the rictus of the guitar player's face as he
struggled with an especially difficult passage, the teamwork
of the road crew as they crouched by the side of the stage,
waiting to change a guitar string or untangle a lead – you
didn't see that kind of stuff in Millburn. I was enormously
impressed.

The next day I bought tickets for the next two gigs of
Central Park's annual summer season. I'd never heard of
either Quicksilver Messenger Service or The James Gang,
both of whom turned out to be West Coast schlep-rockers,
but when I got there I adored the August heat-haze shimmer-
ing across the stage and the blue cannabis smoke drifting into
the twilit sky. I even adored The James Gang and Quicksilver
Messenger Service, dullards though they were, for looking so
long-haired, cowboy-booted and wantable. Not even Millburn High School's top love interest, Mark Winkels, could
hold a candle to these exotics.

By the end of the year, I was going to at least one gig a
fortnight, buying tickets for whatever sounded interesting,
regardless of whether I knew anything about them. I was
profligate, promiscuous, taking in as much music as I could. It
was a fruitful time for rock, the hippie sixties having been
elbowed aside by a whole fresh crop of genres, among them
glam, urban blues (à la Stones on *Exile on Main Street*) and the
bluff testosterone-pop of Rod Stewart, whom I found stunning. So stunning that, learning his favorite drink was brandy,
I had to try it, upon which I upchucked for longer than I
thought possible.

Ma finally got bored with meeting me after each gig and let
me get the 11.30 train back to Millburn alone, high on the
thrill of Alice Cooper, or whatever band's ticket stub was

nestling in my rabbit-fur pocketbook. When I got home, walking the mile from the station with a disregard for safety that's hard to imagine today, I'd write a long concert review in my diary. They typically started, 'I saw Ten Years After tonight at the Academy and they were great. The guitar player, Alvin Lee, was so dynamic' before burbling off into even more breathless description. I was going to copy some of it here, but it's too mortifying.

These were solitary expeditions, mostly, because I didn't know anyone else willing to spend their allowance on going all the way into Manhattan to see what, oh, Black Oak Arkansas sounded like. (Wretched, you'll be surprised to learn.) I rarely spoke to people at the gigs, either. Though I made an effort with pink lipstick and a Revlon eye shadow called Baby Blue, I was too tall, bespectacled and opulent of ass for most guys' tastes, and too dumbstruck to initiate conversation myself.

I did try sometimes. Seated next to an older boy at a Deep Purple show at the Felt Forum, I thought of a no-fail chat-up line, 'How do you tell a guitar apart from a bass?' Guys love explaining technical stuff, right? But I made the mistake of pronouncing 'bass' with a short 'a', like the fish, and the guy rolled his eyes like I was an idiot. 'A *base* has four strings and a guitar has six,' he replied tersely, then resumed his conversation with his friend in the next seat.

Well, at least I'd learned something. I hadn't known it was the number of strings.

All this nurtured a vague desire to get into the music business, though in what capacity I wasn't sure. I couldn't sing or play an instrument, and had no desire to try. Being a rock star's 'lady', as they were called, appealed, but you just had to look at Bianca Jagger and Angie Bowie to appreciate the impossibility of competing with them.

I finally settled on the ambiguous goal of 'working for a record company'. But even then, I knew my inherent laziness would prevent me from pursuing the idea with much vigour. I could have done Millburn High's business studies course, which would perhaps have qualified me for an entry-level job at a record label, but it sounded too much like hard work. It was far easier to just daydream about having my own office at Atlantic Records (home of Led Zep) as I sprawled in one Millburn rec room or another, listening to my friends playing along to *Houses of the Holy* on acoustic guitars.

This insular way of life may not have been productive, but it was a pleasant way to be fifteen. The oil crisis and presidents Ford and Carter managed to completely pass me by as I burrowed into my music-centric lifestyle. I cut pictures out of *Circus* and *Creem* magazines to make a collage of my favorite bass players (four strings good, six strings bad), who included the Zep's John Paul Jones, Boz Burrell of Bad Company and Jimmy Lea of Slade.

I subscribed to *Rolling Stone*, and went to New York every week to buy an extravagantly expensive month-old imported copy of *Melody Maker*. *MM* alerted me to queer English genres like 'pub rock', making me probably the only person in Millburn who knew not just the name of every member of Brinsley Schwarz but also his birthday.

And I listened faithfully to WNEW-FM, New York's main rock station. It allowed its DJs amazing latitude, letting, for instance, star jock Alison 'The Nightbird' Steel open her late-night show by reading her own poetry. It was always soft-focus gibberish about the oneness of the universe and, to compound the nausea, she recited it in a dramatic whisper, always ending with the words, 'Come. Fly with me. Alison Steel, the Nightbird.' That whisper was part of the Nightbird persona, and I was thrilled when her cover was blown at a Jefferson Starship gig. The Nightbird came onstage to introduce the band, and shrieked like a fishwife. Fabulous. It was all grist to my aspiring little music-biz mill.

But apart from my obsession with music, I wouldn't have stood out in a photo of Millburn High's Class of '76. Except, that is, for the fact that I was taller than most of the boys, and had uncontrollably curly hair at a time when dead-straight and center-parted was the only way to go. Otherwise, I was a study in conformity, packed into the same elephantine bell-bottoms, tank top and desert boots as everyone else. That was the uniform of the American student between around 1970–1990; you dressed for comfort, not style. If you wanted style too, you did something to your hair, like a Farrah Fawcett cut. Sadly, that was out of the question for me – all I could do with mine was keep it chin-length and hope I wouldn't wake up in the morning with one side squashed flat and the other springing outward like a bush.

Millburn was just never a place for sartorial extremes, even in the glam-rocking early seventies. We might have been only twenty miles from New York City, but walking down Millburn Avenue, you'd have been hard-pressed to spot a single sequined jumpsuit or Ziggy Stardust haircut. Moreover, the only glittery T-shirt in the whole town, as far as I knew, belonged to me.

I'd filched it at a 1973 concert by singer Todd Rundgren, who had come on stage wearing it, a long-sleeved black number with sparkly purple motif. Midway through the gig – it was a hot August afternoon – he took it off and draped it over an amplifier. Unfortunately for him, a bunch of fans had been allowed to climb on stage to dance, me among them. Before I knew it I'd sidled over and stuffed it into my bag, shocked at myself, but desperate for this personalised souvenir of Rundgren, whose single 'I Saw the Light' was one of my fave songs. The thought of his anger when he found his shirt gone wasn't enough to stay me. I got years of guilty wear out of it.

Rundgren's shirt was one area where my taste diverged from that of my friends. The other major one was my interest in British culture, especially music.

Actually, my interest in the culture began and ended with

music. I was appalled at the non-musical side of Brit culture, which I experienced for the first time when I went to visit a penpal in London in the spring of 1976. TV finished at midnight, and there was no central heating. *No central heating!* What was this, 1945?! The lack of same led to a condition called 'damp', which I encountered for the first time in the freezing terraced house in North London where my penpal lived. It was so shocking I couldn't shut up about it for my entire visit, and when someone invited me one night to a gig by an obscure group called the Sex Pistols, I elected to go to a centrally heated pub I'd discovered instead. 'I'd rather be warm,' I whimpered. That was me – finger on the pulse.

But despite missing the Pistols, I did know my British pop, from Gary Glitter to Traffic. It moved me in a way American rock didn't, being snazzier, cooler and sexier. Basically, American rock had a big image problem in the mid-seventies. Allow me to draw your attention to a photo of Bruce Springsteen on the back cover of his second album, *Greetings from Asbury Park, NJ*. Springsteen was then approaching his breakthrough moment, and was an immensely hot property – about as hip as an American rockster could get. And in this photo, he's wearing a denim shirt he'd obviously slept in the night before, his curly hair is sticking out every which way and matters are worsened by the presence of a beard. The dude's a mess. No matter how good his music was – and it was, cos he was from Jersey – I couldn't respect someone who looked like that. Brit-rockers realised the importance of sartorial detail, not to mention irony. Both qualities were in short supply in US rock, and I simply couldn't fathom the attraction of bands who didn't possess them.

With that sort of cultural divide, most Brit-rock didn't translate very well into American. Consequently, acts who were superstars in the UK, such as Marc Bolan and Roxy Music, could barely fill a New York bar on half-price night. And New York was about the only place you could see them, should you have been among the few who wanted to. Few British artists ventured into the huge central regions, between the East and West Coasts, where cows outnumbered people and English accents were considered evidence of homosexuality.

Those who did, especially the ones who compounded the error by wearing lurex bloomers and weird hair, may as well have saved the locals the trouble by kicking their own faces in. In places like Kansas, musicians who didn't look and sound like Bruce Springsteen could just fuhgeddabaddit. Most quickly did.

As for the Bay City Rollers, they should have flopped dismally in America. By redneck standards they were obviously gay, what with their incomprehensible accents and 34-inch chests (the meagre dimensions were printed for all to see on the sleeve of their first album, *Rollin'*). They were lucky they weren't ridden out of town on a rail. That they became spectacularly successful instead – scoring a number-one single, 'Saturday Night', their first time out and displacing the American teen idols of the time – is to this day one of life's little mysteries.

3

OF COURSE, the Rollers weren't gay. There were always rumors, spread by cruel music journalists who figured any band with chests smaller than most girls' had to be that way inclined. But the rumors were baseless – the Rollers simply weren't the wimps they were perceived to be. They were solid Edinburgh working-class stock, from large families, and left school early to be apprenticed to traditional trades.

Although the *1977 Official Rollers Annual* reveals that Derek Longmuir 'learned about music at Boys' Brigade at Tynecastle Secondary School' (where history, especially the Victorian period, was his best subject), there was little to suggest what lay ahead. When he and older brother Alan decided to form a band, they simply did it out of admiration for The Beatles, whom they'd listened to as teenagers.

They launched The Saxons, with Alan on bass and Derek drumming, around 1969, when they were twenty-one and eighteen, respectively. No Saxons material survives – if the Longmuirs ever preserved one of their gigs on tape, they have never publicised the fact. Judging by what came later, they can't have been very good.

By day Alan was a plumber and Derek a carpenter, and they looked it. They were short and stocky, Derek blessed with Denis Healey eyebrows, Alan with the sort of hair that needed gusts of hairspray to keep it bouffant. Their tastes were equally proletarian: according to the sleeve of *Rollin'*, Derek's favorite food was 'Curries', Alan's 'Well done Steak'. In the '77 *Annual*, Derek expresses his longing for a Mercedes – 'but he's not a snob or a bighead', the text hurriedly reassures us.

The two of them didn't exactly shout 'rock star', which was why they surrounded themselves with people who were closer to the pop ideal. Most of the dozen or so young men who passed through the band before the lineup was finalised were pretty in the effeminate way then fashionable (think David Cassidy, or the way David Cassidy would have looked if he'd grown up on bread and dripping). However, it's doubtful they would have got very far if they hadn't met Tam Paton, an ex-military policeman and door-to-door potato salesman from Prestonpans, a market town a few miles outside Edinburgh.

He was then leading his own dance band on the Top Rank circuit north of the border, but fancied himself something of an entrepreneur. After hearing The Saxons, he brought them to the attention of Bell Records, who were enjoying great success with David Cassidy.

In September 1971, Bell released the first single by the Bay City Rollers, as they now were. 'Keep On Dancing' duly went to number nine despite being – let us be frank – a pile of poo. Cursed by weedy vocals and the tinniest imaginable guitar sound it was terrible. Even the lyric was risible. It was about being in a disco and watching a sexy girl do the latest dances, which had names like the Jerk and the Locomotion.

They might have got away with it if they'd been from Philadelphia or Detroit, where songs about dances were the norm. American music was full of tunes like 'Do the Funky Chicken' in fact, 'Keep on Dancing' was originally a hit for a US group called the Gentries – but that was America. Doing the Jerk in Scottish is a whole 'nother thing. To add to the absurdity, the song was so *un*-funky that even David Cassidy would have laughed.

Lest it seem odd that I should criticise their music, I must explain that I was never under any illusions about their artistic genius. All those rock gigs had instilled a critical faculty that was alert to second-rateness, and I was only too aware that this described the Rollers' music. 'Second-rate' might even have been generous, because their sound was paper-thin and utterly without substance. No wonder they had almost no fans over the age of fifteen. My entire Rollermaniac career was a struggle between knowing they were no Led Zep and loving them anyway.

The Rollers weren't unique in their flimsiness; in fact, a flimsiness clause was written into the contracts of most of the era's other teen idols. But they were singled out for the worst mockery for several reasons. The main one, and you could understand this, was their uniform (calf-length tartan trousers, tartan scarves, striped socks), which they were forced to wear in public at all times. There was also the fact that they were unabashedly romantic, at a time when rivals like Gary Glitter and The Sweet were all about sex (eg, Glitter's 'Do You Wanna Touch?'). Finally, they didn't stand up qualitatively to American competitors like Cassidy, The Jackson 5 and The Osmonds, who simply had better songs.

The much-ridiculed costumes were Paton's idea, a gimmick to distinguish his undistinguished charges, who by early '74 had settled into the classic lineup of the Longmuirs, Faulkner (favorite food: 'Peach Flambé'), guitarist Stuart 'Woody' Wood ('Steak Pie and Chips') and singer Leslie McKeown ('Plaice au Gratin'). The tartan worked on several levels. It emphasised their Scottish roots, the abbreviated trousers were a talking point (and distracted attention from their puny physiques) and the striped socks had sporty associations. Each Roller customised his uniform, with Woody sporting a large W on his jumpers, Eric adorning his jacket with badges and Alan going for a tartan waistcoat that made him look like a puffy-haired accountant. Another trademark was to undo the top button of their pants, a sly little ploy to get the girls steaming. And it worked. On this girl, anyway.

The uniforms, known as Rollergear, were preposterous, but at least they separated the women from the girls. Your love for the band had to be immense to overlook the Rollergear – if you couldn't, you weren't a fan. Of course, many fans wore Rollergear themselves, something I never contemplated. It was a simple decision – the whole aim of my life was to get them to fall in love with me, and they weren't likely to if I dressed like them.

The lineup had stabilised around the time their second hit, 'Remember (Sha-la-la)', began to climb the charts in February 1974. That was when McKeown joined, replacing one Nobby Clarke on vocals, and from that point success was assured.

Leslie was the Robbie Williams of his day – the Roller who smoked, drank and was generally a bit naughty. He was the only one who looked as if he'd probably had sex, though it couldn't have happened very often, given Tam's constant presence. (The idea of sleeping with Leslie – oh, those knowing eyes – was so overwhelming that I can recall the painful longing as if it were yesterday. Perhaps I'd better stop for a moment.)

He drove a blue Mustang, with which, in May 1975, he ran over and killed an old lady. He escaped with a £150 fine which seemed reasonable, because it wasn't as if he'd meant to, was it? Several months later a fifteen-year-old fan was shot in the head with an airgun outside his home in West Lothian. McKeown was not involved, but these were troubled times for him.

He was simply gorgeous, and every sensible fan's top Roller. He was certainly mine, though I had to share him with my friend Cathy, who once had the nerve to suggest that I should fancy Woody instead. 'We don't have anyone for Woody,' was how she put it, as casually as if she were asking whether I wouldn't rather have a cheeseburger instead.

(Cathy and I had been at loggerheads about Leslie since

we'd met at Kennedy Airport in January 1976, waiting for the band to arrive for a promotional visit. I spent much time privately comparing her looks to mine, regretfully conceding that if it came down to it, Leslie would probably prefer her glossy dark hair and pert *tuchas*. Even her Brooklyn accent wasn't as abrasive as it could have been.)

But memory is deceptive. As I write, twenty years on, I'm looking at the sleeve of the second album, *Once Upon a Star*, and I'm stunned. Instead of the young Lothario I remember, there's a skinny character with the pinched features now associated with single parents and council estates. Good lord, did he look like that all along?

None of the others have worn especially well, either. Eric, whom I'd always thought of as beautiful and poetic, seems now to be fey, while little Woody turns out to have Jimmy Hill's chin and the glassy eyes of someone who's suddenly woken up to find himself in the Bay City Rollers. Derek and Alan, meanwhile, look so much like tradesmen that they should be waving spanners.

No, time has done them no favors. But is that because standards of male beauty have changed, or because they were never very attractive in the first place and I somehow never realised it? Will Boyzone fans look at pictures of their boyz in 2019 and shudder too?

I think standards *are* different. The Rollers didn't follow rigorous fitness programs that today are a part of every teen-band's routine. There was no cosmetic enhancement, no styling or designer frocks (apparently, their uniforms were run up on a friend's sewing machine). Their attempts at improving on nature ran only as far as a dab of foundation for photo sessions and gigs – and I have proof in the form of a paper towel streaked with beige makeup (which I'll come to). They were simply allowed to be their whey-faced selves.

Anyway, once Leslie had joined, something in the band dynamic changed. After two hitless years since 'Keep On

Dancing', things suddenly began to happen. 'Remember (Sha-la-la)' reached number six in the UK, beating 'The Wombling Song', Paper Lace's 'Billy, Don't Be a Hero' and 'Ma, He's Making Eyes at Me' by ten-year-old Lena Zavaroni. That was the start of a run of hits that lasted two-and-a-half years. There was 'Shang-a-Lang', then 'Summerlove Sensation', then 'All Of Me Loves All Of You', and that was only '74. By the end of that year, their popularity had eclipsed that of all other teen idols. Even The Wombles couldn't touch them.

4

1975

First UK #1 of 1975: 'Lonely This Christmas'/Mud.
Biggest Roller hit: 'Bye Bye Baby' (UK #3); 'Saturday
Night' (US #1).

1975 WAS THE ROLLERS' pinnacle year. There were two
number-one singles, sold-out tours, their own TV series – the
epochal 'Shang-a-Lang' – and their first foray into America.

But success brought the concomitant downside, with every
member afflicted by nervous exhaustion, stress or tragedy.
McKeown ran over the old lady, and several days later hit a
photographer, for which he was fined £1,192. A few months
later he was knocked unconscious during a stage invasion, and
in December the airgun attack (for which he denied responsibility) took place outside his home. Meanwhile, exhaustion
forced Derek and Eric to take a rest, while Woody was
hospitalised after collapsing on stage in Melbourne. In the
spring of that year, a police sergeant was crushed to death by a
van as he tried to control 800 fans outside the Manchester
studio where the band were recording their TV show.

This last incident provides an idea of the lengths Roller fans
would go to be near the objects of their affection. The first
priority of any fan was to get to the band, and the second was
to stop other females from doing so. Fans were so intolerant of
the idea of women in the group's private lives that the album

Once Upon a Star carried a precautionary footnote on the back cover. Referring to the songs 'Marlina' and 'La Belle Jeane', it reads: 'The names Marlina and Jeane are purely fictional'. It was necessary in order to save every Marlina and Jeane in the country from attacks by fans. I assume that the spelling Jeane, which they pronounced 'Jennay', was an attempt at a little Continental glamour.

I was aware of none of this. The Rollers might have been the biggest thing in Europe, but until they visited America for the first time, in September 1975, the US media ignored their existence. So while they were conquering the rest of the world, I was desultorily attending Millburn High – where, like Derek, my favorite subject was history – and daydreaming about my top succulent love god, Robert Plant.

My own 1975 began with the decision that I should probably find out about drugs, because everyone else seemed to know all about them. I'd always meticulously steered clear, the result of a film I saw at elementary school. It starred Sonny and Cher, who took turns graphically describing what drugs did to you. The most terrifying scene showed the hallucinations an LSD-user might experience, and when Sonny turned into a giant lizard, I was so scared I resolved never to touch any illegal substance. I may be the only person in history who was actually put off drugs by an anti-drug film.

But now, in 1975, I felt sophisticated enough to try an eensy-weensy bit of something or other. Marijuana was the obvious place to start, which I did at a Millburn soirée, but the effect was so negligible that I gave up after a couple of experiments. Then, at the end of January, a girlfriend called JJ gave me some cocaine for my birthday. Wow – a hard-drug opportunity. I plucked up my courage, frightened (I wasn't looking forward to seeing lizards) but determined. 'Just suck it up through your nose like a vacuum cleaner,' directed JJ, after she'd fiddled around for a while with a razor blade I'd swiped from the medicine cabinet. 'That's it.'

Ten minutes later I asked, 'So when does it start happening?'
Because nothing was happening, and nothing did. I suppose I
could have procured some decent coke if I'd wanted to – some
of Millburn High's inmates were rich enough to know real
drug dealers – but I was actually relieved that my attempt to
become a drug addict had failed. I resigned myself to being the
token straight person. At least it meant I was disinclined to
stay up all night analysing Led Zep album covers.

Speaking of whom, I finally got to see them a month after
my birthday, and boy, what an anticlimax. I'd managed to get
a ticket for the first night of a sold-out run at Madison Square
Garden, and went on my own, hoping against hope I'd catch
Robert Plant's eye. Naturally, it turned out that I was just one
of 10,000 similarly inclined females, all of whom had had
more sense than to dress in desert boots and a hand-sewn cape.

After accepting, finally, that he wasn't going to see me back
there in Row W, I settled back to watch the show. Boring? You
can't imagine. Oh, Plant was sexy enough in his little un-
buttoned blouse and skin-tight jeans, blond mane flying in the
breeze created by 20,000 hyperventilating kids. In that sense,
it was worth it. But I hadn't realised that songs would go on
for up to fifteen minutes as Jimmy Page improvised on his
guitar, or that there would be a twenty-minute drum solo.
Nothing on any of their albums had prepared me for the bleak
reality of repeatedly checking my watch, wondering why no
one else was as stupefied as I by the spectacle of John Bonham
pounding his drums to a pulp with no sign he was even
thinking of stopping. And the equally endless guitar solos . . .

In retrospect, you can see why punk had to happen. It was a
very deflated me who got the last train back to Millburn that
night.

I was reminded of that night some months later, when I got
hold of the Rollers' third album, *Wouldn't You Like It?*, and
discovered the last track was, yep, a drum solo. Titled 'Derek's
End Piece' – which I'll bet haunts him to this day – it's easily

the most primitive interface of man and percussion instrument ever committed to record. I urge you to seek out a copy at a jumble sale near you.

The days passed much as they always had, that first half of '75. School, a part-time job at the East Orange Dry Cleaners, another job as a cashier at the Shop-Rite supermarket, occasional gigs in New York. My diary claims I saw Humble Pie, the Climax Blues Band, Journey, Supertramp and Lynyrd Skynyrd, but I have no memory of any of them. I do know that the first two were as prone to long guitar solos as Led Zep, so I've probably blocked them from my memory. They typified the ethos of the day, which sacrificed stuff like decent tunes on the altar of 'progressiveness', or some such tomfoolery.

In May, my former school friend Marcy introduced me to a guy called David, whom she'd met on her philosophy course at Drew University over in Madison. He became an important link in the Roller story, but our first meeting got off on the wrong foot. We were at a birthday party at the college, and apparently he told Marcy he liked the cut of my jib. She advised him that I was 'very single', as she insultingly put it, and suggested, 'She really likes Led Zeppelin, and she'll probably talk to you if you go up and say you work for them.' Like I'd fall for that.

None the less, he sidled over and in a Dick Van Dyke Cockney accent said, 'Ao, hallao, love, Oi'm David. I understand you're a Led Zeppelin fan, sao it might interest you to knaow that Oi'm their manager.' He smiled hopefully.

I looked him up and down, taking in the unfashionably short hair, thick black-rimmed glasses and button-down collar.

'Their manager, huh? So tell me, what happened to Peter Grant?' I asked, repressing a triumphant smirk, because I knew from reading *Circus* that Zep had a manager, and his name was Peter Grant. But David persisted. 'Oi think you must have it wrong, love, we daon't employ a Peter Grahhnt.'

'Give me a break,' I said, irked. Even if he *had* worked for the Zep, did he really think I'd be interested in someone in gray Sta-Prest pants? I might not have been as gorgeous as the school sex bomb, Karen Rothschild, but knew I was worth more than that. I turned to find Marcy to give her a piece of my mind, and David put his hand on my arm. 'Uh . . . all right, I don't work for them. I was just kidding.'

'God,' I muttered, and swept off. I didn't expect to see him again, but, to my displeasure, he called a few days later, and then took to ringing several times a week. At first I was unfailingly rude, more so than his crime warranted. I don't know why he tolerated it, but he did, and eventually I began to warm to him.

At twenty-four, David was a good deal older, but we ended up spending a lot of time together. He became devoted to me, and wanted to be my boyfriend, which he expressed by picking me up after school every day and taking me to the Millburn Diner, where I talked about myself and he listened. I didn't return his feelings, and, unworthy thing that I was, exploited him shamelessly. Still living at home in nearby Summit, and funded by his parents, he always had money and seemed happy to spend it on me. I used his car to practice driving, used his cigarettes to learn to smoke (and, once addicted, expected him to fund my habit), persuaded him to pay for concert tickets, and did it all without an iota of guilt. It took me years to apologise to him.

He's a crucial part of the Roller saga because, as we were to discover, an adult male could sometimes get results where teenage girls couldn't. David was invaluable for booking rooms in hotels and getting information from airline clerks, and when it came to actually pursuing the Rollers, we would have been stuck without his car, a rusting 1967 Oldsmobile known as The Heap.

By mid-'75, I still didn't have a boyfriend – in fact, had never had a proper one – and, David apart, no prospects, either. I'd set my cap for Robert Plant, but, as the Zeppelin gig had demonstrated, I would have to see off a couple of million other chicks first. School didn't exactly offer rich pickings. I had lots of male friends, but when you've watched someone smoke dope to the strains of Crosby, Stills & Nash's 'Marrakesh Express', notions of romance go out the window.

Spring turned into a remarkably hot summer. The humidity was unrelenting, dampening your clothes in the time it took to walk the one block from our apartment to school. Bored with bagging groceries at Shop-Rite, I quit my job and settled in for the usual idle July and August of rec rooms and wondering if I'd ever find a boy who would see beyond what I considered my deeply flawed looks to the romantic pop fan within. I wasn't holding my breath.

My friends were starting to get serious about Life, and writing poetry about it. Marcy showed me one of hers, which went:

'And you/And I/Always/Can it be?/First there is a mountain/ Then there is no mountain/Then there is.'

I recognised the mountain bit as a Donovan song lyric, and was aghast at the rest. But even if I'd been more sentimental I wouldn't have written poetry. Inertia suited me much better than activity. I was uniquely unambitious, unable to picture life after high school, where I was about to start my senior year. I assumed I'd do the usual Jewish girl thing of going to college when school ended, but the idea exhausted me. I had no idea what I wanted to be when I grew up – except 'in music' – and was trying not to think about how I'd make a living. I was happy to just drift.

One of the only subjects that roused much ardor was boys. Deeply tactile, I longed to hold hands with one, and practiced in my room by twisting my own hands around at my side and walking across the carpet that way. When I'd perfected that, I moved on to kissing the mirror, one eye open to gauge how I'd look, should a real person ever kiss me. I also held imaginary conversations to get a feel for witty ripostes, modeling my banter on that of Georgette Smith, a hard-faced girl from my class who always had a retinue of slaves gloomily trudging behind her down Millburn Avenue.

Change was nigh. The Rollers were weeks away.

5

B Y LATE SUMMER 1975, the Rollers' American record company, Arista, was making final preparations for the band's first US visit. Compared with the military precision of present-day boy-band campaigns, which can reap hundreds of millions of dollars (New Kids On The Block, the first group to really exploit the idea of merchandising, were said to have grossed in the area of a billion), marketing was a hit-or-miss affair.

The plan for the Rollers' visit was rudimentary. It was arranged they'd be introduced to the public on TV, which made sense. But what show did they choose? Not an established one with a large audience, but the brand-new 'Saturday Night Live With Howard Cosell' (not to be confused with the comedy show 'Saturday Night Live', which also debuted that year). Also, as you'll appreciate from the name, the show went out on Saturday night, when no one stays in to watch television. Good thinking so far, Arista.

Anyway, the Rollers were to make not one but two appearances on 'Cosell'. The first would be a satellite link-up from London on September 20. Ten days later, they'd fly to New York and do the show again in person. They were to spend five days in Manhattan, during which they would be photographed around the city and do interviews with the local press.

Prior to that, in August, small pieces appeared in teen mags like *Tiger Beat* and *16* ('Top Favorite of Over 7 Million Teeners'). Meanwhile, Arista was throwing together an album called *Bay City Rollers*, which was fashioned from snippets of their first three UK LPs. It was scheduled for release at the end of September, to tie in with the visit.

And that was about it as far as promotion went. The rest was up to the would-be fans. If they read one of the teen-mag pieces and were intrigued enough to call Arista, they were referred to a PR agency, Carol Strauss & Company, whose mission was to whip up excitement for the band's arrival.

I read the little article in *16*, a puff job about this band from exotic Scotland who were coming our way. It was accompanied by a shot of the BCRs grinning sheepishly in full plaid regalia. As a regular reader of the Brit music press, I knew about the Rollers, of course, but seeing them in this fresh context somehow moved me. I'd always dismissed teeny bands, as a good Zep fan was obliged to, but suddenly they looked . . . gosh . . . not gormless as usual, but fresh and fun. Reading further, I noted they were younger than most bands, ranging, the article claimed, from eighteen to twenty-four. That in itself was a novelty. The ages had been doctored a bit, but even Alan, the oldest, was really only twenty-seven.

Moreover, they were smiling. Bands didn't smile in the seventies, in case they looked friendly, but here were the Rollers, giving it their all. I liked that. It made them seem, in their own way, much more radical than Zep or the Grateful Dead or any of the other bands I'd always held to be so individual. So they were coming to America, eh? This warranted further investigation.

I called Carol Strauss & Company, where a harassed-sounding assistant told me they were flying to New York on September 30. If I rang back just before that, she added, they'd give me flight details – the idea being to get as many people as possible to go to Kennedy Airport to give them a Beatles-style greeting.

I was discussing this with David one day in early September as we sat in my room, admiring my new haircut, which I believed made me look like Russell Mael of Sparks (the curly-haired one, not the guy with the Hitler mustache). The cut was a work of art, considering what my hairdresser had had to work with. I'd gone to a Manhattan salon called Davian, which I'd read about in a fashion magazine, determined to do something about the amorphous mass on my head. It was the salon of the moment – Beverly Johnson, the first black model to appear on the cover of Vogue, was leaving as I arrived – and the ringlets the stylist coaxed out of my frizz were worth every penny of the outrageous twenty bucks he charged.

Like all men, David had despised the Rollers on sight, but had already agreed to drive me to Kennedy on the thirtieth. But I was starting to think it might be fun to do more than just see them at the airport. What about actually meeting these approachable-looking guys who were only a few years older than me? Girls in England swooned over them, so why not find out how swoonable they were?

'What if we told Strauss we were from a magazine and asked for an interview?' I mused.

'She's not gonna believe us,' David replied, placing two cigarettes in his mouth, lighting them and passing me one. Surreptitiously wiping the end before taking a drag, I came up with a solution. 'But what if we had press cards and business cards, and stuff?'

As we soon learned, press cards weren't easy to get – you needed to have produced three issues of a publication before you could be considered for press accreditation. Business cards, though – all you needed was $10, and any printer would whip up a batch in their own little box. By the end of the week, we had 250 white cards engraved with 'Backstage Magazine' – cos backstage was where we wanted to be – and our phone numbers.

David made the approach to Strauss – new magazine, interested in pop phenomena like the Rollers, love to inter-view them, blah blah. Strauss said she'd let us know, but in the end, as I noted in my diary on September 5, we got the brush-off.

> Carol Strauss called Dave at home last night. Rather than the Rollers being overbooked with interviews, as we'd feared, she said they're probably only going to be doing very few. But she said she'd keep in touch, and Dave said she sounded very friendly.

Backstage magazine did wangle us a couple of tickets to the September 20 Howard Cosell show, the one where they were to perform via satellite. I was so pleased I didn't realise till the day of the show that the tickets were for the afternoon dress rehearsal, which the Rollers weren't taking part in. So Cosell, a famously laconic sportscaster who was out of his depth hosting a variety show, did a little spiel about 'the hottest new group in Britain', the stagehands rolled down a screen, and – nothing. Three minutes of Rollerless silence, much to my disgust.

I watched the proper satellite broadcast at home that night, though, and that was when my fate was irrevocably sealed. Having only ever seen them on the printed page, the sight of them live, singing their first American single, 'Saturday Night', was a shock. They were, I decided in a millisecond, the most gorgeous things I'd ever laid eyes on. From that moment on, I belonged to Leslie, he of the appraising smile and wagging butt. My Lord, but he was cute, frolicking and leading the rest of the band in the chant, 'Saturday night!' I'd never seen a band with such exuberance and *joie de vivre*. Robert Plant? Robert Schmant.

I knelt in front of the screen, pressing my hands against it whenever Leslie waggled into view. 'Look at them!' I screeched at David, who was slouched on the sofa with his lip curled. He made no attempt to join me, lighting a cigarette and blowing moody smoke-rings at the ceiling.

They induced similar hysteria in the studio audience in London that night. After they finished 'Saturday Night', there was a stage invasion that resulted in Leslie briefly being knocked unconscious. This was after the satellite link-up had ended, so we didn't see it, but I knew how those girls felt. I wanted to invade that stage myself.

The moment the show ended, my bud Sue J rang. 'My God,' she breathed. 'Eric.' When she said that, I knew something weird was happening to us. Sue, who was five voluptuous years older and even more of a music fanatic than me, wasn't a girl who fell for teenybopper groups. We'd met six months before at a Queen gig, and had taken to going to shows together, she always with her camera in tow. She was trying to build a portfolio that she hoped would get her work as a professional photographer. I'd been to her house in Bayonne, near Newark Airport, and seen her numerous photo albums. She'd managed to snap everyone from Paul McCartney to Brian Jones, the latter of whom she'd actually convinced to smile as she caught him leaving some hotel. As a result she had a thing for Jones, and had visited his grave in Cheltenham a few years before.

Just two weeks earlier, Sue had dragged me to see heavy-rock grunters Uriah Heep. Now she was hyperventilating over a Bay City Roller. What was going on?

That night I wrote: 'We just watched them on TV and I screamed like a maniac. I never thought I could scream at some teenybopper group, but I LOVED them! Leslie!! We just have to get into the *Cosell* show when they come over, we just have to.'

Carol Strauss came through with flight details. They were arriving on TWA flight 703 at 2.35 p.m. on September 30. 'Dave was in touch with Carol Strauss, and she said there are going to be zillions of kids there, because WPIX has been announcing it all weekend,' I wrote the day before. 'Melanie Mackin's father's *is co-producer of the Cosell show*!! But since she and I hardly know each other, I can't bring myself to ask her for a ticket. Anyway, Dave called the TV station and said we were from *Backstage*, and they said they'd try to find a couple for us.'

But they didn't, so we never did get tickets for the October 4 show, the climax of their five-day visit.

No matter. September 30 found me, Sue J and a very reluctant David at Kennedy Airport. I had dressed carefully for this little expedition: pale blue corduroy flares, a short polyester trenchcoat for that cazh-but-smart look and a beret that was the last word in Paris-via-New Jersey chic. I was all set for Leslie, should our eyes meet across a crowded airport.

Tragically, they didn't. Strauss had done a good job of creating a commotion about their arrival; around 200 girls were there, along with crews from all the local radio and TV stations. Hence, there were too many people packed into a small arrivals area for Sue or me to get anywhere near a Roller. The band probably wouldn't have appreciated it, anyway, after a seven-hour flight that had been preceded by a Heathrow send-off that resembled those old newsreels of The Beatles flying off abroad.

We milled around, waiting for them to appear. An Arista employee wandered through the crowd, handing out tartan scarves, which I stuffed into my bag in case it looked like I was wearing Rollergear. Someone else was distributing the just-released debut American album, *Bay City Rollers*. Its cheap design – a photo of the Rollers with a tartan border on the front, a list of songs on the back and no other information – suggested it had been a rush job. Accustomed to the painstaking artwork of the Zep and Yes, I sneered. An older girl nearby smiled sympathetically, and we fell into conversation. She was covering the event for a real magazine, and knew where the band were staying. 'It's the Westbury Hotel in Manhattan. In the East Seventies somewhere. Don't tell anyone,' she whispered, glaring at a drippy-nosed twelve-year-old eavesdropper.

They finally made their appearance, flanked by Tam and a few heavies, and we surged as close as the crash-barriers allowed us. Scrumptious, I thought, staring reverentially at Leslie, who was cautiously sizing things up, a little smile playing about his slit of a mouth. He was much better-looking than in pictures, which didn't convey his litheness and self-possession. I snapped one Instamatic shot after another, grimly standing my ground as 200 girl-children drummed little hooves as they tried to knock over the barriers.

The other Rollers, who were smaller than I'd expected, cavorted around, transparently delighted to be in New York. All except poor Woody, who, as ever, looked dazed and out of place. Inappropriately dressed in BCR cold-weather gear – a tartan-trimmed heavy overcoat – he roamed around the enclosure as if waiting for a train.

After ten minutes, they were led out, and as they passed us I reached out wildly and was rewarded with a quick feel of Alan's stiffly-gelled bouffant. They clambered into a black limousine and roared off. We scrambled for The Heap and followed, arriving at the Westbury Hotel on the Upper East Side minutes after they checked in.

Because of David's presence, we were able to stroll right past the doorman into the plush hotel. 'Go to the phone and ask for Tam Paton's room,' I instructed David, who was rolling his eyes and muttering about how he hoped he wouldn't run into anyone he knew.

'But what'll I say to him?' he asked dubiously.

'We don't wanna talk to him, we just wanna find out what floor they're on,' I explained, mastering the situation. Once he found out Tam was in room 1409 Sue and I left him in the lobby, reading *The New York Times*, as we slipped up to the fourteenth floor.

At 1409, we pressed our ears to the door. Yep, those were definitely Scottish accents in there. At this point, we should have pulled one of the classic meeting-your-idol ruses. I'd heard about things like pretending you're from room service – 'Hey, Leslie, are you hungry? Well, here I am, big guy' – or having yourself delivered in a huge box. But after hanging around for a while, listening to the muffled conversation within, we were too nervous about being discovered, and slunk off.

'The Rollers did all the radio stations. They sounded very perky. Dave called Strauss, who said there's gonna be a big press conference, and she might be able to get us in. We're supposed to "call back tomorrow", as usual. I'd like to meet them in a relaxed situation. I can't stand crowds of little kids,' I wrote on October 1.

The day after that, a grey, autumnal Thursday, Strauss, no doubt on to us, said we couldn't go to the press conference. 'But they're doing a photo shoot in Rockefeller Center tonight, and I guess you can come to that,' she reluctantly added.

They arrived as dusk was setting in, obediently lining up for a phalanx of photographers in front of the massive gold statue of Prometheus. This time I got an unimpeded look at them. Sue and I managed to nudge our way in front of the photographers, and for ten lustrous minutes we were no more than four feet from the band. Down at my end, Woody and I were separated by mere inches, and I happily noted that he had acne. I could relate to that.

He and his comrades shuffled their feet and managed a credible impression of cheerfulness. In fact, they were exhausted from the relentless promotional schedule that had begun the moment they'd stepped off the plane. As Derek told *New York* magazine, 'It's like those old army films where you're being interrogated in a little room with a light in your eyes.'

I stood there studying them, my attention captivated by Eric's nethers. Was he wearing bloomers or not under those white trousers? There was an unmistakable convex outline under there that suggested not, but surely he wouldn't be so brash? Then a little girl interrupted my reverie by stepping on my foot and sobbing, 'Derek, you're beautiful.'

Derek? Beautiful? Abruptly I snapped back to reality. It was so far-fetched that anyone would fancy the beetle-browed Ringo of the group that I rudely said to the girl, 'Honey, look at him. That's beautiful?'

Tam, who'd been hovering at Woody's shoulder, overheard me and snapped. 'That's really nasty. You're the first nasty American I've met.' I matched him glare for glare and boldly continued taking pictures, but I was a bit shaken. Incurring the manager's wrath, I knew, could stand in the way of my marrying Leslie.

'He told me I was nasty,' I wrote defiantly before I went to bed. 'I'm honoured [*sometimes I used British spellings to seem chic*] to have that distinction. I knew I'd hate him even before I met him. Those boys are virtual prisoners – they're not even allowed out of their hotelrooms alone, and then they're put on display for writers and photographers and, geez, not even allowed to have girlfriends. I feel sorry for them. I wonder if they enjoy themselves.'

On Saturday October 4, their last day in America, they were ferried out to a New Jersey shopping mall for an autograph session. David, The Heap and I were there, waiting for them in the parking lot when they arrived. A few hundred adolescents were lined up inside the building, but we were the only ones outside, so I had them to myself when they arrived.

Woody was first out of their car, and for a moment we were alone, blinking at each other. He warily waited, a rabbit in my headlights. 'Your jeans are undone,' I finally blurted. The perfect opening line, right? Helpful but slightly sexy. He fumbled at his top button, but before he could do it up, Tam appeared at his side and barked, 'Leave it.' So his pants were *supposed* to be open? Behind me, David mumbled, 'Jesus.'

They were led into a side entrance, and we trotted behind, passing the mall security guard as if we were with the band. Suddenly we were all in a narrow corridor, and I found myself next to Woody. 'All this must be so crazy for you,' I said, trying to sound sympathetic and un-fannish. As he began to reply, Tam loomed out of nowhere. 'You again,' he said in his singsong accent. Catching a guard's eye, he pointed at me. 'Can you get her out? She's been pestering the boys all week.'

'Pestering'! Even now, it inflames me to remember it. If you call turning up at a band's public appearances and attempting to talk to them 'pestering', heaven knew what he called really obsessive behaviour.

The guard hustled David and me out of the corridor and into the crowd, where I defiantly took up a position just behind the raised platform where they were sitting down to sign autographs. From this vantage point I was able to keep a close eye on the band's backs as all the other fans queued up in front of the table. I took one of my best-ever Roller photos right there, a close-up study of Woody's tiny tush.

Presently, they lumbered back to the limo and, to piteous adolescent cries, rolled off toward Manhattan. We went to my place and watched them perform two songs on the 'Cosell' show. The next morning, they left New York.

I was no longer a girl, I was a woman. A Roller woman. Led Zeppelin? You could keep 'em.

6

I SPENT THE AUTUMN sheepishly buying and reading teen magazines to keep up with the band, who were now starting to colonise the US press.

In November, a New York newspaper carried an unfavorable article by Lisa Robinson, the doyenne of American music journalists. I had a bit of a bone to pick with her – not only was she friends with Led Zeppelin, which used to move me to wild heights of jealousy, but now she was dissing the Rollers.

'Y'know what we should do to her?' I asked David.

'What?' he apprehensively replied.

'Why don't you call her and pretend to be Tam, and tell her you're really pissed off?'

Five minutes later, he was asking for her at the paper's switchboard. I only heard his end of the conversation, but he managed a credible approximation of hurt and dismay, delivered in a fabulously implausible Scottish accent. He sounded so ridiculous I can't believe she didn't see through him.

But she didn't; quite the contrary. 'You've got to understand, Lisa, we're trying to break America, and the boys' feelings were injured by your article,' he wailed, and there was a rapid flow of words on the other end as she tried to placate him.

'She said she was sorry and she hadn't meant to be mean about them,' he said when he finally hung up. I removed the pillow I'd stuffed in my mouth. I was sure the Rollers would have appreciated what we'd done.

That same month, I also quit school. My senior year had started in September, and I was idling through a schedule that included potentially interesting courses, like Film Studies, but I couldn't engage. Even worse, because I'd skipped almost all my gym classes the previous year, I was forced to do an hour of gym every day, instead of the usual twice a week. Five hours of volleyball every single week, from now till next June. For a klutz like me who tripped over her own shoelaces, that was bad news indeed.

Quitting was the most rebellious act of my life, because middle-class Jewish girls don't quit school, they graduate and go on to college and end up in high-flying jobs in retail and the media. I wanted the job, just without the intervening college part. So there seemed no great reason to stay at Millburn High, other than the thought of my mother's face when I told her I was leaving.

Quitting has highly negative associations in America, where most people stay in school till eighteen – in Millburn, the only people who left early were boys who moved their lips when they read. I was amazed and a little frightened that I was even contemplating something so taboo. But I'd come to the realisation that I wanted to be in the music business, and couldn't envisage four years of college helping me get there.

My decision met with surprisingly little resistance from Ma, whose only condition was that I took the test for the General Equivalency Diploma, without which it would have been impossible to get a job anywhere other than McDonald's. In late November, armed with said diploma, I left academia forever.

'This is so great,' I confidently announced to David. 'I'll have so much time to see the Rollers the next time they come.'

'Yeah,' he agreed, far less enthusiastically.

Looking back, it's plain that something substantial was lacking in my life to make me devote so much energy to them.

The suddenness with which I'd embraced them, the importance they'd quickly assumed, bespeaks a lack of something somewhere else. But why them, and why then? I'd certainly never, before or since, had a crush so breathless and overwhelming. The obvious explanations – dearth of real boyfriends, boredom with school – only partly account for it. I still can't entirely understand why I watched 'The Howard Cosell Show' one day in 1975, saw the Bay City Rollers and fell for them. It seemed so random that I fully believe that if I'd seen them two days before, or four days later, I would have barely noticed them.

The BCRs' ascension to the top of the teenybopper elite that autumn had been swift. It looked like this:

September: trip to New York, 'Cosell' show, release of 'Saturday Night' and *Bay City Rollers*.

October: 'Saturday Night' begins to climb charts, thanks to heavy airplay and major coverage in the teen mags.

November: newspapers devote tracts to the Roller phenomenon (which was really still more a phenomenonette, as they had yet to impinge on the consciousness of anyone other than teenage girls).

December: 'Saturday Night' reaches Number One in the Billboard Hot 100.

It was quite an achievement. Few bands had ever made it to the top of the US chart their first time out, let alone a band who'd been completely unknown in the US until three months before. It must have been a very happy Christmas in Edinburgh. I know it was in Millburn, where I was considering taking down my 'Does your mama know you've been keepin' Bad Company?' poster to devote more room to Leslie. You can see what he was starting to mean to me.

7

1976

First UK #1 of 1976: 'Bohemian Rhapsody'/Queen
Biggest Roller hit: 'Money Honey' (UK #3); 'I Only
Wanna Be With You' (US#10)

IN JANUARY of 1976, the Rollers returned to New York
to do another 'Saturday Night Live with Howard Cosell'. American success had come just in time. In Britain
they were now past their peak, and with something called
punk rumbling in the distance, their fresh-faced aura was
beginning to look old-hat. But in America their prospects
seemed boundless, and their handlers were set on cashing
in. Their January visit was the first of four that year.

Waiting for them at Kennedy Airport on January 15, I got
talking to three girls who, like me, were older than the other
fans. My ensuing friendship with Emma, Cathy and Sue P
would outlast our Roller obsession, but that day we were
drawn together because we were the only females not wearing
Rollergear. In fact, I was quite proud of my outfit, a man's suit
and tie, which I'd chosen for its ambiguity. It was the kind of
thing David Bowie, who was currently in his *Young Americans* soul phase, would have appreciated.

My new friends didn't agree. 'We thought you looked really
weird,' Emma told me much later. She should talk. She was
wearing a blue satin jumpsuit and stack-heeled shoes, but the

glam-rock effect was spoiled by the T-shirt under the jumpsuit, which said 'St Mary's R.C. High School'. The other two were in light-colored sweaters and what Brooklynites call 'dress pants' – fancyish slacks with buckles and pleats. Sue P's monumental bosom was straining against her sweater, threatening to imminently burst forth, and her rear end was straining in the other direction.

They were very friendly, volunteering the information that Emma, who was from the Bronx, had met Cathy and Sue P, who were schoolmates in Brooklyn, during the Rollers' first visit, and they'd all become inseparable. Sue and Cathy had taken a day off school for this, while Emma, who was nineteen and a secretary at the impressive-sounding American Society of Composers, Authors and Publishers, had called in sick.

'It's embarrassing, isn't it?' I said, nodding toward the worried-looking kids pressed against barriers that had been erected in the Pan Am arrivals area. Although there were still fifteen minutes till the band were due, they had staked out their places and were clinging to them, faces set grimly. God help any security guards who tried to move them. Many were holding home-made banners and signs with slogans like 'Les, I wanna spend Saturday night with you!!'

'Yeah,' Emma nodded, long straight hair falling across her face. She pushed it out of the way with a gesture I still associate with her. 'I couldn't imagine waving a banner.' We sat primly, out of the way of the mob, congratulating ourselves for being so adult.

The band duly appeared, and, of course, we made more of a spectacle of ourselves than the little kids, shoving ten-year-olds aside so we could get a better view. The Rollers were whisked through the terminal and into a black limousine, which took off before we were even out of the building.

'Come with me! I've got a car!' I bellowed. We caught up with the limo at the lights near the airport entrance, and drove behind it all the way into Manhattan, where they bounced to a halt outside the ultra-swank Hotel Pierre. A cluster of kids outside stared longingly at the Rollers, who dashed into reception.

This was where not looking like a fan helped. Straightening my tie, I strode past the security guards, who didn't give me a second look. And then I was in the cubbyhole marble lobby, just me, the Rollers and Tam. Anxious to avoid Tam, I made my way to Derek, who was standing off to the side behind a pillar.

'What a sweet boy,' I swooned in my diary later. 'He was a doll. And so short! We chatted about New York for about 10 mins before he had to go up to his room.' I seemed to have forgotten that little incident at Rockefeller Center a few months before, when I'd found him so uglette. All any Roller had to do was look at me and I automatically thought he was gorgeous. I was that undiscriminating.

After I got home and gave David his tie back, I tuned into WXLO, 'your official Roller station', where the band were answering calls from listeners. I phoned and found myself connected to Eric. 'Ask Derek if he remembers Caroline from the hotel lobby this afternoon,' I begged. He did, and replied, 'He remembers you, baby.'

'Baby'! A Roller had called me 'baby'! How sexlicious could you get?! Never mind the fact that I didn't actually fancy either Derek or Eric, it was the principle. Being called 'baby' by a Bay City Roller was tantamount to being kissed by him.

But despite the promising start to their visit, I didn't see much of them this time around. There were no photo opportunities or public appearances. They ventured out to do the Cosell show, where they played 'Saturday Night' and their new single, 'Money Honey', but spent most of the next four days holed up inside the Pierre in meetings.

Undaunted, David dreamed up a way to sort of get in touch with them. Vigorously egged on by me, he rang Carol Strauss & Company, posing as the lawyer for a millionaire who wanted to book the Rollers to play at his daughter's birthday party. Word came back that Tam thought it was 'feasible', and they'd get back to us.

They didn't. That was obviously for the best, because at some point we'd have had to reveal ourselves as pranksters, but I enjoyed the vicarious thrill of almost making contact. Just knowing that Strauss had been in touch with them on our behalf was exciting, almost like talking to them myself.

The Rollers left on 18 January for a short tour of the East Coast and Midwest, hitting places like Philadelphia, Atlanta and Detroit. There were local TV appearances promoting 'Money Honey', which ultimately reached number ten in the US chart (and three in the UK, which wasn't bad – till you remember that their last two British singles hit number one). The album *Bay City Rollers* reached number nineteen, by the way – good going for a new act.

The band finished their American mini-tour in late January and flew back to Scotland. We didn't hear much about them for the next few months, which they spent touring other bits of the world and preparing to record their next album, *Dedication*. Meanwhile, Cathy, Emma, Sue P and I began to talk on the phone most days. It was a relief to broaden my network, because until then Sue J had been my only other Roller confederate, and even she often refused to discuss them, claiming they were 'too stupid'.

We arranged Roller activities in their absence. On March 20, the day after Derek's 'twenty-first' birthday (actually his twenty-fifth), we met in Manhattan for a party. Converging on the stage door of the Ed Sullivan Theatre, where 'Cosell' was taped, we spread a sheet of tartan wrapping paper on the steps, on which we carefully arranged a chocolate cake with a photo of Derek poking out of the icing. Birthday cards and little cartons of milk, the band's favorite tipple, completed our tableau. We looked at it reverently for a few minutes, took pictures of each of us next to it, sang Happy Birthday, then ate the cake. What a bonding moment. The only fly in the ointment was Sue P, who insisted on telling passers-by it was Derek's birthday. I didn't mind going public about my love for the Rollers, but I didn't want people thinking I had a thing for Derek.

In April, worn down by months of pleading, Ma paid for me to go to London to visit my penpal, Denzil. Introduced by a mutual friend, we'd been writing for the past year, so I was looking forward to meeting him – a real English guy! With an accent! I was even more excited about finally seeing London. It had been my ambition since I'd bought my very first record ('Layla' by Derek & The Dominoes, since you ask), and now, of course, there was an extra carrot in the form of the Rollers, who spent a lot of time there when they weren't right around the corner in Scotland.

London, and England, turned out to be a surprise in more ways than one. I've already mentioned my disbelief at the lack of central heating. There were also the shops, which all closed at 5.30 in the afternoon, and the way a request for a 'sandwich' brought a slice of ham and two limp pieces of white bread. There were strange potato chips, known as crisps, which you were forced to salt yourself with a tiny bag that came with the pack. Like it was too much trouble for them to do it at the factory? And there was Smash, the instant-potato powder that, along with sausages, formed the bulk of meals at Denzil's. Why would anyone be so desperate for mashed potatoes that they couldn't wait for them to cook in the normal way?

Then there was Denzil himself, a math student at nearby Middlesex Polytechnic. Though warm and effusive in his letters, which tended to dwell on his favorite band, Wishbone Ash, he was so withdrawn in the flesh, he refused to either meet my eyes or sit anywhere near me. Our hackles rose at the sight of each other, almost as soon as I arrived at his house from Heathrow on April 19. After our first uneasy evening together – 'Well, if you want bloody heating, you should have stayed in America' – he pretty much ignored me for the rest of my three-week visit.

It was too bad, because I'd harbored hopes for him. During our year-long correspondence, he'd been keen enough on me to have mailed me an Indian cheesecloth blouse *and* a sweatshirt advertising the newly launched Capital Radio. I'd sent him a silver wishbone pendant, and the letter he wrote in return began 'Darling Caroline . . .' He'd looked cute in his pictures, too, with long, shaggy hair and languorous David Essex eyes. Shame, really.

I ended up hanging out with his housemates, who occupied the other three bedrooms of a terraced house in North London's Colindale. The name still evokes net curtains – another queer Britism – and quiet suburban streets and the sense of being miles from wherever the action was.

By and large, though, I enjoyed London. You could go to gigs every night, record shops were stuffed with albums I'd only ever read about, and you could buy *Melody Maker* and *NME* on every corner. I spent an entire morning at the Virgin Records shop on Oxford Street, buying exotica like the Brotherhood of Man single 'Save Your Kisses For Me', which was number one the week I arrived, and Abba's 'Fernando', and 'Girls, Girls, Girls' by a band called Sailor, who dressed up as, yes, sailors. My joy was compounded by the discovery that the Rollers had just released a new single, 'Love Me Like I Love You', which wasn't available in America. It was like being inside a chocolate cake. With custard (my one happy Brit food discovery).

Denzil didn't approve of my music-centric existence. 'Don't you have any other interests, girl?' he inquired irascibly one night. To appease him, I made an effort to take in the non-musical side of London the next day. I spent the afternoon doing the House of Commons, Buckingham Palace and Whitehall, and returned to Colindale wondering why Parliament couldn't be replaced by something a bit sleeker, perhaps along the lines of the United Nations building in New York.

Punk was making its first inroads, with the Sex Pistols playing the seminal gigs that would make their name. Unfortunately for my future credibility, I was oblivious to both them and the scene unfolding around Seditionaries, the King's Road shop owned by Malcolm McLaren and Vivienne Westwood. As related earlier, I refused a chance to see the Pistols in favor of staying in a centrally heated pub, something that causes my friends no end of hilarity these days.

No, I was there for the Rollers, and one May morning I dropped by their UK publicist's office, using the *Backstage* magazine pretext, and asked if there was any chance of an interview. I thought it might be easier to nail them on their home turf, but it didn't work – the BCRs had just left for California, minus Eric, who was in hospital following an accidental overdose of sleeping pills. 'Just to get some kip, I just took too many downers. Yeah, I was just some guy who took too many uppers and took too many downers,' he explained years later in a British television documentary. He'd been using amphetamines to control his weight and needed 'downers' to counteract the stimulants.

The incident took place at Tam's house and as Eric says, 'I'm told, whether it's true or not . . . that before he called the ambulance he called the *Daily Record* or the *Scottish Daily Express* or something.' He was packed off to rest while his bandmates flew to America for their third promotional trip in seven months.

At the same time, April 1976, there were rumours that Alan also attempted suicide. Eric and Alan dismissed this in the same programme, 'It was like "Alan stuck his head in a gas oven." I mean, no way . . . "Alan drowns himself in beer" perhaps, "in the bath" . . . I'd believe that one.' And Alan on the subject said, 'I was druffed that night. I got pie-eyed. I just felt so depressed, I said, "What am I doin'? How can I no' just be myself? How can I no' just be a plumber again?" ' Alan, in a 1979 *Sunday People* exposé, admitted he had always been one for the booze. 'During the Japanese tour I would take a Coca Cola can on stage with me, but it would be full of whiskey and lemonade. I've had a smoke of cannabis, but I didn't go for it. I much prefer drink. I'll probably finish up an alcoholic.'

Whatever the true story, he was sick of incessant touring and opted out. He retired, at the age of twenty-seven, to the quiet life of a farm outside Edinburgh, and was instantly replaced by a seventeen-year-old Belfast boy called Ian Mitchell of a group called The Young City Stars.

Alan stuck around long enough to pose for a press shot depicting him handing over to Mitchell. The kid is in brand-new Rollergear and Longmuir is wearing a pinstriped suit and tie, obviously delighted to be back in civilian attire. He's shaking Mitchell's hand with an expression of relief as the younger man smiles, unaware of the torment awaiting him.

But the PR woman, Bess Coleman, didn't tell me about Eric or Alan, of course. Rather, she blandly explained that the band were in the US, but would I like some glossy eight-by-ten photos and a lavish press kit?

As an afterthought, she also advised me to find out about a new Scottish boy band called Slik. 'They'd be perfect for your magazine,' she said helpfully, which was how I found myself the next day in a white-fronted Belgravia terraced house, chatting to Slik's publicists. They were pleased to meet an American 'journalist', and loaded me up with booty on the group, who are now remembered only for having been Midge Ure's first band.

I was about to leave when another PR agent clattered downstairs. 'I've heard you're from an American magazine,' he called from the stairway. 'Yes,' I lied. 'Do you like Marc Bolan?' he asked hopefully.

It turned out Bolan was upstairs at that moment and

available for interview, if I was interested. Hmmm. I wasn't a fan of the glam-rock icon – his englittered feyness had never really tooted my flute – but hey, he was a celeb, and if I talked to him maybe I could sell the interview somewhere and actually get closer to being a real journalist.

I didn't realise that Bolan's career was in desperate doldrums at that point, which was why he was willing to meet any hack who dropped by. He would make a partial comeback with his own TV show before his death in a car crash eighteen months later, but on that sparkling May morning, he was a has-been.

However, I didn't know that, and keenly trotted up to see him. The publicist supplied me with a pen and notebook and then we were on our own, the ol' Bopping Elf and me.

What an egomaniac. The point of an interview is to allow the subject to talk about himself, but the man took liberties. Me-me-me for an entire frigging hour. Check this out:

Caroline: 'Do you still get mobbed by girls?'

Bolan: 'They can't get enough of me. I was dancing at this club a couple of weeks ago and these girls just wouldn't leave me alone.'

Me: 'Oh, you like dancing?'

Him: 'I'm probably the best dancer you've ever seen.'

And on and on. With hindsight, it's plain it was pure bravado, but at the time I thought he was one of the most irritating people I'd ever met. And he didn't even have any redeeming sexiness, his delicate features were blurred by the extra fifteen pounds he was carrying on his slight frame. I got an exclusive, though: taking out his wallet, he showed me a photo of his eight-month-old son, Rolan (yes, he'd named the poor creature Rolan Bolan).

I left feeling like a proper journalist, with every intention of writing up the piece when I got back to Denzil's that night, and trying to sell it to an American magazine when I returned home. But my plans fell by the wayside. I had a date with a particularly cute friend of Denzil's, and spent that evening and the rest of my remaining week in London moping around the Hendon squat where he lived, lovesick. Just as well I was lovesick, as I had no option but to stay in the squat. The day after the Bolan interview, Denzil and I had had another argument, sparked off by my complaints about the watery liquid that passed for a British milkshake, and he invited me to leave his house. Once I'd moved my things to the squat, I never saw Denzil again.

By the time I flew back to New York, on May 11, Bolan felt like a distant memory. And once home there was other stuff to occupy me, like the announcement that the Rollers were to play their first American gig on June 26 in Atlantic City, New Jersey.

They'd picked *Jersey* for their first gig!!! It didn't get much better than this.

8

A TLANTIC CITY was the equivalent of an English seaside town – it was bruised around the edges, and its glory days were a long time gone. Its fortunes were about to be dramatically reversed by the introduction of gambling, which would make it the only city in America, other than Las Vegas, where it was legal. But the casinos, hotels and the Trump Taj Mahal were still two years away. In June of 1976, it was a rusting coastal town with a pier and a hundred stalls selling cotton candy and chili dogs. And this was where the bright hopes of British boy-pop were making their American debut. There was something so Rollers about that.

The day before the gig, Sue J and I went to the Plaza Hotel in Manhattan, where the band were resting up before their big night. We shot the breeze on the sidewalk for an hour or two, then abruptly snapped to attention as Leslie and Tam walked out, the former in a brown T-shirt and tight jeans. Tight *full-length* jeans, with not a hint of tartan anywhere.

'No Rollergear,' gasped Sue, while I desperately searched my bag for my camera. 'What's going on?'

My heart was pattering queerly, and a little flame began to smolder somewhere around my solar plexus. No Rollergear. The seeds of rebellion were in that Leslie boy, and I was hooked like I'd never been on anyone else – not Robert Plant, not even Denzil's friend in London. But I realised, with one of the first adult emotions I'd ever had, that the chances of snaring him were almost nil, and the tragedy of it was unbearable.

Up till that moment, I'd nurtured a vague idea that if something was desirable enough, it was attainable. I didn't often get as far as considering exactly how I'd attain it, leaving it up to a childlike faith that things would simply work out without my intervention. Most of the things I'd longed for, save straight hair and a boyfriend, had come about without my ever being troubled by abstract concepts like cause and effect, responsibility or accountability. Now I'd run up against my first brick wall, and reality was biting triumphantly. As sure as Leslie stood there, I knew I hadn't a chance. The unfairness tore through me savagely.

As I ruminated, he and Tam stepped into a limousine, and that yanked me out of my trance. 'Haul ass!' roared Sue, fumbling for her car keys. We piled into her own version of The Heap and stayed nose to tail behind the limo through rush-hour traffic all the way to Little Italy, where they stopped at a restaurant called Paolucci's. It took us fifteen minutes to find a parking space, by which time the restaurant had filled up. If there'd been a table we'd have grabbed it, but instead were consigned to sitting on the steps outside till whenever they finished their meal. There was no question of not waiting – Leslie was in there, practically alone and wearing long pants. Anything could happen.

'Let's talk to the chauffeur,' Sue suggested, smiling at the uniformed brute leaning against the long black car. To our surprise, Frank, as he turned out to be called, seemed delighted to have company. He invited us to sit in the car, and we didn't need to be asked twice. Once we'd settled into the plush brown seats, he was happy to chat about his clients. We were pantingly attentive, but it turned out that his potential as a Deep Throat was limited. There was something of a communication problem between Brooklyn Italians and inner-city Scots. Basically, he couldn't understand a word they said.

Glancing around the car, I noticed a squashed-out cigarette in the ashtray. 'Whose is this?' I inquired. 'Oh, that's the skinny guy, the singer,' rasped Frank. Overjoyed at obtaining my very first personal effect, I wrapped it in a tissue and carefully zipped it into my bag. That Marlboro had touched his lips, and I was aching to get it into my scrapbook.

Frank checked his watch. They were due out at 11.30, but it was only 11.15. 'Wanna ride for a coupla minutes?' he offered. Well, of course we did. We cruised around the block, looking at the world from behind the same tinted glass that had lately encased Leslie, and thought that life was good.

Then we heard Frank's mumbled 'Oh, shit'. We looked and there were Leslie and Tam cooling their heels on the pavement. 'Out,' Frank barked, all friendliness gone, and out we stumbled in front of the bemused pair. I'd love to know what Frank told them.

We chased them back to the hotel, but lost them when we missed a light on Park Avenue. But I had Leslie's cigarette to keep me company on the way back to Sue's house in Bayonne. Almost as good as the man himself.

The next day, I wrote:

The show started to the LOUDEST SCREAMING I've ever heard. I got right down the front, on Ian's side. He looked out of it. By the way, they do play their instruments. Very poorly. Leslie played organ on one number, with one finger. Woody wore a blue jumpsuit (nice) and looked thinner than ever. Eric was sweaty and appears to be gaining weight, and Derek was Derek. At one point it was so crazy they had to go off and Tam came out to tell everyone to sit down. Creep. We left in the middle of 'Saturday Night' (last #) and drove to Philly, beating 'em there by an hour.

Frank had confided that the band would be staying in Philadelphia after the concert, and we sped across the flatlands of South Jersey to get there first. We'd been sitting for a good while in the parking lot of the Spectrum Hilton, a dreary glass tower overlooking an expressway, when their limo pulled up. They clambered out stiffly and disappeared into the hotel, occasioning a furious debate between Sue and me. Should we sit tight in the hope that some of them would come out to grab a late dinner or something, or should we go home? We voted to sit. And we did – all night. They never did resurface, but we sat rooted to the spot, watching the moon rise and set, and, many hours later, a clear summer dawn break. I'd never kept my contact lenses in so long, and was feeling grubby and wretched by the time they trooped out at 6 a.m., bound for the airport.

The group looked as exhausted as we felt. Not surprising, as they were being worked without respite, every waking moment accounted for. At that point, they were midway through recording their fourth album, *Dedication*, in Toronto, and had interrupted work just for the Atlantic City gig. Now they were returning to Toronto, without even a day off to savor their concert triumph. No wonder they looked pale and miserable in the struggling sun.

'I just feel that one of the Rollers – probably Eric or Leslie – has got to give way under the pressure,' I wrote morosely the week after Atlantic City. My diary is full of similar gloomy predictions; later in the summer I foresaw 'something bad happening to Leslie'. Nothing ever did, but I was melodramatic, and frequently fantasised about McKeown being in some sort of danger that only I could rescue him from.

Keen to learn where in Toronto they were recording, I phoned Arista Records, pretending to be Tam's elderly mother in Edinburgh. My Scottish accent wouldn't have passed muster with the Royal Shakespeare Company, but it fooled the secretary at Arista. Her boss, who knew the band's whereabouts, was at lunch, but she promised he'd ring as soon as he returned. I made up an Edinburgh number where he could reach me. I wonder if he ever rang.

While all this was going on, punk was continuing apace in the UK. Bands like The Clash and The Damned were forming, and by summer 1976 there were enough to stage a soon-to-be-legendary festival at the 100 Club in London. The old order, had it but known, was in the process of being overturned by the new, though nothing really cataclysmic would happen until December, when the Pistols made their career-defining appearance on the 'Today' show. That was the one on which they used bad language and made the cover of the next day's *Mirror* under the famous headline 'The Filth and The Fury'.

I mention this because I was starting to be intrigued by punk. The coverage in the English rock press was piquing my interest, and I wondered where I could hear a punk band. Not in America, that was for sure. The US hadn't taken any notice of glam rock, and it damn sure wasn't going to acknowledge punk. Two things gripped the nation during the summer of '76 – the Bicentennial and *Frampton Comes Alive!* The former was celebrated with monumental fanfare, but to some of us *Frampton* was the bigger event. For one thing, once the Fourth of July was over, it was over, but *Frampton* went on for the rest of the year. Curiously for such a landmark, it's little-remembered today, proving its success was due to an accident of time and place rather than greatness.

It's telling that Frampton, who was English, got a much better reception in the States than at home. He did so well in America that he actually moved to upstate New York and married a local girl, and just as well, for by the time *Frampton* came out, long-winded guitarists like him couldn't get arrested in England.

It was also as well that the Rollers decided to expend most of their energies on America in '76. Like Frampton, they were just about spent in the UK. Despite two chart-topping records the year before, their biggest 1976 single, 'Money Honey', only reached number three in the UK charts. It was inescapable evidence of their audience getting older and moving on.

But it was doubtful they even realised what was happening in Britain, because they spent so little of that year at home. They were in Toronto the rest of the summer, finishing *Dedication*, then did a short US concert tour in late August. It took in only a few cities, with Philadelphia the nearest they got to New York. We bought tickets the day they went on sale.

On August 31, Cathy – who by this point was calling herself Cathy McKeown – the two Sues and I took the train to Philadelphia, then a cab to the airport to meet their flight. We followed them back to the Spectrum Hilton, the same hotel they'd used after Atlantic City.

Cathy prepared to dash in after them and was only stopped by my bellowed, 'YO!'

'What!' she shouted, poised for flight.

'They're never gonna let us in there like this. We've gotta call David and get him to book us a room!' I shouted back, clamping both hands around her wrist. We slipped into the hotel's side entrance and I phoned David, instructing him to ask for a room for 'my wife and her friends'.

'You owe me for this, Sullivan,' he grumbled, but did my bidding. He must have told them his wife was seventy-five, because when we checked in, they gave us a room on the same floor as the Rollers. We were sensible enough not to abuse the privilege, staying put in our room rather than sneaking down the corridor to listen at doors. We figured we'd leave that till after the gig, when it would be party time. Except it wasn't, because by then they'd got wind of us and moved to the eighth floor.

We arrived back from the show ('Woody's bass-playing has improved, and Eric sounded quite fine. He's lost about 10 lbs and looks better. Nice stage costumes, too') and piled into the bar, hoping they'd come in for a post-gig digestif. But they immediately went to their rooms and it seemed they were all out for the count.

As we slouched around a table, sipping an economical two Cokes between the four of us, a little fan approached us, moist-eyed.

'I just called Eric,' she faltered. That got our attention. 'He said, "I can't get no sleep; people keep calling and I'm getting pissed off." ' Her voice cracked with misery.

Of course! Why didn't *we* think of phoning them? Back in our room, I dialed every room on the eighth floor till an unmistakably Scottish voice answered.

'Hi,' I purred.

'Hi,' he purred back encouragingly.

'Who's this?' I asked, crossing my fingers.

'It's Tam. Who's *this*?'

Typical. He was feeling benevolent, though – you could never predict his moods – and willing to chat. We spent an entertaining fifteen minutes discussing the film he was watching, the sci-fi classic *The Fly*, before he snapped back into Tam-mode and abruptly said goodbye. I mentally filed away the conversation – yet more contact with a Roller associate, if not an actual Roller.

When they left the next morning for their next gig, we waited till they were safely gone, then headed to the eighth floor. The maids were already starting on some of the rooms, and most of the doors were open. We poked our noses into a couple, and on the third try we found the one Eric and Leslie had shared. There was no doubt whose it was because of the little heap of fan letters on the desk.

There was all sorts of junk lying around. It was a dream come true – stuff they'd used so recently it was still warm – literally. A cup of tea on the bedside table hadn't even had time to get cold. Sue J plucked the bag from the cup, squeezed the liquid out and reverently wrapped it in a tissue.

The rest of us swarmed around, cats attacking an especially succulent mouse. In the bathroom I found a plastic razor, which gave me pause, for surely neither Eric nor Leslie actually shaved. Into my bag it went, anyway, along with an unlabeled bottle of what looked like shampoo. Sue P helped herself to a damp bath towel, wondering aloud which Roller behind it had been in contact with, and Cathy was overjoyed to find half a slice of buttered toast. All told, a satisfying haul.

We were in high spirits as we drove to the train station, but our happiness began to ebb as soon as we rolled out of Philadelphia. By the time we reached New York's Penn Station ninety minutes later, we were much deflated. Each encounter with them was painfully intense, and the more we saw of them, the more perversely depressed we were afterward. The high of being around them was always counterbalanced by aching lows as we returned to real life.

It wasn't that we didn't have any other men in our lives. Emma had a boyfriend, and I had David, who wanted to be my boyfriend. But American guys, we agreed, just weren't a patch on the maddening, gorgeous otherness of these Scots with their blurry accents and slinky ways.

I suspect that if I hadn't met Emma, Cathy and Sue P, I'd never have become as deeply involved with the band as I did. Pursuing them alone would have been too daunting, and anyway just plain embarrassing at my age. It was a relief to come across girls the same age as me or, in nineteen-year-old Emma's case, even older.

We became dependent on each other, a tight little unit that also included Sue J when she wasn't saying things like, 'I need my head examined for even having their records in my house.' The oldest of our gang, Sue J was often assailed by doubts about the whole thing, though she usually managed to quell them when the band were in town. I had similar doubts, stemming from frustration with their musical limitations.

If Sue J and I were Doubters, Emma and Cathy were Believers. They found beauty and inspiration in songs like 'Saturday Night', refusing to accept that Eric Faulkner wasn't a talent on a par with Eric Clapton. As for Sue P, she was a happy-go-lucky disco girl from Brooklyn who simply enjoyed the music for what it was. There was always a little distance between the Doubters and the Believers, but our co-dependency was such – because we knew we'd never find anyone else to hang out with – that we lived with it.

Being as antiquated as we were, we attracted attention. Journalist Lisa Robinson, the one David had phoned, described us as 'the strange older girls who hang around for the Bay City Rollers', which had the sting of truth. When everyone else is eleven, a bunch of seventeen-year-olds stands out.

There *was* another group of older New York fans, a much flashier crowd than us. Each faction jealously guarded all information, and only consorted with the other bunch when it couldn't be avoided. We distrusted them, and likewise, because none of us was above sending the others on a wild goose chase. We cordially disliked our rivals because not only were they deceitful, they couldn't be trusted to honor gentlemen's agreements.

Once, in April 1977, we drove to Philadelphia to queue for gig tickets. We arrived about midnight, ten hours before they went on sale, because we wanted to be first in line. We were, but it quickly got so cold that we decided to go see a porn movie to keep warm (honestly, it was the only place open at that hour). Leaving a note stuck to the car windshield, we left for a couple of hours.

And who should be there, hogging the front of the line, when we got back from *Here, Pussy, Pussy*? 'We didn't see a note,' smirked their leader, Joey, a squat Italian guy from Queens who had a camera permanently affixed to his barrel chest.

That was another reason we hated them, their acceptance of men into their clique. As we saw it, loving the Rollers was strictly a she-thing. Who wanted guys around? Joey and the other boy in his bunch, Barbarino, weren't even gay, they just liked the Rollers, which struck even us as too bizarre for words.

Anyway, back in early September '76, two weeks after we ransacked the Philadelphia hotel room, the horror of real life caught up with me as Ma announced that the time had come for me to find a job. The idea wasn't without merit, as having an income meant I'd be able to afford to move to New York – no more rushing for the 12.30 a.m. train back to Millburn! – but the notion of actually working was very distressing.

Two depressingly short days later, I was a 'teller trainee' at the Greenwich Savings Bank on 34th Street in Manhattan. The bank had a dozen branches around the city, and once you'd completed the week-long training, you were assigned at random to a branch. I was sent to West 57th Street, which happened to be – I could hardly believe my luck – directly across the street from Arista Records. If the Rollers came or went I couldn't help but see them. Maybe working wouldn't be so terrible after all.

9

I T WAS, of course. My co-workers were amiable, but I had no aptitude for handling money all day, other than my own. My mistakes were numerous, and I knew within days I was in the wrong job. I cried when I woke each morning, thinking of the work day to come and the leisurely life now receding into the distance. David, who had recently started working at a Manhattan insurance broker's, escorted me to the bank each day so I wouldn't be tempted to turn tail and get the next train back to Jersey. All this misery for $85 a week after tax. Moreover, the Rollers never turned up at Arista. I used to crane over my till, watching the doorway across the street, but there was neither hide nor hair.

After a month or so of commuting into the city, David proposed we get an apartment there. It had never occurred to me to live with him, but it was a sensible idea, given that neither of us could afford a place on our own. Within weeks, we were installed in a tiny studio pad on West 23rd Street and 7th Avenue, right next door to the Chelsea Hotel, where Sid Vicious and Nancy Spungen would come to such grief two years later.

It was handily located for all Manhattan's attractions, and there was a pleasantly raffish air about 23rd Street itself, which was lined with Spanish restaurants and small shops. We quickly adapted to living together after a few uncomfortable moments when the realities of sharing one room hit home. One of them was having to use the same bed, which we dealt with by sleeping side-by-side under separate blankets, like cocoons. But the drawbacks were greatly outweighed by the pleasure of not having to make the ninety-minute journey from Jersey every day.

In November, after two months at the bank, I threw in the towel, much to both my and my employers' relief. At around the same time, new Roller Ian Mitchell did the same, quitting the band because, as Eric put it, 'it was doing his head in a bit'. He didn't elaborate, and we could only speculate about his meaning.

Like Alan before him, Ian was swiftly replaced by one Pat McGlynn, a nondescript Edinburgh youth that none of us fancied. His main qualification for the job seemed to be that he was willing to do it. It was asking a lot of someone to be a Bay City Roller, especially now that they were quitting like flies.

A few days after I left the bank, Emma found me a job in her office at the American Society of Composers, Authors and Publishers. This was definitely a step in the right direction of a music biz career. ASCAP was one of the USA's two main performing-rights societies, charged with the dull but important job of collecting and distributing royalties on behalf of songwriters and publishers. While my position in the membership department was mainly typing, it was exciting to come across files for the likes of David Byrne of Talking Heads and other big rock names. You'd even meet the odd composer, though the ones who dropped by tended to be old-school Broadway types.

I had quite a bit of free time, and during one slow afternoon I came up with the idea of a Rollers newsletter. Its title was inspired by a fanzine written by Emma and Cathy for the benefit of some young kids they corresponded with. Theirs was called *The Tartan Alert*; mine ended up *The Tartan Pervert*. The subtitle was 'The Official Newsletter of the Tacky Tartan Tarts' (the Tacky Tartan Tarts being, I'm afraid, us – Sue J came up with that), and its purpose was to disseminate as much scurrilous gossip and speculation as possible, preferably with a sexual slant. I went out of my way to be as crude as possible, with many references to schtupping and nudity. Issue One contained a picture I found in a magazine, a crane with the words 'Bay City' on the side. Underneath I typed, 'Something to help the Rollers get it up'.

I photocopied it and sent it to my sister Tacky Tartan Tarts, who were gratifyingly enthusiastic. It lasted twenty-four issues, and I hope I'm not being immodest in saying that it became a bit of a cult, with copies finding their way across the country and even, reportedly, to the Rollers themselves.

Shortly after I started at ASCAP, the Rollers announced they'd be doing their first New York gig on 8 January 1977, at the Academy of Music. This was of no little import for the simple reason that, once we had them on our home turf, we'd be able to stake out the hotel from dawn to dusk, and follow them everywhere.

Tickets went on sale just before Christmas, and, as usual, we camped out the night before. When we arrived, we were disgruntled to see that our rival faction had beaten us there, leaving their boy Barbarino as a sentinel. We'd anticipated something like this, and come up with a plot in the form of chocolate-flavored laxatives. The plan was to offer some to whoever was there first, then take their place in line when nature called. But Barbarino smelled a rat and refused our gift.

We nagged, coerced and finally begged him to let us go first, but he stood his ground. Finally, resigned, we sat in silence behind him. A few minutes later, he turned to Emma, who was second in line, and whispered something.

'Dream on, you creep!' she replied in disgust, and inched away from him.

'What did he say?' we demanded.

Her face curdled. 'He said he'd let us go first if . . . never mind, I'm not going to repeat it.'

'Pig!' shouted Cathy, impotently swinging her bag at him as he cawed dementedly.

If any of us had been willing to go that far for a Roller ticket, it certainly wouldn't have been with Barbarino. Not only was he short, skinny and just seventeen, he was the most obnoxious kid imaginable. He had a high-pitched laugh he constantly deployed at his own jokes, he pretended to have insider knowledge about the band and he was absolutely desperate to lose his virginity. Joey had once told us Barbarino had never even kissed a girl. Hardly surprising with that laugh.

Barbarino stood his ground till the rest of his gang returned, at about 6 a.m., and when the tickets went on sale at nine, they got the first ones. We still managed to get front row, making for a particularly happy Christmas and New Year's Eve.

Sue J and I saw in 1977 by going to see Patti Smith, whose caterwauling did more to put us off than any other act we'd seen since the Rollers. 'I'm sure she's doing that on purpose,' Sue decided after a few painful minutes. We agreed that an artist's right to express herself ended where our eardrums began, and left after the second number, finishing off New Year's Eve at my place with pizza and TV. I expect the Rollers did the same.

10

1977

First UK #1 of the year: 'When a Child is Born'/Johnny
Mathis
Biggest Roller hits: 'It's a Game' (UK, #16); 'You Made
Me Believe in Magic' (US, #9)

W E LEARNED FROM Carol Strauss that the band
were doing a gig in Los Angeles on Friday, 7
January, then flying straight to New York in the
early hours of Saturday. The Tacky Tartan Tarts assembled on
Friday night at my pad, whence we left for the airport at four
in the morning.

It was a horrible hour to be out; the city was frozen and
lifeless, and the roads slick with black ice. We huddled in The
Heap, which was none too warm at the best of times, and
shared a cup of coffee from the all-night diner on 23rd and
7th. Before heading for the Midtown Tunnel and Kennedy
Airport, we stopped at the Rollers' limo-hire company to try
and extract details about what flight they were on. We took
this desperate measure because Strauss, whom I'd called the
day before posing as a French radio DJ, wouldn't release
details.

'You guys are going out to the airport at this hour?' honked
the dispatcher, hugely amused. 'Whadayouse, nuts?' Our
pleading faces confirmed it. 'Uhright, I guess you deserve a

break. They're coming in on –' he consulted his book, 'TWA 702, little after 6.30.'

Armed with that knowledge, we set off for the airport. Something inexplicable happened on the way. Just before entering the Midtown Tunnel on East 37th Street, we noticed a clock on the side of a building reading 4.15. 'Synchronise watches,' Cathy ordered. Now, the route from midtown Manhattan to Kennedy Airport meanders through the borough of Queens, first via the Long Island Expressway, then along the major artery of Queens Boulevard, and finally down the Van Wyck Expressway and into the airport. Depending on traffic, it takes anywhere from forty-five to ninety minutes. When we pulled up outside the TWA terminal, we checked our watches. Only sixteen minutes had passed since leaving Manhattan – a physical impossibility. Spooksome. We excitedly discussed the possibility we'd been caught in a time warp till someone pointed out that it just gave us more time to wait in the cold.

Frank the chauffeur turned up a little after six, so at least we knew we were in the right place. The Rollers shuffled out half an hour later, sleepy and blank-faced. We were the only fans around, but we'd agreed not to get out of the car so we could leave as soon as they did. Leslie wandered toward us, mistaking the long, boxy Heap for a limo in the darkness. He was actually reaching for the door handle when one of the others hauled him away.

'The car chase will go down in Tacky Tartan Tart legend,' says my diary:

I stuck with them, 2 inches behind, at 80 mph all the way back to the city. I was cutting cars off all over the place, and at one point I bumped the limo. Frank told us later that Tam closed his eyes and the BCRs opened theirs very wide. Anyway, they checked into the Warwick Hotel on 54th, and David got us a room. We spent the morning trying to find them. They were on the 18th floor, which we didn't find out till about 2.00.

The knowledge didn't do us much good. We were too conspicuous skulking around the eighteenth floor, and the hotel was at any rate unable to cope with all the fans both inside and outside its doors. By mid-afternoon, it had asked the band to leave. They moved uptown to the Essex House, while we were stuck in the Warwick, having already paid for the room.

The gig at the Academy was mayhem. The place was an old vaudeville hall on East 14th Street, and while it had hosted numerous rock gigs, it wasn't designed to cope with infants in full pop arousal. The audience jumped on seats till they broke, made the balcony bounce and blindly hurled themselves at the stage. Even the bouncers were scared.

The Tacky Tartan Tarts were in the front row, and we'd dressed to catch the band's eye. I'd even bought some expensive silk pantyhose to go with the black skirt and red high heels I'd deemed it necessary to wear. The pantyhose were goners in seconds, shredded by a kid behind me as she climbed from her seat into mine. I shoved her back into her seat none too politely, but moments later she was joined by scores of other brats, all determined to reach the band. I gave up defending my place and watched the show crushed against the stage, one leg bent for leverage. The other Tarts did the same. Sue J even used her elbows to fend kids off, but she was too short and they were too many.

I never really enjoyed the shows, not just because of the crowds but because my mind was always on following them afterward. The gig was just the starter; the main course came when they left the venue and we hared off after them. I was never sure what we'd do if, just once, we'd followed them and got them on their own. We were a bit like those dogs who chase cars – what would they do if they caught one?

After this particular gig we followed them up Central Park

South to the Essex House, through whose door they swept without so much as a glance at us. After grumbling about this for a while, Sue J suggested going back to the Academy. Her brother-in-law worked there as a stagehand, and she figured he'd let us into their dressing room so we could see what they'd left behind.

Which he did, admonishing, 'Be cool.' He didn't have to worry; there was almost no one around, anyway, now that the band had left.

We struck lucky. On the table was a hairbrush full of long, dark-brown hair and a bit of gel, which the Rollers used by the hundredweight to keep their distinctive 'tuftie' hairdos sticking up. Near it were two paper towels streaked with beige foundation. They used makeup? Applied with paper towels? This was a thing. It was understandable that they needed the camouflage – they really did have pimple problems. But there was something gross about the idea of them shoveling it on with towels.

We moved into the Essex House the next afternoon. The hotel was one of a row of grand 1920s behemoths facing Central Park, and accordingly cost a fortune even for our small twin. Split five ways it was just about affordable, and we picked up an extra ten bucks by charging Sue J's friend Karen for hanging-out privileges.

Karen actually proved an asset. 'She went down to Eric's room and listened at the door. He was watching TV and once blew his nose – hey! The rest of them returned from dinner at 11.30 and caught Karen sitting outside the door and Tam raved at her. By midnight everyone was in bed including us, cos we had to be up for work.'

11

I KNOW WHAT you're thinking. What fueled our obsession? Did we ever get to sleep with them? Did we want to?

I can't speak for the others, but I certainly wanted to. And I believe Cathy would have laid down her virginity for Leslie (she and I were still bickering over who owned him, by the way). I had an urge for Leslie that was more intense than my love for Robert Plant, deeper than my lingering crush on the best-looking boy in Millburn, Mark Winkels. I knew from the first time I saw McKeown that, if the circumstances were ever right – though I couldn't imagine how they ever would be – I'd do it. I wouldn't have to think twice.

That was the tragedy of it. We were desperate to join the sexual revolution but our potential schtupees were thwarting us by being unattainable. We were at the peak of our youth and were squandering it on men who barely knew we existed.

Psychologists have it that girls idolise teen bands because it's a safe way of exploring their sexuality without actually having sex – because, of course, most girls never get to meet their idols. With us it was different. We *wanted* to meet them, wanted to sleep with them. Ideally, we wanted to be their girlfriends, but sleeping with them would do. If that sounds cut and dried, let me remind you that it was the seventies, when abstinence was almost abnormal. I wonder if the Rollers ever knew what they were ignoring.

But they, I suppose, were spoiled for choice. It appeared

they did conduct some sort of discreet sex life; Tam had told *Rolling Stone* magazine, 'They're very choosy about who they sleep with.' Presumably, they even indulged on tour now and then. But with whom? Thirteen-year-old fans were out of the question, but where did they meet women their own age? Here we were, only a few years younger – we were perfect for them.

But it was obviously a buyer's market, and we, the would-be sellers, had no leverage. The most we could do was hope they would notice us. It didn't matter that after a year we'd never properly spoken to them and were unlikely to have anything in common with them. We just wanted, badly, to possess them.

12

THEY WERE IN NEW YORK for six days, during which we frequently saw them trundling in and out of the Essex House. ASCAP was only a few blocks from the hotel, so Emma and I spent our lunch hours sitting outside – separately, because we'd fallen out at the gig. She alleged – in fact, still alleges, twenty-two years later – that I'd deliberately stepped on her in the crush next to the stage. I probably *had* squashed her, but who could have helped it in that mob? She spurned all my apologies, icily ignoring me in the office and at our lunchtime vigils.

The situation grew so tense the rest of the Tarts were forced to take sides. By now the five of us – Emma, Cathy, the Sues and I – were so closely knit that it was impossible to avoid each other, and when two argued, everyone got embroiled. Emma finally relented, but has never hesitated to bring it up since. 'What can I expect from you?' she'll say. 'You used me as a stepladder.'

Our little clique was originally based on the assumption that it would be easier to get to the Rollers in numbers than individually. For the first couple of months the band were the glue keeping the Tacky Tartan Tarts together, but as we developed a history, something permanent emerged that gradually rivaled the Rollers in importance. The bonds established when you wait outside a hotel at midnight in January are strong, and the simple sharing of experience became as meaningful as our actual sightings of the Rollers. Men don't seem to form the same bonds that come of fantasising and mutual encouragement ('Eric will love you in that skirt'), yet they have the nerve to joke about the passion girls expend on teen idols. My own disloyal boyfriend refers to my BCR years as 'tragic'. Would that he knew.

My first mission after the Rollers left town was to buy a silver metallic jacket like the one Leslie had worn for most of their visit. I tracked the thing down to Bloomingdale's and unhesitatingly handed over $65, two-thirds of a week's salary. It was really naff – made of some sort of heavy nylon and studded with patches emblazoned 'Pontiac'. I was incredibly proud of it, and bought a shiny gold handbag from hip Fiorucci to match.

I was in particularly fine fettle that Saturday afternoon, because in the morning I'd found out something delicious regarding Leslie. I was listening to my tape recording of the Academy gig, and when they got to the song 'You're A Woman', written by Faulkner and Wood, Leslie changed one of the lines.

Instead of 'What happened to the girl I used to know?' he sang, 'What happened to the boy I used to know?' Shiver me timbers, what was this? Was he just bored with singing the usual drippy lyrics? Or – ooh! – was a different side of his sexuality rearing its head? He was a man of profound mystery. I was utterly enthralled. Take me, for God's sake, I'm yours.

Life continued Roller-centrically. One night a month or so later, the Sues, Cathy and I went to see the Electric Light Orchestra, the flute-tootling, cello-sawing Brit-rockers then at the height of their popularity. Honesty compels me to admit that that was still the kind of music we enjoyed when the Rollers weren't around. Get a load of my gig list for January and February 1977: The Rollers, January 8, The Kinks, 29, Average White Band, 30, Sutherland Brothers & Quiver, February 1, 2 and 9 (I must have really liked them), Electric Light Orchestra, 11, Mr Big, whoever they were, 13, and

Renaissance (an English ensemble who fused classical music and rock, back in the days when rock was forever hooking up with more refined genres to try and gain respectability), 18.

I mention ELO because while we were in the bar at the gig, we happened to come across Danny Fields, the editor of the biggest teen mag in the country, *16*. We recognised him from the picture on the Letters to Danny page, so naturally we eavesdropped on his conversation, and were electrified to hear him say he was going to Florida the next day to see the Rollers tape a TV show.

We figured that if we could find where Fields was staying, we'd find the Rollers. The next morning I got on the phone, and I'm still impressed by my cunning. Surprisingly, Fields was listed in the phone book, so I waited till he'd probably left for the airport, then rang his number, hoping he'd left his where-abouts on an answering machine. Instead, a male voice answered.

Me: 'Is Mr Danny Fields there, please?'

Voice: 'Sorry, he's away this weekend.'

Me: 'Do you have a number where I can reach him, sir? It's Western Union. Telegram for him.'

Voice: 'Uh . . . [muffled sound of paper being shuffled] . . . he's at the North Bay Village Holiday Inn in Miami, but I haven't got the number.'

Me: 'Don't worry, sir, we'll look it up.'

Which I did, congratulating myself on my cleverness. Then I called the Holiday Inn, and had the following exchange.

Me: 'Has Mr Danny Fields arrived yet?'

Holiday Inn woman with generic singsong operator tones: 'Checking for you . . . yes, Mr Fields is registered. Would you like me to connect you?'

Me[hastily]: 'Oh, no, not yet . . . could you check to see if you've got a Mr Leslie McKeown – M-C-K-E-O-W-N?'

Operator: 'One moment . . . no, ma'am, no one by that name.'

Me [worriedly]: 'What about Stuart Wood?'

Operator: 'No, ma'am.'

Me [in harrassed-executive voice]: 'Can you check again, please? My secretary made those reservations, and they're confirmed. They must be there.'

Operator [after short pause while she consulted with someone in background]: 'Sorry about that, ma'am. I have to be careful who I give this information to, but yes, Mr Wood and Mr McKeown are expected later.'

Me: 'I'll call later. Thanks.'

I was absurdly pleased for having traced them so adeptly. I wrote: 'I found them myself with no help from anyone – I conned the info out of everyone myself! It was great – I just felt so clever! Now that we know where they are, I don't know what good it'll do, though.'

No good at all, as it happened. We weren't about to call any of the band because our tacit rule was that all encounters with them were to be face-to-face. Phoning was a no-no, because it was sure to annoy them. But I did call the hotel receptionist daily for the next six days, just to see if they were still there. That month's phone bill came to $54, an absolute fortune.

'The Rollers are now so much a part of me that if I suddenly stopped caring, there wouldn't be anything to put in their place. But I'm not ready to give them up,' I scrawled on February 19, the week after they left Miami.

February 25 was Woody's twentieth birthday. David and I celebrated with chocolate cream pie and party hats, David donning his only after bullying and threats. The next day I packaged up a few of my better photographs of Woody and sent them by registered mail to his mother. Though he himself was now living with Eric on a farm in remote countryside outside Edinburgh, his family address was an open secret among fans, and Mrs Wood was said to be good about answering letters. She didn't answer mine, but at least she signed the delivery receipt, which went straight into the scrapbook.

When I told Cathy about it, she also decided to befriend a Roller mother. She was craftier, though. She wrote to Pat McGlynn's mother, correctly guessing that the newest addition to the band would have fewer fans. She promptly received a letter back from Mrs McGlynn, which turned into a regular correspondence. Mrs M used girlish floral notepaper, writing a few lines on each page in a cluttered script (most of the Rollers also had cramped, old-fashioned hands, as if they'd been taught penmanship by a Victorian headmaster). She seemed more interested in hearing about Cathy's swinging life in Brooklyn than in discussing her son, greatly disappointing us.

In any case, their budding relationship didn't last, because in April, Pat left the band. 'He just didn't cut the mustard,' said the PR company mysteriously, and as with Ian Mitchell's departure, no other explanation was forthcoming. Frankly, we weren't surprised. McGlynn had never fitted in, never lost the slack-jawed look of shock that was his habitual expression. When they decided he had to go, they liquidated him swiftly and then maintained a Stalinist silence, so that after a few months you weren't sure whether he'd ever really existed. In his five-month hitch, the poor thing had only done a couple of gigs and never even got to make a record.

Or did he? Twenty years later he popped up in the news again, claiming he *had* played on their fifth album, *It's a Game*, which they recorded in early 1977. He alleged that not only was he not credited on the sleeve, they'd even cut his picture out of the cover shot. Even if true, it's probably been a good thing for McGlynn in the long run. None of the BCRs' records was anywhere near good enough that you'd actually want your name on it, and some of them were so terrible that you'd have paid to have it removed.

As I write, I'm listening to 1976's *Dedication* album. It opens with an Eric Carmen song, 'Let's Pretend', which climaxes, and I use the word advisedly, with a verse about not being able to wait to seduce some little charmer. Leslie's frail voice cracks on the high notes, and his simulation of adolescent lovemaking is so hideously embarrassing that I've had to skip to the next song.

But the next song, an Eric-Woody ballad called 'You're A Woman', is just as wet. 'Oh, you're a woman, and you know what love is for/You say you don't need me/You're not a little girl any more'.

And then, a change of pace – a noisy guitar number, 'Rock 'n' Roller'. Another Eric 'n' Woody job. (They were the group's creative nucleus, gradually taking over most of the songwriting from professional songwriters Bill Martin and Phil Coulter, who wrote much of their early material.) It opens with a burst of squealing guitar and walloping drums, and Leslie grunts, 'Get my kicks from rock 'n' roll/ Twelve-bar boogie gonna bless my soul/Gonna dance to that rockin' beat/I wanna be a rock 'n' roll star/Make my money from playin' guitar . . .'

There's something unspeakably pitiful about those lines and their archaic reference to 'twelve-bar boogie'. It explained the bleakness that often attended them. They really did want to be rock 'n' roll stars. Proper rock 'n' roll stars, that is, respected by their peers and fancied by women over the age of consent. They'd never set out to be teen idols – no band did back then.

Eric felt it especially keenly, having once revealed that in embryonic incarnations of the Rollers he loved nothing more than inflicting 'five-minute guitar solos' on audiences (if only Led Zeppelin had restricted their guitar solos to just five minutes). Fate made him a teen star, and his frustration was writ large.

But the most poignant song on *Dedication* is side one's closer, 'Yesterday's Hero'. This track is, as far as I'm aware, the only recorded instance of a teen act acknowledging that stardom is inevitably transient.

When I walk down the street
See the people stop and stare, and say
Haven't I seen your face somewhere a long time ago?
We don't wanna be yesterday's hero, yesterday's hero
That's all that we're gonna be if we don't get it together
Make a new plan and be constantly better . . .

You have to admire them for facing up to their obsolescence so unflinchingly – even if, when they recorded it, it seemed a long way off.

Anyway, back to McGlynn. He was gone by April, but there was little time to mourn him, because his departure coincided with news of a major tour the following month, starting May 9. It would be their first cross-country jaunt, taking in both coasts and lots of virgin territory in the middle. We bought tickets for the four closest gigs – Westchester, Poughkeepsie, Philadelphia and Pittsburgh – and then, in a moment of madness, for Chicago, too. Chicago is two hours' flying time from New York, almost a third of the way across the country. Were we nuts? Undoubtedly.

It took a lot of careful co-ordination, and more money than we could afford. There was also the problem of persuading David to lend us The Heap for a week, and of getting time off work. The latter was actually the least of my worries, as I was thoroughly sick of my ASCAP job and its endless typing, and was hoping to get fired so I could collect unemployment.

The whole tour was thrown into jeopardy in mid-April when we heard a rumor that Eric had quit the group. We took the news with a pinch of salt because it came from Barbarino, who was always coming out with stuff like that. Improbably, since the night we'd queued with him – y'know, when he'd invited Emma to make the acquaintance of his nasty little pecker – we had become friends with him. He was still chummy with the other fan-faction, but he hung around with us most of the time now, and was always full of outlandish gossip. He had some never-explained connection at Arista, and was frequently privy to juicy bits of information. But he was unreliable, getting it wrong more often than he got it right. This time he was wrong, but he threw us into such an uproar that Sue J threatened to kick his ass, frightening him so much that we didn't hear from him for the best part of a week.

A Pat McGlynn eulogy:

Just before he quit the band, he had turned nineteen. Obviously, we had had to celebrate, but he was so faceless we'd been at a loss. My diary records: 'Since we don't have a clearly developed personality for him, we just sang Happy Birthday and each had a Twinkie.'

13

I REMEMBER THAT PERIOD as an unbroken Roller-thon, but in fact my interest in punk was beginning to rival my devotion to the Rollers. 'The whole idea of punk is very cute. Anyway, it's better than disco', remarks my diary, failing to grasp that punk was more than 'cute', it was a musical and cultural watershed. To me, it was just better than disco, which was anathema to little suburban girls.

I went to see Blondie open for Iggy Pop, and was perplexed by Debbie Harry. Didn't she realise she'd forgotten to bleach the whole back of her head, and it was dark brown? Oh, that was punk. I see. Cool!

Sue J and I went to see The Damned, our first experience of a genuine spitting, pogoing English punk group. We were very impressed, especially when the vampire-like singer, Dave Vanian (as in Transyl . . .), denounced the crowd as 'fucking tossers'. Enchanting.

Punk had dominated the UK music press for the last year, but predictably America was slow to warm to it. The average American just had a thing against groups with safety pins in their faces. They didn't mind American punks, embodied by the burgeoning New York scene founded by Blondie, The Ramones and Television; it was the more political Brit-punks they had a problem with.

Hence, few of them toured the States. Many of them had (or purported to have) convenient anti-American sentiments, so it was a mutually satisfactory arrangement. They didn't want to come to America, and America sure as hell didn't want them.

But I did. I was deeply curious to see the Sex Pistols, The Clash and the other groups I kept reading about. So imagine my excitement when I heard the Sex Pistols were planning a whole week of gigs in New York in June. At least, that's what I was told by a girl named Barbara, whose rock-promoter boyfriend was supposedly behind the event.

I met Barbara at ASCAP. She was a songwriter-member whose name I'd come to recognise from filing her cards. Each time a writer wrote a new song, we were obliged to note the fact on filecards, and hers had stood out for having titles like 'Hot Chocolate Cock'. So when Barbara dropped by the office one April afternoon, I knew who she was, and was surprised to find she seemed quite normal. We got talking, and she mentioned that her boyfriend was putting together a month-long punk festival, the highlight of which was to be the Pistols' first American appearance. The boyfriend needed people to help get it all together, she added. Did I want to get involved?

Did I?! I went down the venue, a dilapidated downtown movie theatre called The Elgin, that very night. The boyfriend, Harry, had set up an office in the basement and put me to work answering the phone. It wasn't much, but I was proud to be doing my bit to bring the Sex Pistols to New York. As Harry explained it, their gigs would be the cherry on the cake of three weeks of shows by big punk names. And which names were those? Well, the only ones confirmed so far were a handful of unknown New York bands. But he was working on getting Patti Smith, Television and lots of others. It was all but definite.

He felt sufficiently confident to place an ad in the *Village Voice*, which brought dozens of calls. But by the week before opening night, the slipshod nature of the whole operation had become obvious. In a final act of disorganisation the night before we opened, Harry failed to return a call from the Pistols' manager, Malcolm McLaren. Not that it mattered, really, as the Pistols had never officially been confirmed, and in any case never intended to play.

Amazingly, the festival actually went ahead, though in severely truncated form. Opening night, which was also closing night, saw a host of bedraggled unknowns playing to fewer than 100 paying customers. Most of the many journalists and radio people Harry had invited failed to attend – I knew, because I was in charge of the guest list. The last I saw of old Harry, he and Barbara were arguing at the back of the auditorium about whether she should step in and do a quick set of her own. 'Hot Chocolate Cock' probably would have gone down well.

But it wasn't a total loss. I had been inspired by my conversation with McLaren the night before, which had gone thus:

Me: 'Hello, Elgin Punk Festival.'

McLaren [in nasal Cockney accent]: 'May I speak to Harry?'

Me: 'I'm sorry, he's not here right now.'

McLaren: 'Would you tell him to ring Malcolm McLaren? He's got the number.'

The Malcolm McLaren – and I'd talked to him. Fired up by it, I decided to buy some punk clothes. The only shop in Manhattan that stocked anything of the sort was a joint called Ian's – there was supposedly no Ian, they just used the name because it sounded English – in the West Village. Going there after work one night, I was pleased to find a T-shirt with a picture of a safety pin and the legend 'Anarchy in the UK'. Almost as groovishly, they also had black straight-leg jeans. Straight-legs were all but impossible to find in that flarey era, and owning a pair meant you were so hip you probably came from London – exactly the impression I was trying to give.

The shirt and jeans were a timely purchase because, with the Roller tour just weeks away, we had to start thinking about what we called our 'tour wardrobes'. We always bought new stuff for their gigs, on the off-chance that we'd meet them, and this time we went all-out. We'd be needing two separate wardrobes – one for the gigs and one for the long hours we'd be spending in The Heap, driving from show to show. Emma went rural-English with floral pinafores, Cathy was minimal in lots of white and I opted for the Bianca Jagger look with the straight-leg pants, antique chiffon tops and silk flower brooches.

As an afterthought, I made up little 'tour passes'. On white index cards I typed 'Tacky Tartan Tarts On Tour', with each person's self-chosen Tart pseudonym underneath. (Emma was Angie Wooburn, Sue J was P H O'Tographer and the rest of us had similarly foolish names. No, I'm not divulging mine.) There was a space for their signature and my own 'counter-signature', and when each Tart had signed her card I glued a strip of tartan ribbon to the bottom of the card, then took the whole lot to Woolworth's and used their laminating machine to seal them. Then I glued a safety pin on the back so we could wear them.

They looked amazingly realistic. While they'd never have passed muster for getting backstage, if they made bouncers at the venues think we worked for Arista and they let us stand right at the front, we weren't going to argue.

The tour started on Monday, May 9, at the Westchester Premiere Theatre, thirty-odd miles north of Manhattan. We assembled at my place, because that was where The Heap was, and after we'd finished primping, Sue J took a picture of us in my living room. It's in front of me now. Sue P and Cathy are wearing the white jacket/black shirt combo that John Travolta would later immortalise in *Saturday Night Fever*, Emma is pretty in a long flowery dress and I'm, well, exotic in a black kimono I'd picked up in Chinatown. Our hair, flicked and wedge-cut, is gleaming flossily, and the tour passes are proudly affixed to our tops. We look grand.

The show, which started at the surprisingly adult hour of 9 p.m., was more interesting than usual in a musical sense.

And in a sartorial sense, too, since only Woody was sporting what you could call Rollergear. The others, presumably to their great relief, were wearing normal clothes, with only a discreet hint of plaid on the hems of their jackets.

And musically – yes, things were different, all right. For a start, the first half of the show consisted entirely of songs from their as-yet unreleased new album, *It's a Game*. And these new songs weren't your typical shang-a-langers, either. There was a decidedly disco-ish edge to some of them, and cosmicky lyrics on others ('The faces all around me, they are running everywhere/But everywhere is nowhere, and nowhere isn't there').

There was a number by the Rollers called 'Sweet Virginia' that seemed to be about a lesbian (the pertinent bit went 'Is it really such a crime/To be loving your own kind?') and they even covered David Bowie's 'Rebel Rebel', which went unrecognised by most of the audience. Eric sang lead on that one in quite the most unmelodious voice you can imagine.

It gave us plenty to think about on the drive back to Manhattan. Obviously, the new clothes and new songs were a valiant attempt to break out of the teen-band ghetto. The funny thing, we agreed as we slowly cruised down Park Avenue, trying to find their hotel, was that they might just do it. Led Zep wouldn't be losing any sleep, but these new tunes of Woody and Eric's had much more *oomph* than anything they'd done before. They were, dare I say it, verging on the sexy.

'Roller at nine o'clock!' Sue P suddenly bayed. Our heads simultaneously snapped to the left. There, entering the swanky Waldorf-Astoria Hotel, was Eric. We parked around the corner and followed him in, expecting them all to be in the lobby. Strangely, there was no sign of anyone except Eric, who was disappearing into an elevator.

We figured the rest would be along soon, and settled down on one of the Waldorf's velvet sofas, trying to look as though we weren't desperately hoping to encounter the Bay City Rollers. Eric reappeared five minutes later, stalking over to the reception desk to collect some messages. He met our gaze levelly, and we smiled. Ignoring us, he got back into the elevator.

He could only have been gone a few minutes before he rematerialised, this time to buy cigarettes. Again the glance at us and the hurriedly averted face. This happened twice more – the disappearance and reappearance – and we were at a loss to understand his behaviour. Was he testing us to see how long we'd wait? Reassuring himself that he had fans? (Hmmph – if he'd asked, I would have informed him I was there for Leslie.) Simply drawn to our collective gorgeousness but too shy to talk to us?

As we were speculating, Joey from our rival faction wandered in. 'You looking for the others?' he inquired, in his irritatingly superior way. 'They're at Maxwell's Plum. I've just been there.'

We trusted him like Kennedy had trusted Khrushchev, but we'd been sitting in the lobby for half an hour, and figured we might as well take a drive. Off we went to Maxwell's Plum, a tacky Upper East Side singles bar populated by Queens secretaries and their male counterparts. Not the sort of place you'd expect to find the Rollers, but there they were, sprawled around a large table and chowing down on the remnants of jumbo lobsters. Derek was drinking milk. (So all that business about the Rollers and milk wasn't entirely fictitious.)

Although we positioned ourselves a discreet twenty feet away at the bar, they were aware of us almost immediately. Leslie, finishing his dinner, lit a cigarette and fixed us with a very hard stare. We tried to blend into the background, which wasn't difficult; it was midnight and the joint was heaving. But each time we glanced over, we found Leslie glaring, arms folded across his chest, like a bouncer dying to introduce his boot to the nearest head. After twenty minutes we were embarrassed into leaving.

The next four days are a blur. I took the rest of the week off work, not least in the hope of getting fired. The Rollers went to Boston for a gig on Wednesday, and we consoled ourselves by listening to an advance copy of their new single, 'You Made Me Believe in Magic', which Barbarino had procured from his mysterious Arista source.

The B-side, 'Dance, Dance, Dance', was highly intriguing. Contrary to the title, it wasn't a dance song, but a soul-searching meditation on a love affair written by the Bay City Rollers. And the lyric was very grown up, for them: 'I heard the words you said inside my loving bed [they said "bed"!!], I've seen the scars I left inside your loving head'. The words were clumsy, but the meaning was clear: they were writing adult songs about adult emotions.

The problem was, they weren't reaching an adult audience. At the next three gigs, Poughkeepsie, Philadelphia and Pittsburgh, the Tacky Tartan Tarts were the only people other than the group themselves who didn't have to be in bed by 9 p.m. The Pittsburgh show was even a matinee, for Christ's sake.

The band were tangibly frustrated. In Poughkeepsie, the shrieking girls vexed McKeown to the point that he hissed at them to shut up, which of course incited them to sob even more relentlessly. In Philadelphia, he tried another tack. As if it would bestow credibility, he and Eric mimicked David Bowie and Mick Ronson's famous homoerotic stage routine. Leslie, as Bowie, knelt in front of Eric/Ronson and nibbled at his guitar, then looked at the kids, who were foaming at the mouth, and winked. But the reference went over most heads, and he shrugged.

The stage set was another manifestation of their – as we rock critics put it – new direction. The backdrop and floor were a giant black-and-white chessboard, augmented by four huge chess pieces at the front of the stage. When the stagelights went on, the Rollers stepped out from behind the chess pieces (please stop laughing), the implication being, I suppose, that we are all players in the chess game of life.

If that sounds preposterous, I assume you haven't seen the sleeve of the album *It's a Game*. 'Sleeve concept by the Rollers', it says, which explains a few things. The front cover used the chessboard theme, the board stretching into infinity, which was represented by celestial lightning in a night sky. The back was even better. More lightning, and in one corner the Rollers, naked from the waist up and not a chest hair between them. You ached with sympathy.

In a piece of wretched timing, the album hadn't yet been released when they toured. The whole point of any band going on the road is to persuade fans to buy their latest record, which should be in the shops from the start of the tour. But *It's a Game* didn't come out until July; a month after the tour had ended.

In the meantime, we clocked up close to 1,000 miles traipsing from Westchester and Poughkeepsie in upstate New York to Pittsburgh, at the extreme western end of Pennsylvania, with Philadelphia in between. As self-appointed admiral of our little expedition – because I semi-owned the Heap – I ran a tight ship. We travelled mostly at night, and I insisted we always leave gigs before the encore so we could pull The Heap up to the stage door and follow when they exited. In so doing we always managed to discover where they were staying, which was generally the local Hilton or Holiday Inn.

Sometime during the week, Barbarino said, 'I was talking to Leslie backstage [yeah, he wished] and he goes, "When I see Caroline driving, I hide my head in my hands and pray for my life." ' Knowing Barbarino, Leslie probably hadn't said anything of the sort, but if he had, I was flattered beyond words that he knew my name. Any recognition, no matter how unverifiable, sustained me for days.

Poughkeepsie and Philadelphia passed without incident, which was a drag, because we were panting for incident. But they were maddeningly elusive in both cities, failing to show their faces once they'd returned to their hotel each night.

They seemed to be deliberately snubbing us, or at least they were no longer making eye contact or smiling. There could have been any number of reasons for this, such as tension resulting from McGlynn's sacking, or a falling-out with Tam Paton, who, extraordinarily, wasn't on the tour.

Even worse than their puzzling remoteness was the introduction of a new tour manager. His name, Larry Packer, was soon changed by us to Pecker because of his ill-treatment of fans. Where Tam sometimes allowed you to exchange a few words with the band, Pecker was set on preventing all contact. Cathy and I composed a song about him, set to the tune of Leo Sayer's current hit, 'When I Need You'. It went, in part,

> When we want you
> We just read *16* and we're with you
> But all that we try to do to you
> Is stopped by Pecker every day
> When we need sex
> Pecker does his best to break our necks
> Never knew so many roadies were struggling to keep
>   us away . . .

The Pittsburgh show on May 14 was a sort of watershed. It began and ended peculiarly, and by the time it was over, our perception of the Rollers had changed.

Faced with a 350-mile drive to Pittsburgh, we left Philadelphia at three in the morning. None of us had slept, and we were short-tempered and bleary. When dawn broke we were in the mountainous country of central Pennsylvania, where tunnels with Indian names like Tuscarora and Kittatinny were hewn through solid granite. These rural mountain tunnels struck us as unspeakably odd, and for the first time we realised how far we were from home.

Sue P and I took turns driving while Cathy and Emma slept in the back. A few miles outside Pittsburgh, we pulled into a

Howard Johnson's Motor Lodge for breakfast. We'd been driving for eight hours, and were pretty well spaced out by then. There's a picture of us in the restaurant parking lot, leaning on each other's shoulders as we dazedly looked at the camera. If only the Rollers knew what we went through for them. In fact, they did know, but chose to ignore it, our tenacity damning us in their eyes. But if we hadn't been persistent, they'd never have noticed us at all. Damned if we were, damned if we weren't.

We wearily pressed on to the airport, meeting their plane and following them to a Hilton in the middle of the city, where the driver briefly stopped, then drove off with the band. Assuming they were staying at this hotel, we went in and got a room. Not such a good idea, because after we'd checked in and paid, we discovered they weren't there after all. Pigs-will.

Cathy resolutely got out the Yellow Pages. She got lucky on the second attempt, finding Pecker registered at the Hyatt. But we couldn't afford to lose the fifty bucks we'd just coughed up, so we were stuck where we were.

The gig, which commenced at the ungodly hour of 3 p.m., was disappointing. We'd been awake for nearly thirty hours, but the Rollers' lack of enthusiasm penetrated our stupor. They were in the lowest spirits we'd ever witnessed, going through the motions with blank apathy. When Leslie played guitar on one number – he did this every show, to prove he could – he stared at the floor, marking time till the song ended.

Maybe playing in the middle of the afternoon, a time when most bands would just be starting to think about breakfast, was for them cruel confirmation that they were, and would ever be, a teenybopper band.

Naturally, it didn't stop us from going over to the Hyatt afterwards. No sign of the Rollers – they'd already gone to their rooms – but the reception was full of middle-aged Middle Americans in animated conversation. At least, they seemed to be conversing, but the lobby was silent. In the packed cocktail lounge, an eerie stillness prevailed, broken by a whisper of fluttering fingers. Then we saw the badges: 'American Association for the Deaf'. It was their convention. As queer days went, this was certainly one of the queerest we'd had in a while.

The Tarts were the only fans around, unless some of the deaf people were Rollermaniacs. So it was just us 'n' them, and we decided to be proactive. Leslie was in Room 1138, the receptionist had told us, and the four of us hovered at his door, trying to summon the courage to knock. A door on the other side of the corridor suddenly opened, and there was Eric, clutching an ice bucket. Startled, he took a step back, then sauntered down the hall toward the Coke machine, pretending not to see us. I galumphed after him, with our Eric-fancier, Sue P, just behind.

'Did you enjoy the gig?' I asked. Without stopping, he replied, 'I was a bit tired.'

You're telling me, I thought. You hardly even made an effort. 'Are the kids outside all the hotels getting on your nerves?' I continued – inane question, admittedly, but the point was to keep him talking.

'Oh, they're all right,' Eric answered, his voice scraped raw from barking out 'Rebel Rebel' every night. (The song was his big moment of the set and he always made the most of it, pulling anguished faces, jerking his guitar around and doing everything he could to prove that he was a real musician.)

'They're quite sweet, most of them. It's just when they ring up when I'm trying to sleep.'

I made sympathetic noises that implied that *we'd* never call when he was sleeping, because we were older and more sensible. Know what I mean, Eric? Older, more sensible . . . might I even say sexier? In other words, perfect girlfriend material.

I glanced at him covertly. Gosh, he was pretty. Not as gorge as Leslie, obviously, but he had glossy hair and eyelashes any girl would kill for.

But when he'd got his Coke and ice cubes, he headed back to his room. 'Why don't you come down and have a drink?' Sue suggested, desperation triumphing over shyness. 'Thanks, but I'd better not. I'm just going to watch some TV. Night-night.' The door shut and we heard the chain-lock slipping into place.

At least we'd made contact. It was probably the longest conversation we'd had with any of them. Much encouraged, we returned to the lobby.

'Why don't we send him a bottle of champagne?' Cathy proposed, half-joking.

'So he'll come down and thank us, you mean?'

'No, just because he was sweet.'

So we did, scraping up enough cash between us for a litre of Château l'Hyatt, which we dispatched with a note reading, 'Sleep well. Love, the Girls in the Lobby'.

Then we collapsed on to a sofa and wondered what to do. It was so rare to find the Rollers unbesieged by other fans that we wanted to take advantage of it, but what could we do, other than pray they'd come down to the bar?

And there we were, Cathy, Emma, Sue and me. It was around 10 p.m., and we'd last slept thirty-six hours ago. I felt alert in that brittle way you sometimes get when you're exhausted. With the alertness came a sudden pitiless realisation of how we must look sitting there, arrayed directly opposite the elevator so we could see everyone getting on and off.

We looked like . . . like . . . groupies. Or, worse, fans.

In our minds, we were neither. What we were was . . . well, special fans. Fans old enough to relate to the Rollers in a woman-to-man way. We seriously saw them as potential boyfriends – and such a thing wasn't inconceivable. Many a pop star has met his future wife on the road, and we were probably the only females chasing the Rollers who were close to them in age. We had lives and jobs, and we weren't unattractive. We felt sure that if we could only meet them and have a proper chat, they'd like us.

But suddenly, sitting there in the lobby of the Pittsburgh Hyatt, I saw what the Rollers must have seen – four girls who tailed them relentlessly and were prepared to spend entire nights sleeping in cars to see them. Girls who didn't fit in – too old to be fans, not employed by Arista, no real reason to be there. We were so demeaningly conspicuous that it was no wonder they weren't interested.

The train of thought was mortifying, and I abruptly said, 'Look, they're not coming down. Let's go.'

'Let's just give it another fifteen minutes,' pleaded Cathy.

'Well, I don't think –'

Sue silenced me with an elbow to the chest. 'Look.'

Leslie and Pecker got off the elevator and strode outside and into a taxi. Even if we'd been able to reach The Heap in time, I wasn't about to follow, considering my recent revelations. But I felt, with a mixture of despair and relief, the same adrenaline rush induced by any Roller-sighting, no matter how brief.

'I'm staying here till he gets back,' Cathy announced, setting her mouth like a Victorian spinster. I wavered, then thought, No, I'm not gonna do this any more. I said I'd see them later, and drove back to the Hilton.

The phone woke me a couple of hours later. It was Sue, saying they were bored and about to leave. 'We haven't seen anybody. It's been – what?' There were voices in the back-ground and she suddenly seemed to drop the phone. Then she returned. 'I'll have to call you back. Leslie's just come in with a girl.' She hung up.

'Whaaat?' I screeched, forgetting that I was no longer a fan. Wide awake and burning with curiosity, I waited for her call. But ten minutes later they were back in our room. I opened the door to find Cathy in tears and Emma trying to comfort her. They went into the bathroom and shut the door, but Cathy's sobs were audible.

Sue explained that Leslie and Pecker had returned, accompanied by a blonde girl of around twenty-two. It was clear from the way she snuggled up to him when they got in the elevator that she was with Leslie. That alone was enough to make Cathy burst into tears, and Sue and Emma decided they'd better get her back to our room.

She eventually came out of the bathroom, pale but relatively composed. 'How can I get back at Leslie?' she asked miserably. 'Point at his crotch and laugh?' I suggested.

I don't know why I wasn't just as upset. After all, I was as nuts about Leslie as she was, and this graphic proof that he did indeed go out with girls – just not us – should have hurt me just as much. That it didn't I can only attribute to my prurient streak – I wasn't happy that he was with someone else, particularly someone who obviously wasn't even a fan, but that being the case, I wanted to find out every detail I could.

'She was plain, kinda chubby and she was wearing like a sort of knitted sweater-coat,' was all Sue remembered. 'Oh, yeah, and she works in the newsstand in the hotel.'

'How on earth do you know?'

'Because when they came in the desk clerk goes, "Hi, Debbie", so I went up to him and casually asked if he knew her, and he goes, "That's Debbie Bottom from the newsstand." '

Debbie Bottom, eh? I consolingly told Cathy, who had put on her nightie and was now lying in the other bed, staring at the ceiling, 'Hey, at least your name's not Debbie Bottom.' A sniffle was the only response.

We lingered abed for a long time the next morning, each of us probably thinking more or less the same thing. The Debbie Bottom Affair had put a whole different complexion on things. It was one thing to assume that the Rollers, being healthy young men, probably had sex lives, quite another to actually see evidence of it.

It shook us up more than any of us could have imagined.

Firstly, our devotion to the group was predicated on the idea that they were unattainable. We couldn't get them, but neither could anybody else. And here was Leslie breaking his side of the agreement.

Secondly, the fundamental innocence of the chase was irreparably damaged. If they were picking up chicks on the road, what was there to distinguish them from proper rock bands? And we didn't want a proper band, we wanted the Rollers, who were untouched by the hedonism of the times. If Leslie was picking up girls, did that mean the others were, too?

And lastly, why Miss Bottom and not us?

After breakfast, we headed for the Hyatt to check it out before we started the long drive home. A couple of New York fans were in the lobby. They'd apparently arrived late the night before, and had also seen Leslie and his little friend. Following them to the eleventh floor, they'd sat and listened outside his door for almost six hours, which struck even us as a bit much.

'We heard them talking till about five o'clock – no, we couldn't tell about what – and then they played Eagles tapes till six and then we couldn't hear anything.'

We received this intelligence with varying degrees of dismay. I was more distressed about the Eagles than anything else. If they'd said he'd played *Frampton* I couldn't have been more appalled by his taste.

We were chewing this over when the elevator opened and disgorged what could only have been Debbie Bottom. She ambled across the lobby, lost in thought, and didn't notice Cathy till the latter planted herself in her path.

We watched transfixed, for Cathy was normally the gentlest of souls, but right now she was clearly not herself. 'Did you have a good time?' she demanded, her voice trembling. Debbie Bottom eyed her with alarm and whispered, 'It was all right,' then darted around her, out the door and into a taxi, as if Cathy was waving a machete.

14

I T WAS A LONG DRIVE back to New York – ten hours, not counting time off for lunch, coffee and an hour when the car overheated in the middle of the Pocono Mountains. It happened without warning in the late afternoon, as we were traveling through the Amish country, the rural region of lush cropfields and hex symbols. Steam began to issue dramatically from under the hood, so I pulled over, and as soon as we'd stopped, the other three, fearing an imminent explosion, scrambled out and up a bank. 'Come back here!' I shouted, furious that they were abandoning The Heap in its hour of need.

We eventually got it going again and crawled into Manhattan at midnight. We were quieter than usual as we good-byed and see-you-latered, Sue and Cathy heading for Brooklyn, Emma for The Bronx. The trip home had been more reflective than usual, once we'd exhausted the subject of Debbie Bottom and what we'd like to do to her. We were preoccupied with adjusting our thinking to encompass this new version of Leslie and, by extension, the other BCRs.

Despite the events of the previous twenty-four hours, there was no possibility of our calling it a day. The idea of life without them was unimaginable. Oh, we'd have survived, and eventually even found proper boyfriends. In fact, Emma had just started seeing a guy she'd met on a bus in The Bronx. 'You're going out with a guy from The *Bronx*?' we said, aghast. 'Yeah, but he wears black velvet jackets,' she swooned.

Ah. Black velvet jackets. We could understand that. That was class.

At some level, we realised that this fatalistic devotion was a one-time-only thing that, once gone, could never be recreated, and none of us was ready to stop. At one point during that week, Cathy had said, 'I'll never be this happy again.' Of course, all four of us have been that happy and more since – Emma and Sue at their weddings, Cathy when she got a job at a record company in Los Angeles, me the first time I saw something I'd written in print. But I must say, latter-day happiness has lacked that chocolate-sauce-and-cherry-on-top that was Roller-happiness. A fan summed it up recently on a Roller internet site: 'Life was so simple then.' Quite. For as long as we loved them, real life was a place we only had to visit now and then. Rollerland was our refuge from the adult lives we weren't ready for.

But we had one more gig to attend – Chicago, the next weekend. If it hadn't already been arranged, we might have given it a miss, but Sue P, Cathy and I found ourselves on a Friday-evening flight to O'Hare Airport. After landing – it was almost the furthest I'd ever been from home – we went to the Arie Crown Theatre, where they'd be playing the next night. It was deserted, and we wandered around, scoping out the stage door and equipment entrance, working out how we'd follow them the next day.

The following morning we went to the airport. The ensuing chase was the usual hysterical mêlée of squealing brakes and corners taken on two wheels, which never failed to make us cackle with glee. God knows what the Rollers must have thought each time we raced after them, a gaggle of mad-eyed girls with a grim-faced redhead – me – at the wheel, leaning on the horn to warn the other traffic. We must have looked scary as hell. Anyway, we found a hotel a couple of blocks from theirs, then made for Wrigley Field, home of the White Sox, where they were to judge a dance contest. Of all things.

It was some promotional tie-in with a local radio station, although asking the Rollers to judge dancing was like asking a cook at the local greasy spoon to choose the best monkfish cassoulet. None of them had ever shown any sign of dancing ability. Leslie was probably the best mover (a risibly skinny 8 stone 8 lbs, he was light on his feet), but he didn't have great rhythm, maybe because their music was so unrhythmic.

That didn't stop them from standing way up in the bleachers and pointing to various kids dancing on the field, one of whom was eventually declared the winner and taken up to meet the band. As for us, we were stuck on the field, sixty feet below.

And that was the closest we got to them in Chicago. After the show, we followed their car till their driver jumped a light at Michigan Avenue and lost us. But that was okay, we thought, because we knew where they were staying. At their hotel we did the usual stationing-ourselves-in-the-bar thing and sure enough, half an hour later their limo pulled up. But the people who emerged were Arista employees.

Never mind, maybe they'd gone to a party and would be back. We ordered another round of our new favorite drink, Tab – Coke without the calories – and settled in for the long haul.

At midnight we walked across the street to admire Lake Michigan, sparkling in its hugeness, and resolved to give it another hour. At 1.00, as we nursed our fifth Tabs, the limo returned. Yowsah! The door opened. A foot appeared. It was followed by the Hawaiian-shirted torso and bespectacled face of Pecker. Shit. He was the only passenger, so after he went inside we approached the chauffeur.

Like, where are the pigging Rollers, my good man?

'They're staying at the promoter's house in the suburbs,' he said, sounding so matter-of-fact that we believed him.

In a last-ditch attempt, we returned to their hotel for break-fast in the morning. There was no sign of the Rollers, or of anyone connected with them. They had clearly left Chicago. We felt abandoned and sheepish. 'This has been a complete waste,' said Cathy. 'Completely,' we agreed. It was so dis-appointing.

Work was as dreary as ever Monday morning, so I decided to take the next day off. I got home Tuesday afternoon from seeing a movie to the not unexpected news that I'd been fired. Well, it was about time. No more typing, no more filing, no more waking up at seven, and especially no more spending good Roller-time closeted in an airless little office. The only thing I'd miss was the typewriter, which had come in handy for *The Tartan Pervert*.

I went downtown the next morning to apply for unemploy-ment, and there discovered that I hadn't worked at ASCAP long enough to qualify for benefits. Now, this put a spanner in the so-called works. I'd been counting on unemployment to tide me over till I could force myself to look for a new job. Instead, I was going to have to start looking there and then.

I began a half-hearted search at the end of the week, trawling around all the major record companies to fill out applications for secretarial jobs. But there wasn't much going for someone of my skills, which amounted to an ability to type without too many mistakes if I went slowly enough. After a couple of days, I realised that no record company would take me on, even if I did know absolutely everything about the current British music scene. I'd have to go back to my bank job, if they'd have me, which they probably wouldn't, or try something like waitressing.

To cheer me up, David gave Pecker one of his special phoney phonecalls. Tracking him down in Oklahoma City, David informed him that our fourteen-year-old daughter had gone missing, and we believed she was travelling with one of the Rollers. I don't know how he thought 'em up.

Pecker's protests were audible as David thundered that he'd take a very dim view of Pecker allowing such a young girl to hang around a rock band. His irate parent act was perfect – I often wondered why he'd never considered going into acting.

Pecker finally convinced him that he hadn't seen our kid, and then, improbably, the two of them lapsed into guy-chat about life on the road. 'I'm just in the middle of booking the Japanese tour,' I could hear him saying. 'And I'm also writing an article for *16* magazine about being on the road with these guys.'

I frantically scribbled a note: 'Get some dirt!!!'

David obligingly said, 'I guess they can get pretty wild when they're on tour, huh?'

'Nah,' he chuckled. 'The wildest they get is that Les smokes. Hey, he's not your daughter's favorite, is he, Dave?' ('Dave'!!)

Thank God David was so well-versed on the Rollers, because he was able to confidently reply, 'No, she likes Woody, 'cause he's the youngest.'

Pecker chuckled richly. 'Well, in that case I can definitely assure you that she's not with us, because Woody doesn't fool around on the road.'

A few more pleasantries and they hung up. 'Seems like a really nice guy,' David commented. 'Nice! That's Pecker you're talking about!' I spluttered, betrayed. Jeez. Men, huh? Not worth the paper they're printed on.

Two weeks later I still hadn't found a job, so, dispirited, I decided to curtail my search for a while. During my working months I'd saved about $1,000, so there was enough to live on, especially since David bought the groceries and paid the bills.

I spent most days lounging on the couch, stupefied by the June heat, or hanging around Bleecker Bob's record shop in the Village. Bob's was one of the few places you could get imports, and he was so on-the-ball that he had stuff like the Pistols' 'God Save the Queen' the same week it was released in Britain.

Increasingly fascinated by punk, on one visit that month I bought 'God Save the Queen' and the first Jam single, 'In The City', to add to my collection, which consisted of The

Damned's debut album and a Nick Lowe single, 'So It Goes'.
While I was in the shop I also read *Melody Maker*, taking care
not to crease the pages so Bob would make me buy it, and
noted that 'God Save the Queen' was causing a bit of fuss in
England, where the Queen was about to celebrate her jubilee.
It seemed the record was deemed offensive because of the lyric,
which contained observations to the effect that the monarchy
was fascist. I tried to imagine an American group having the
guts to come up with something called 'The President Sucks',
couldn't, and decided the Sex Pistols were eminently worth the
$10 Bob had just soaked me for for the single.

15

'GET UP HERE immediately,' commanded Sue J as soon as I picked up the phone. 'I'm at the Plaza, and Tam is here. How should I know what he's doing? You'd better get over here right now.'

It was a muggy, overcast Saturday in mid-June. The Rollers' tour was over and they were safely back in Scotland, so there didn't seem any reason for Tam to be in New York. I got a cab – hang the expense – and arrived five minutes before Tam left the hotel in the customary long black car. Sues P and J and I followed in a taxi, and a dozen other fans crammed into two more cabs behind us. He alighted at Bloomingdale's, the posho department store on Lexington Avenue, and pretended not to notice us as we piled on to the escalator three feet behind him, but by the time he reached the men's department he decided to acknowledge us.

'Are you a Pat fan, then?' he asked a chubby girl in a T-shirt with 'Pat' printed on it. 'No, it's my name,' she said, much offended but none the less delighted that he'd actually addressed a friendly remark to her.

One of the younger kids ventured to ask whether the Rollers were in New York. 'No, sweetheart, Eric's in Honolulu and the rest of them are back home. I'm just here on business,' he replied, fingering a peat-colored safari shirt. Very stylish.

'It was a pretty hectic tour, wasn't it?' I piped up, thinking, My God, he's talking to us – what's gotten into him?

'Why don't you piss off?' he said without glancing at me. Surprised, I bristled, 'Oh, thanks, charming.'

'Piss off,' he repeated, holding the shirt against himself, then returning it to the rail. Sue J shot me a pitying look, appalled on my behalf but transparently grateful that it was me rather than her. I knew he must remember me from our very first encounter, way back in October '75, or at least recognise my face and sense that he didn't like me for some reason.

One of the kids asked him something about the Rollers, and he went out of his way to be polite to her. Yeah, rub it in how much you dislike me, you old bastard, I thought.

Fifteen minutes of aimless wandering later, he announced, 'I'm going to try Macy's.' Back downstairs he went and into the limo, which pulled slowly into traffic-choked Lexington Avenue. The Sues and I were the only ones with enough money left to hail a cab and follow.

I know, I know – why was I pursuing someone who'd made it exquisitely clear that he didn't want me to follow him?

A) because I was very, very sad.

and

B) because I was so intrigued by his sudden accessibility that I couldn't help it.

We arrived at Macy's, the huge 34th Street department store, to find him just getting out of the limo. He noticed us and waited till we'd paid the cab, then the four of us walked in together. 'I'm sorry,' he immediately told me. 'I was just in a bad mood.' And then he led us, chatting cheerily, to the men's department. In a fit of gallantry, he even held my elbow on the escalator. Why the turnaround? He simply seemed glad to have an audience, even if I was part of it. Even better for us, he was in an expansive, gossipy mood.

After we helped him choose three shirts – we talked him out of a khaki leisure blouson he was set on – and a pair of sunglasses, he proposed we go to the coffee shop for a milkshake. 'My treat,' he added, in case the expense deterred us.

By the time we reached the coffee shop, we were all on giggly first-name terms. Knowing we'd probably never have such access again, we seized the opportunity to ask him the most lurid questions we could think of.

Sue P ventured, 'Eric's not really twenty-one, is he?' No, said Tam, he was actually twenty-three. 'And sex-mad,' he giggled.

Sue J was more forthright. 'Are any of them gay?'

He sighed, rolled his eyes and launched into a spiel about who was and wasn't. Discretion prevents me from naming names, but he claimed that one Roller was more gay than straight and liked butch guys, another swung both ways and yet another was basically straight but sometimes went for older men. Pasta fazool.

Of course, he was probably having us on. He'd have been pretty silly to spill the beans to nosy girls like us. He even went into detail about the size of their undercarriages, waving a pinkie to describe one, holding his hands a foot apart to depict another. If only I'd had a video camera.

'So, Tam,' I began, basking in our new best-friendhood, 'what about you? Are you gay?' This was something we'd always wondered about, mostly on the basis that many teen-band managers were.

'No way,' he responded warmly, punctuating it by grabbing a handful of first my then Sue J's bosom. 'I love to feel a woman's boobs,' he chortled.

The gentleman did protest too much, methought, but there had been a lot of enthusiasm in his grip, so who knows? And when he autographed our placemats at the end of the meal, he was even more macho. Mine read 'Thanks for a lovely day and a dirty night'.

Whatever the truth about his or the Rollers' sexual orientation, we didn't mind. We were just pleased that this whole incredible episode was happening. Previously Tam had rarely been less than intimidating, dedicating himself to maintaining a wide *cordon sanitaire* between fans and his boys. Now here we were, drinking milkshakes like old buddies. In the space of an hour he'd completely shattered the impression we'd formed over the last two years. Most disconcerting.

Damnably, he soon had to return to the Plaza. We saw him back to his car, where he thanked us for our company, adding, 'Keep in touch.' (Yeah, like how?) As he chugged off into the traffic, the three of us clung to each other to keep from sinking on to the sidewalk. For at least five minutes all we managed was, 'Did you *believe* that?' Short of sharing a milkshake with an actual Roller, this was the greatest thing we could have asked for.

Still, I'd sobered up enough by that night to write: 'I told him I'd met Bess Coleman [their UK PR woman] in London last year and he seemed pleased and said how nice she was. In fact, he seemed to like everyone else a lot more than the Rollers.'

His whole attitude, now that I thought about it, had certainly been contemptuous toward his band. Even if he was kidding about their sex lives, it wasn't very respectful.

When I got home from Tam, I called Cathy to gloat, which she endured with remarkably good grace. After a post-mortem, she asked where the Rollers were. Eric was in Honolulu, I told her, and the others were back in Scotland. 'I wonder where Eric's staying,' she mused, and then had a brainstorm.

'If Tam's called Eric in the last few days, the number must be on his hotel bill. So how about if we get David to call the Plaza and pretend to be Tam and say he wants to check his bill?'

A classic ploy. It wasn't that we especially cared about finding Eric, it was just a good way of keeping the wheels oiled. We only had to hear the words 'Bay City Rollers' and, like good doggies, we went to fetch.

So I dragged David away from a TV baseball game, and he

did his thing. By now he'd stopped attempting a Scottish accent when impersonating Tam, his manner being so plausible people believed him anyway. This time he simply asked the hotel operator for a record of the long-distance calls 'he' had made and she unhesitatingly read them out to him.

Puzzling – no calls to Honolulu, but there was one to Illinois and another to Scotland.

'I know,' I told him, 'call the Illinois one and tell them you're calling from the Plaza Hotel 'cause he's left some luggage here.'

He did, and duly discovered that the woman who answered was Tam's sister, who'd emigrated to Illinois years before. She was naturally puzzled by the call, but we couldn't help that. He suavely apologised for the mistake, then called the Scottish number.

That night, I filled my diary with a feverish account of the call. 'Apparently, it was Tam's home number, cos we got a young dolt saying Tam wasn't back yet. So I called back later, saying I worked for 16 magazine and wanted to leave a message for Tam. The same young dolt answered, took the message (something about wanting to do a photo shoot with the group) and then, as I was hoping, began talking. It turned out he was in one of Tam's other bands, and was staying at his house.'

What an opportunity to pick up some gossip. I told the kid, 'Well, as long as I've got you on the line, maybe we can have a little chat. I'm the assistant editor of 16 magazine, and we're always interested in all of Tam's bands.' (Wrong – we were interested in just one of Tam's bands.)

'You want to interview me?' he asked, after a long, dim pause.

'That's right!' I replied, magazine-editor perky. 'You'd like to be in 16, wouldn't you?'

Another silence as he considered. 'Uh, yes,' he said at length, his viscous Edinburgh accent rendering his words a muffle-vowel jamboree.

Goodness, this was turning into a chore. 'So, how about a

few details?' I chirped. 'What's your name and what's your band called?'

He was called Martin, and was in a band called Keep, along with 'Pat, Malcolm and John', whose last names he didn't know. There were more silences as he groped for answers to basic questions. He suddenly brightened as he remembered a fact about his group. 'We're quite well-known in Japan, you know.'

'Oh, so you're popular there,' I said encouragingly. He thought it over, and eventually replied, 'No, not really.' I gave up the 'interview' as a lost cause. But hey, I'd discovered Tam's home number.

The rift between Tam and the Rollers, if there was one, must have been growing, because the band were suddenly speaking out more openly in interviews, not to mention asserting themselves sartorially. During June, the British pop mag *Record Mirror* carried a picture of Eric on the cover – an unrecognisable Eric, dressed and made up as a Japanese geisha girl. Seriously – red lipstick, kimono, the works. He was the only Roller pretty enough to get away with something like that, but if he thought it would shore up their popularity in the UK, he was wrong. The accompanying interview, which unaccountably failed to explain why he was in drag, was full of quotes that would have been unimaginable mere months before: 'If I'm sleeping with an Alsatian dog, it's my business.' There was no way Tam would have permitted this if it had been up to him alone.

I displayed the article to the other Tarts at an emergency meeting. By the time we'd each examined it minutely, the cover was torn from Sues P and J bickering over it, and the ink was smudged with sweaty fingerprints. As for the Alsatian quote, we were ambivalent. Their new openness was ostensibly what we'd been praying for, but it seemed the more they changed, the further they slipped away.

16

D AVID WAS CALLED into phone service again at the end of June. My new English penpal, Brenda, an eighteen-year-old Londoner who had written to Emma till the latter got too busy with her new boyfriend – the velvet-jacket guy – to keep up the correspondence, sent a number purporting to be Pat McGlynn's. David's mission was to 'interview' McGlynn on his reason for leaving the Rollers. He rang the number, using as his alias Bill Hodgson of the fictitious *New York Herald*. Sure enough, it was McGlynn on the other end, surprised that an American reporter wanted to talk to him. Yes, he was willing to do an interview. Right now, if you like.

'Oh . . . oh, right,' said David, taken aback. He hadn't anticipated such co-operation, so he hadn't prepared any questions. No matter, for McGlynn was happy to do the talking.

He claimed he was fired because he'd complained about his wages, which were, he maintained, a princely £20 a week. 'That was all I got,' he said. 'The rest of them were making thousands and I was on twenty quid.' Furthermore – he was working up a head of steam here – his vocal and guitar tracks allegedly had been removed from the still-unreleased *It's a Game* album, and he hadn't been credited for a song he'd supposedly written, 'Sweet Virginia'.

This was better than I'd dared hope. I was agog as I pressed my head next to David's in an effort to hear.

'After they sacked me, I wanted to give up music altogether,' he went on. 'Eric told me over the phone. Why couldn't he have told me face-to-face? It's a bit hard to get it over the phone.'

'Did drugs play a part in your getting fired?' David asked, now as riveted as I.

'No, no,' he replied, aghast. 'I don't take drugs, I've got weak blood.' Then, boringly, he changed the subject to his new group, who were called Pat McGlynn's Scottie. I caught the phrases 'Much better than the Rollers . . . really happy . . . quite promising . . . America in October'.

I perked up a bit at that last. I was so shameless that, if they did come to America, I'd have had to go see them. Thankfully, they didn't, and nothing more was ever heard of Scottie. McGlynn himself disappeared for the next twenty years, only resurfacing in 1997 at a Roller convention in Las Vegas.

An hour after the 'interview', the doorman buzzed that a Mr Barbarino was on the way up. He was at the door a moment later, gibbering with excitement, because he'd obtained an advance copy of *It's a Game*, and had come to my place because I was the nearest person with a record player. I put it on and we flopped on to the floor with the last of a family-sized box of Hostess Snoballs, small chocolate cakes covered with a coconut-marshmallow topping that looked like a rabbit pelt. Stuffing one down in one piece, I grabbed the sleeve and examined it as the record started.

'The photos are gorgeous, and the one of Eric is breath-taking,' I scribbled lustfully that night. 'It's possibly the best I've ever seen of him. He's wearing leather and looking to the side very pensively, and for the first time he looks like a grown-up instead of a cute little cuddly thingie.'

The others were equally jawdropping – Leslie in full-length jeans – it was still a novelty to see them in normal trousers – Woody posing cheekily with his bass, Derek looking . . . well, Dereky.

And the music! Opening with 'Love Fever', a haunting number about a bewitching Japanese woman, and closing with a raw-sounding 'Rebel Rebel', the whole thing was so stunningly mature, for them, that Barbarino and I were speechless. The Rollers had finally come up with a record that would compare favorably with albums by 'real' groups. Even David was mildly impressed.

' "Love Fever", even after 15 or 20 listens, still amazes me. Everything from Eric's Framptonesque guitar to Leslie singing some of the verses in Japanese is excellent. It's just such a progression. [You can see the future rock critic in me trying to get out.] On "Sweet Virginia", they go, "Is it really such a crime to be loving your own kind/She blew her mind out in the rain." Heavy, at least for them.'

It *was* heavy. To quote one of their own earlier songs, what happened to the boys we used to know? It was more and more obvious that these weren't the little bunnikins we had adored; these were testosterone-packed, fuel-injected men who probably had to shave at least twice a week.

We hardly knew what to think. If you buy the theory about teenagers fancying teen bands because of their unattainability, you'll understand our ambivalence. This new incarnation of the BCRs was hovering on the edge of availability. If they were now singing about Oriental temptresses and lesbians, it was a fair assumption that in real life they were also sampling forbidden fruits: sex, booze – drugs? – and maybe even staying up past their bedtimes.

We could hardly imagine what their next tour would be like, but it would unarguably be interesting.

17

THE HEAP PASSED AWAY. We were on the way
home, Cathy, Sue P and I, from a Roller-friend's
graduation party in New Jersey when we hit a slippery
patch of road near Newark Airport. The car hit a guard rail
and shook us up a bit, but we were undamaged, which was
more than could be said for the poor Heap. The dear thing was
mangled beyond repair.

David took the news with remarkable equanimity, considering it had been his car. 'I guess from now on you'll have to
rent a car if you're gonna chase the Rollers,' he said, and I
could have sworn he was suppressing a mocking laugh.

As fate would have it, a few days later, in early July, a tour
was announced. It was set for August, and would see the Rollers
doing a series of outdoor shows in the South and Midwest.
There was no New York show (indeed, their Academy of Music
show in January '77 turned out to be the only time they ever
played New York during their peak years), and the closest they
would get to us was Youngstown, Ohio. We went for broke,
buying tickets for the three final dates, Youngstown, Detroit
and Charlotte, North Carolina, on August 25, 26 and 27. It
would entail a lot of flying – six times in four days – but there
was no alternative. That is, there was no alternative to going.
The idea of not going was out of the question. We had too much
invested, especially now that they seemed to be on a longer
leash; there was a sense that if we were ever going to get near
them, it would be this time. How right we were.

In the meantime, there was the question of earning a living. By mid-July, nearly two months after getting fired from ASCAP, I was still unemployed. 'I have no inclination whatsoever to look for a job,' I wrote. 'I must be the sort of person who can't adjust to routine and discipline. Probably cos I'm spoiled and immature.'

Obviously, unemployment in itself didn't bother me, but I was low on cash and didn't want to dig into $1,000 I had in the bank, which I was saving for the tour. The immediate answer seemed to be to sell something. The only piece of jewellery I owned that was worth more than a couple of bucks was a gold necklace David had given me for my birthday. With regret, I went up to 47th Street in the jewellery district, and walked into the first place I saw.

The rip-off merchant behind the counter gave me $9, about a tenth of what it was worth, but I was too broke to quibble. I must have looked pretty pathetic as I put away the fiver and four singles, because he leaned across the counter and lowered his voice. 'If you really need money, I might be able to help,' he whispered, trashy-novel style. 'I can introduce you to a couple of people.'

'I'm not that desperate,' I sniffed, turning and leaving with what I hoped was a flounce.

The encounter was depressing; not only had I been propositioned, I only had nine bucks to show for it. To cheer myself up, I bought three English music papers, all of which carried reviews of Alan Longmuir's first solo single. Yes, the old boy – remember him? – had grown bored with retirement and was relaunching his career. Barbarino had already played me the single, titled 'I'm Confessing', and it was terrible. Poor Alan was never the most spirited soul, but on this weak-kneed little tune his negligible voice was so weary you wondered how he'd stayed awake till the end of the song. It did absolutely nothing in the charts, failing to even make the Top 75. If there was a follow-up single, I never heard about it.

A couple of days later, a chance encounter with a Millburn friend got me a job as a barmaid in a small neighborhood place in Newark, New Jersey. The bar, which I christened El Tackio, was in the Portuguese section, which meant I was in great favor with the locals. Latin men are great admirers of hips and butts, and I was amply blessed in both departments – so much so that I earned $35 in tips my first night. Unfortunately, I spent most of it on a taxi home – that very night, New York suffered a city-wide power blackout, and the trains weren't running. It was a fabulous blackout, though. The electricity wasn't restored for almost twenty-four hours, during which shops were lit by candles, cars gleefully pranged each other at junctions and the absence of air-conditioning made itself felt in the most odoriferous ways.

My career at El Tackio was shortlived. The work was easy enough – my customers weren't fussy, and mostly wanted Miller beer – it was the strain of being a love goddess for all these Portuguese guys, few of whom would take no for an answer. It was as if I were being paid back for all the times I'd whined to Cathy or Emma about not having a boyfriend. Well, every one of these dudes wanted to remedy that. 'Mama, mama! *Mira, mira*,' they'd hiss as I poured their Millers. 'Nice beeg ass. I loooove that beeg ass.' So flatteringly put, sir.

The first night, one of them followed my taxi all the way back to Manhattan, and I only lost him because the streets were pitch-black thanks to the blackout. My third and last night, another customer offered me a ride back to the city, which I accepted with impunity because he was so much shorter than me.

As we joined the approach road to the Holland Tunnel he suddenly said, 'You geev me some or I don't take you home.' He didn't have to explain what 'some' was. I got out of the car right there on the elevated highway and started to walk. The creep's chivalrous instincts belatedly kicked in, and he sheep-ishly offered me a lift to the train station, which I warily accepted. I sat as far away from him as possible, but he didn't try anything else – lucky, because I was prepared to bite his hand off.

I didn't return to El Tackio, and decided not to look for another job till after the Roller tour. So I was in a worrying financial state, and at the same time, things weren't happy on the domestic front. David and I weren't getting on at all well, mostly due to the strain of two people with conflicting aims – I wanted to stay platonic, he didn't – sharing one small room for nearly a year.

In July he went back to his parents' place, leaving a terse note stating that he no longer intended to pay his share of our rent. When I called him to tell him what I thought of that, he retaliated by having the phone cut off. The phone company was kind enough to inform me they'd be turning it off at seven that night, so I spent the afternoon making long distance calls to everyone I could think of to run up the bill. Then David announced that he'd be staying at his parents' for the rest of the summer, and that on his return he wanted me to be out of the apartment, which was technically his. We didn't speak for six weeks after that conversation.

Just as annoyingly, in late July Barbarino learned that the Rollers were chartering a private plane for their tour, which scotched our plans to travel on their flights. I was particularly disappointed, because in one of my most brilliant pieces of detective work, I had uncovered what I thought were all their travel arrangements.

Actually, it was a complete accident. I rang Eastern Airlines to make reservations for Sue P, Cathy and me on a flight from Detroit (where they'd be playing on August 26) to Charlotte (27). As it happened, Sue's last name was the same as one of the Roller's roadies, and the airline clerk got her wires crossed. She thought I was checking on an existing reservation rather than making a new one. So she fed Sue's name into the computer and a moment later said, 'Yes, we do have her confirmed for that flight. She's travelling with Mr Duncan, Mr Allen, Mr Fuson . . . ?' – all names I recognised as BCR crew.

'Yes, that's her,' I chirped. 'You couldn't just remind me of the rest of her itinerary, could you?' And she did, reading off the entire flight schedule for the four weeks of the tour. If only airline clerks were as helpful nowadays.

It was a significant achievement, because we had figured that whither goest the roadies goest the band. Accordingly, I had booked us on to the Detroit-Charlotte flight and one from Charlotte to New York on August 28, the day after the last gig. But if Barbarino was right about the private jet, our reservations were now useless. 'So we're gonna be flying with the roadies only, which would be great if I had a crush on one of them,' I wrote peevishly.

Each day was hotter than the one before, and time trudged by. The apartment, where I spent most of my days because it was too humid to go out, was so airless that I got damp just from the exertion of getting dressed. I went out in the morning, when it was coolest, to buy my meager food ration for the day – I was subsisting on Snoballs, coffee cake and pizza – and a newspaper. Back upstairs, I'd listlessly alternate between watching newly introduced cable TV and reading the paper, which was full of the antics of a serial killer dubbed Son of Sam. They caught him, through sheer happenstance, about three weeks later, and he turned out to be a nebbishy Jewish guy called David Berkowitz, who looked exactly like the few boys who had liked me at school.

Occasionally I got the energy to go downtown to Bleecker Bob's, where I read *Melody Maker*. The Brits were all in a flap about the twenty-fifth anniversary of the Queen's Queenship. The Sex Pistols' Jubilee single, 'God Save the Queen', had become a big hit – number two, in fact – but 'Top of the Pops' was refusing to play it because of its supposedly insulting lyric. I couldn't see the problem. Surely the stuff about morons and

H-bombs referred to her subjects rather than to the old girl herself?

American music wasn't producing anything nearly as exciting. The chart was dominated by disco – space-fillers like 'I Feel Love' by Donna Summer, and 'The Shuffle' by Van McCoy, which was the follow-up to his other hit, 'The Hustle'. Jeez. Both Shuffle and Hustle were dances, but you weren't gonna catch me doing them. Like nearly all middle-class types, I despised disco, believing its simplistic rhythms and hedonistic philosophy to be far inferior to the more complex rumblings of white guitar bands. I even proudly wore a T-shirt with the slogan 'Shoot the Bee Gees'. Little did we know that, two decades later, every one of those middle-class types, me included, would suddenly decide that those simplistic tunes had been epochal classics all along. I even own a compilation CD called *The Old Skool Reunion*, which features thirty-eight songs I wouldn't have listened to if you'd paid me in 1977. 'Yeah, I loved these when I was a kid,' I tell people now without a glimmer of shame.

My stupor was interrupted at the end of July by a hunkster called Michael. God had finally answered my prayers. He was an English guy I'd met a couple of months earlier at some prog-rock gig at the Academy. Sue J had been with me, and her radar had picked up his London accent before we even spotted him. We'd had a hilarious conversation that lasted half the night, and when his holiday ended we exchanged a few letters. I was nurturing a small crush on him, and was extremely pleased when he phoned in July to say he had business in New York and would be coming over for a few days.

But he arrived during a particularly Roller-heavy week, when I'd been playing *It's a Game* a lot and dreaming about a private audience with Leslie. Poor Michael just couldn't compete with my fantasies. I was inattentive and pretty poor company – and hence felt doubly guilty when, at the end of the third day, he awkwardly confessed, 'You know, I didn't really come on business, I came to see you.' Whatever spark had existed between us had been extinguished by then, at least on his side, and I could only berate myself for not realising that he'd, like, dug me. If I had realised, maybe I'd have become involved with him and the definitive Roller moment that lay just around the corner wouldn't have happened.

18

I DON'T KNOW WHERE I got the chutzpah, but throughout the summer I'd been desultorily pursuing a claim against ASCAP for unfair dismissal. I knew that they'd been well within their rights to fire me – my work was woefully below par, as sheaves of file cards blotchy with Tippexed corrections eloquently attested. And even if I'd been more competent, my attendance record was spotty due to all those Roller-related days off. So I hadn't a leg to stand on, and can only admire my gall in thinking I had. But I kept at it in the hope of winning a settlement, as money was running short. Paying for my plane tickets had left me with just over $500, every penny of which I'd need for the tour.

Of course, the tribunal threw out my claim. But by then, early August, the tour was but weeks away, and there was no point looking for a job till after I got back. The tour occupied so many of my thoughts it was easy to postpone worrying about money.

All sorts of scintillating reports were coming in from friends who'd managed to get to some of the early dates. A postcard from the first gig, in Montana, sprang the news that Eric's stage costume was a football shirt and pair of shorts with 'Spank Me' embroidered on the back. Now, if that wasn't an invitation . . .

I got to see this spectacle for myself when they appeared on 'The Midnight Special', a 'credible' rock TV show they wouldn't have been welcome on even two months ago. Things *were* changing.

'They were amazing,' I wrote at 2 a.m., completely unable
to sleep:

> They sang and played live (a first) and looked quite
> edible. Even though Eric, in his shiny blue eyeshadow,
> leather jacket, shorts and leg-warmers, was a bit ludi-
> crous, specially when he tapped his foot and all that flab
> on his leg shook. He and Leslie (in very tight jeans) kept
> goofing around and sang a bit of 'Deep in the Heart of
> Texas', and then before an ad break Leslie said, 'Don't
> you DARE go away', and the camera panned to Eric,
> who was busy zipping his fly up and down. Hahaha! I
> think it was the best TV show they've ever done.

The titillation of the tight jeans and unzipped shorts was
compounded, of course, by the astonishment of seeing them
act like grown-ups, with grown-up personalities, humor and
the usual grown-up attributes. It was a sensation that had
become more and more familiar in the past few months, but
each time was just as incredible as the last. Yet despite their
increasingly laddish behaviour, they still weren't quite real to
us.

I'm not sure what would have happened, to them or to us, if
the Rollers had clung to their old sexless, juiceless image.
Commercially, they couldn't have survived much longer as
tartaned teen-throbs. In Britain punk had rendered cuddly toy-
boys obsolete overnight. (The Rollers' one UK single that
summer, 'You Made Me Believe In Magic', only reached
34 in the charts, the lowest placing of their career – and
was the last BCR single ever to make the Brit chart.) So their
change of image, which they were nudging along, probably
kept them going longer than they otherwise would have.

As for the Tacky Tartan Tarts, we'd likely have lost
interest sometime that summer if the band hadn't begun
to grow up. It had been two years of intense adoration by

that point, forsaking all others for them, and we would have inevitably reached burn-out if they'd remained as cloistered as before.

I had other interests that were beginning to compete with the Rollers, like my punk collection, which now included most of the major bands who'd released records – the Pistols, The Damned, The Clash, The Jam. Though punk's politics failed to move me – demands for anarchy in the UK meant nothing to me – I loved its mad, incandescent energy. Moreover, it was the first movement ever invented by and for people my age. Even when it got out that Joe Strummer of The Clash, my favorite band, was actually pushing twenty-five in 1977, I wasn't deterred.

The other Tarts were branching out as well. Emma was spending a lot of time with her boyfriend, Cathy was focused on leaving her dull job at a trucking company, Sue J was going through one of her periodic spells of Roller-indifference. So if the band hadn't adopted this intriguing new persona, we'd have been outta there well before the middle of '77. Instead, here we were, planning our biggest expedition yet.

I was even captivated enough to buy what we referred to as a 'Debbie Bottom coat' – a long white sweater-coat of the sort worn by the chick Leslie picked up in Pittsburgh. They were all over the shops that summer, and although they were deeply unflattering to anyone with hips, I got one because, as I wrote, 'subconsciously I think if Leslie wanted her, anything she wore must be okay'. I deplored my weakness.

Mid-August, I moved out of the apartment I'd shared with David. My departure was expedited by the fact that my mother had just moved from Millburn to a studio apartment on 5th Avenue in Manhattan. I rang her a week before she moved and announced I was coming to share the place with her. Her reaction isn't fit for a family book. She'd been looking forward to her own little bachelor pad in the city after nineteen years in the suburbs, and she hadn't counted on anyone else being there. I overrode her frantic objections, promising, 'You'll hardly notice me, I swear.'

A week later I moved in. Ma watched inscrutably as boxes and crates piled up from one end of the room to the other. 'Just let me get the stereo in and I'll be done,' I cheerily called over the boxes. 'Oh, and can I move your records? Mine won't fit otherwise.'

'How long are you planning to stay?' she asked quietly.

'I dunno. Till I can afford my own place, I guess. Hey, should I sleep on the bed or this couch?'

It was fortunate that on that day neither of us knew that my stay would last two-and-a-half years. We started with the assumption that I would move out as soon as I got a job, and maintained that fiction as weeks turned into months and months into years. It was the only way we could tolerate each other. I can attest from experience that the parent-child bond is not strengthened by living in one room. I got the couch, by the way.

Still, there were advantages to having your mother as a roommate – she always fussed over me when I was sick, bringing chicken soup right to my couch, and was usually willing to call in sick for me at work when I finally did get a job. In return, I kept the place relatively clean and imparted a lively teenage atmosphere. That was what I told her, anyway, whenever she asked when I'd be leaving, which was every couple of weeks.

But for the first few weeks I was there we got on well, once she'd recovered from the shock. I was so busy making plans for the tour that I didn't have time to get in her hair. And for her part, Ma kept her thoughts to herself except to comment on the clothes I bought for the gigs. They set me back $100 I could ill afford, but if they made a Roller notice me it would be money well spent.

'Are you sure about these?' she inquired when I displayed my purchases.

'What do you mean?' I asked, miffed. I had some zappy little numbers this time around – silver sandals, an 'ironic' Betty Boop T-shirt, a white vest top with a big metallic silver star – very Studio 54 – and two pairs of hugely flared jeans with novelty zippers on the pockets. Oh, yeah, and a pair of oversized shades with rhinestone stars glued on to the lenses.

I was very pleased with everything. They made me look as sexy as I ever had in my life, I thought – I was sure to catch a Roller's eye, assuming I could get near enough.

It was with this newfound confidence that I rang David – we had slowly begun speaking again – and asked if he could lend me some money for the tour. 'Lend' actually meant 'give', as I could see no way of ever being able to repay him, but, good soul that he was, he agreed. I went up to his place, shot the breeze for a while and pocketed five $20 bills.

And then, as I was leaving, he did the most out-of-character thing. I went to the bathroom, and when I emerged he'd taken off all his clothes except his underpants, which were small, tight and tiger-striped. He approached with a merry smile, and I screamed, 'What are you *doing*?'

I beat a quick retreat and headed home, deeply disturbed – not so much by the disrobing, but the motive. He'd clearly done it to get back at me – but why?

I could think of a dozen possibilities. For treating him like a loan service, expecting him to pay all the costs of running our apartment, wrecking The Heap, roping him in when we needed him during our Roller adventures (though I felt he sort of enjoyed that), refusing to take seriously the fact that he was 'fond' of me . . .

It struck me that perhaps I wasn't a very nice person. ('You weren't,' Emma told me recently. 'You were really selfish, and we always used to talk about how badly you treated him.')

I didn't like the idea that I was insensitive to his feelings, particularly as I'd always been terribly sensitive to my own. So there I was, confronted by an uncomfortable truth – that I wasn't as nice as I thought I was. 'Still,' I comforted myself, 'acknowledging it is the first step to solving it.' And I would have done something about it if I hadn't been so busy.

The day after David stripped to his skivvies, Elvis Presley died. The King's passing made the front page of the evening papers, the local oldies station devoted itself to playing his records for the rest of the day, but otherwise New York was unruffled. Elvis had left the building for good, but . . . well, there were other things to be getting on with.

This contradicts what's been written in the many tomes that have appeared since 1977, which claim his death had a substantial impact in America. This overlooks the fact that by then he was of small consequence to anyone younger than himself – as proof, I point to the fact that I hadn't even known he had been scheduled to play Madison Square Garden the week after he died. When his departure was announced in a London punk club, apparently there were loud cheers. In Manhattan it didn't even merit that reaction.

All quite a contrast to the reaction to John Lennon's death three years later. The genuine grief then owed much to the fact that Lennon was still a contemporary artist who was then in the process of rediscovering his fire. The awful circumstances touched many who hadn't been moved by Presley's self-inflicted demise; on the subway the next day everyone was silent, absorbed in the *Daily News*'s front page headline, 'John Lennon Shot Dead In New York', and picture of Yoko Ono crumpled on the arm of David Geffen.

For me, the day of Elvis's death passed in a flurry of phone calls as I tried to track Barbarino down. Two days before, he and his friend Kim, an Eric fan from the rival clique, had gone to Columbus, Ohio, with the intention of seeing the Rollers there and at the next stop, Louisville, Kentucky. He'd promised to call me from Columbus, and hadn't. I was mucho pissed off, because I was dying to know what was going on.

Although we had the tour pretty well covered, with informants attending shows all over the place – Montana, Toronto, Milwaukee, Des Moines – the gossip coming back had been disappointingly sketchy. But Barbarino, I knew, would have tons to tell.

Quite how he got his information we never knew. He was hardly the sort the Rollers would take into their confidence, what with that whiny little voice that had moved all of us at some point to threaten to kill him if he didn't shut it. And his capacity for irksomeness was great; after propositioning Emma while queueing for tickets back in December, his courage had grown to the point where he regularly begged us to assist in his struggle against virginity. We never succumbed, but it never stopped him trying.

I couldn't smoke him out in either Columbus or Louisville, so I turned my attention to attempting to discover the band's itinerary for August 24, the day before we were flying out. We already knew they were going to Bay City, Michigan, to be presented with the keys to the city (they'd supposedly got their name by sticking a pin in a map, which landed on said small town near Detroit. I believe its other claim to fame is that Madonna grew up there. Wonder if she was into the Rollers). But it would be helpful to find out what they'd do afterward – would they stay in Bay City overnight or go on to the next city, Youngstown?

I phoned Pecker's travel agent in California – Barbarino gave me the number – and pretended to be his wife. Afterwards, embarrassed, I wrote: 'Pecker must be a big account there, cos the girl who answered knew who he was immediately, and switched me to a bitch called Deborah, who handles him. I said I was Liz Packer, and the bitch said, "I know his wife and that's not her name." Bitch.'

The next day I finally got hold of Barbarino. He was back home in Queens, and he had a tale to tell. Oh, yes.

He'd been to Columbus and Louisville and seen a lot of the Rollers. He related with relish that Leslie had spent most of his time in Louisville driving around in a Cutlass Supreme with a local girl called Candy. One of the others had apparently been bragging about wanting to see how many women he could bed in his life, and another Roller had said he wanted to break his record of how many times he could do it in one night.

'Were they all talking like that?' I breathed, groping blindly for a pen to write it all down. He tittered his Barbarinoey titter and refused to say more.

I phoned his friend Kim, a laboratory technician who lived near Barbarino in the euphoniously-named Far Rockaway. She wasn't part of our circle, so we weren't on proper gossiping terms, but the situation transcended protocol.

She confirmed everything Barbarino had said, then added, 'They're screwing around pretty openly, there's no two ways about it.'

'My God.' I absorbed the implications for a few moments, then asked, as an afterthought, 'What was Eric up to?' There was a silence, and she changed the subject. The actual gigs had been excellent, she declared, and the band had become a tight little onstage unit. That was almost as hard to believe as all the rest.

'But after the show the last night, everyone was sort of tired and upset,' she went on. 'They're just so . . . different now. Not fun any more.'

'But,' I persisted, sensing I was on to something, 'where was Eric?'

She seemed to be about to say something, then sighed, 'I'll tell you when I see you.'

Recounting all this took up two solid diary pages. I wasn't at all happy. Their sluttish behaviour, the vulgarity, Kim's reticence when Eric was mentioned ('I think she may have gotten what she wanted from him,' I wrote, unable to believe I was talking about a girl I actually knew), none of it was what I'd expected.

Gawd, was that what they were really like? Had those

tartan suits been concealing Led Zeppish rock beasts? Or was it all just an exaggerated reaction to finally being let off the leash?

After writing it all down, I nearly broke my finger dialing the other Tarts, who were equally shocked.

'Whaddaya expect? They're normal guys, and girls throw themselves at them,' was David's unsympathetic assessment the next day. It was a week after his impromptu striptease, which we had never discussed by unspoken agreement. We were entertaining two clients who had just concluded a major deal at David's insurance company, taking them first to dinner, then to a football game across the river at Meadowlands Stadium. David had asked me to accompany him as a girlfriend-figure, but I ended up talking to the twelve-year-old son of one of the clients because we were closest in age.

'Do I have to do the football game?' I'd complained. 'Just think of that hundred bucks,' he'd replied; ergo there I found myself, watching the New York Jets and the Pittsburgh Steelers at the first and last football game I ever attended. The twelve-year-old tried to explain, but I just couldn't get it.

At last it was the day before the tour. We spent it variously. Barbarino hung around outside Madison Square Garden, selling tickets at triple face value for that night's Peter Frampton gig. Kim, who was going with us, spent it lying on the roof of her apartment building, working on her tan. Sue P stayed home in Brooklyn, trying to decide which of three dozen outfits to pack. And Sue J and I paid a call to the Rollers' former A&R guy, whom I'll call Norman.

A&R people are the record company employees who assist musicians in choosing material, producers and all the other thousand-and-one details of making an album. We detested this particular A&R guy from way back – whenever the band had been in New York, Norman had always been there, imposing his considerable girth between us and the band in case, heaven forfend, we tried to talk to them. Bastard. But he had latterly moved to Atlantic Records, and was no longer a threat.

The receptionist summoned Norman, who lumbered into the reception room, did a double-take and left. Moments later we heard hysterical female laughter, and a woman's voice gasped, 'But *how* did they find this *floor*?' A job well done, if we did say so ourselves.

The plan was for all of us to meet at La Guardia Airport at seven the next morning, August 25. I spent the night at Sue P's, which was closest to the airport. We sat up talking till two in the morning, lewdly discussing plans for our respective Rollers. I was full of vim because I'd weighed myself on Sue's scale and discovered, to my ecstasy, that I'd lost fourteen pounds over the summer through being too broke to eat. I was the thinnest I'd been since I was fifteen.

'All right, already,' Sue said after enduring my squeals for a while. 'Let's get some sleep.' She turned off the light and we lay there wakefully, waiting for daylight.

19

T 7.30 A.M. we assembled at La Guardia's Eastern Airlines terminal, Sue P, Barbarino, Kim and me. I'd given a lot of thought to what to wear for this first tour-day, and had finally decided on the Betty Boop T-shirt, denim shorts and high-heeled platform shoes. The shorts were pretty short and the heels were pretty high, and I looked, well, less than demure. Sue took a picture in the departure lounge. I'm standing there with a come-hither smile while a businessman in the background goggles at my newly slenderised rump.

Two hours and a change of plane in Pittsburgh later, we were in Youngstown. Although we didn't see much of it, and I've never been back, the place has held a nostalgic glow for me ever since. I believe it was once the subject of a Bruce Springsteen song about its former mining industry, but it looked to us like a typical small Midwestern city, with a leafy downtown shopping area and arid strip malls on the outskirts.

The distance between the airport, where you were greeted by a large sign warning that anyone who joked about hijacking would be arrested, and the venue, Idora Park, was great enough to necessitate renting a car. We were issued with a slick new Chevy, and after 'designated driver' Kim (the only one old enough to rent) finally worked out how to make the thing go, we hit the road. We had hours before the show, which began at 4 p.m., so, first things first, we set off to find the Rollers.

An hour of cruising all the Holiday Inns and Day's Inns in town was fruitless and we began to worry. For once it was actually crucial that we found them, because our next move depended on theirs. If they were leaving for the next city straight after the show – something they'd apparently taken to doing – we needed to know, and if they were planning to stay in Youngstown we needed to know that, too.

The only thing for it would be to follow them after the show, so after debating it over lunch in a Day's Inn coffee shop we headed for Idora Park.

If you've seen the 1984 film *This Is Spinal Tap*, the spoof rockumentary about a fictitious English rock group, you'll remember a scene where the band, who are very much has-beens, arrive for a gig at a Midwestern amusement park and find a marquee reading 'Puppet Show/Spinal Tap'. When I saw it, I was immediately reminded of Idora Park – the sign there said 'Thursday Rollers/WHOT Day/Friday Buddy Rich'. Poor schmucks – not even the dignity of their own marquee.

I wasn't especially looking forward to this show – it was more of an obstacle to be got through so we could get on with the real business of tracking down the Rollers. It would be my ninth BCR gig, and by the time you'd seen nine Roller gigs, you'd pretty much got the point. As we lined up outside the grassy arena, I was already planning our pursuit afterwards. Despite the fact that only Kim was insured, I'd been elected post-gig driver because she didn't feel confident about follow-ing them. The responsibility made me walk taller in my silver sandals, which I'd changed into from the high heels because they were giving me blisters.

The gig was the first time we'd seen them since May, so we were curious to check out their new look. Eric was indeed wearing shorts, which were so brief they were almost hot pants, and Leslie was naked but for white drawstring pants. Sigh. Say what you wanted about him, he could certainly wear a pair of pants. Woody and Derek wore something or other; I was too captivated by Leslie to look. I did notice Woody's new white bass guitar, which was carved into a horse shape, a rock-star affectation that seemed very out of character.

As usual I'd brought my tape recorder, which in those lo-tech days weighed about five pounds. It was worth dragging it along, though, because during 'Rebel Rebel', Eric was seized by madness. When he got to the last line he changed it to 'Hot tramp, suck my toe', punctuating it with a ferocious grimace. Thank God I got it on tape, because nobody at home would've ever believed me.

I was standing near the mixing desk, halfway between the stage and the back of the arena, where a sound engineer was vainly trying to make the clanging noise emanating from the band's instruments sound like music. He saw my tape recorder and remarked that I'd be lucky to get much apart from static and crowd noise.

'Oh, do you work for the Rollers?' I asked innocently. The ensuing conversation provided two bits of valuable information – that the road crew were staying at a Holiday Inn a mile away, and the band were at another Holiday Inn outside town. 'Why don't you and your friends come over for a drink later?' he suggested, with what was undoubtedly an innocent wink. I filed it away as a possibility – if we failed to hook up with the band, we could always hang out with this guy and pick up lots of gossip.

As the first notes of the traditional show-closer, 'Saturday Night', thumped across the field, we hot-footed it out of the arena and into the parking lot. We planned to station ourselves at the backstage gate, ready to take off as soon as they went by. Except that when we piled into the car, it wouldn't start. I turned the key and the strains of the current Foreigner hit, 'Cold As Ice', issued from the radio, but no sound from the engine. I tried again, and then a third time. Nothing. We sat there in silence. 'The song's ending,' Kim suddenly observed, as the last chorus of 'Saturday Night' wafted out toward the parking lot. As Leslie sang 'Saturday . . .' we automatically added 'Night!'

I tried again, pressing the accelerator to the floor. The engine emitted a polite cough, then lapsed back into silence.

'Shit,' said Sue.

'SHIT!' said Barbarino, much more loudly. A camper van shot through the backstage gate and out of the park. We watched helplessly. This was like some pathetic sitcom – quarry speeds off as hunters fume in broken-down Chevy.

'I met the sound guy and he told us to come over for a drink,' I said, trying to cheer us up in our helplessness. 'I ain't hangin' out with no fuckin' roadies,' Kim muttered out of the side of her mouth, like a gangster.

The car finally started, but by the time we reached the main road, they were out of sight. I floored the gas and we screeched down the tree-shaded street, pausing at intersections to check the side roads.

As we approached a main junction, the light changed and we had to stop. 'Every fuckin' red light!' Kim hissed, digging her nails into my neck like it was my fault. 'What's with these scumbag motherfuckers?'

Suddenly Barbarino, who was hanging halfway out the back window for a better view, shrieked, 'They're down there!' And so they were, about a quarter mile down the road, emitting a cloud of exhaust as they rocketed past small shops and one-story houses.

We closed the gap, jumping red lights till the camper was only a few car-lengths away. Thank God practically every cop in town was over at Idora Park, dealing with the post-gig traffic there.

The camper did a left into a highway mall and stopped outside a small pizza joint. Leslie, Eric and a portly dude hopped out and headed into the restaurant. The big boy was their security guard, Big Bob – Kim had told us about him that morning. It seemed they'd met at the Columbus show the week before and he'd taken a bit of a fancy to her, probably because she had been wearing her standard summer uniform of spaghetti-strap leotard top and tight jeans. He'd proved a useful ally, divulging not just where they were staying in Columbus but in Louisville, too.

Barbarino leapt out and ran toward the pizzeria, and after a millisecond's hesitation I opened the door. 'Aren't you coming?' I asked Sue and Kim. The latter vigorously shook her head. 'I ain't going nowhere, not with my fat legs.' Actually, they weren't fat at all; if anything they were enviably skinny. It suddenly dawned that she just didn't want Eric to see her.

For there had indeed been some hanky-panky the previous week. She'd told me about it on the plane. They'd been together in Columbus and Louisville, and while she didn't go into particulars, she was clearly smitten. That was why she didn't want to follow him into the pizzeria, and she was wise not to, considering what happened when Barbarino and I did.

Eric and Leslie were at the counter, waiting for slices of square Sicilian-style pizza, and glanced at us with what you couldn't possibly mistake for enthusiasm. Barbarino took a few quick photos, and I assessed the situation. There they were, no Tam, no Pecker, not another fan for miles. This was my big chance. So I addressed Leslie with the first thing that came to mind. 'I hope you don't mind us following you,' I laughed tentatively, hoping he'd laugh back. Instead, he favored me with one cool glance and witheringly replied, 'You can do whatever the fuck you like.'

Not encouraging. Here I am, finally talking to Leslie one-to-one for the first time ever and he swears and makes it obvious he thinks we're schmucks. Correction. That *I'm* a schmuck. Not good at all.

'Uh . . . sorry! But we've come all the way from New York,' I babbled, as if our dedication would impress him. He rolled his eyes and left the shop, leaving Eric and Bob to collect the pizza. Appalling. My world was collapsing. I've bugged Leslie and he thinks I'm an idiot. Two years of devotion and he swears and tells me to get lost.

I loped back to the car and blurted to Sue and Kim, 'I can't believe the way he talked to me! He said, "You can do whatever the fuck you like"! I can't believe it!'

Barbarino slid into the car and we pulled out after the camper, which turned back on to the highway. I was retelling the whole story, but Barbarino interrupted. 'They're just tired,' he comforted me. 'Bob was saying they didn't get much sleep last night.' This was some small consolation. On second thought, no it wasn't.

We had no trouble keeping up with them as they drove through the lush eastern Ohio farmland. A few minutes later a Holiday Inn sign directed us into a parking lot on the right side of the road. This time we sat tight in the car as the band piled out of the van and entered the hotel. 'So what now?' Sue inquired.

'I guess we get a room.' We couldn't troop in en masse, so Sue and Barbarino volunteered to stay in the car. Crouching behind it, I changed from my shorts into more respectable-looking light-blue corduroy jeans, and Kim and I went inside. It was your typical motel lobby, with a reception desk, some sofas and a dimly lit bar. Leslie and Bob were in the bar, playing pool. Not about to approach them again, I went to the front desk just as Bob spotted Kim and waved her over.

Dismayingly, there were no vacancies. I was about to go find Kim when she reappeared, and I told her the bad news. 'It don't matter, 'cos they're not staying here. They're going to Detroit, and Bob told me the hotel,' she chortled triumphantly.

Hasta la vista! Rock 'n' roll!

Minutes later we were at the airport, finding out about flights to Detroit. But there were no direct ones from Youngstown, and it transpired that the only way to get there that night was to drive to either Pittsburgh or Cleveland – about an hour-and-a-half either way – and fly from there. We opted for Cleveland because it was closer to Detroit and headed for the interstate. The sun was setting as we left Youngstown, and night had completely fallen by the time we hit Cleveland, whence it was a twenty-minute hop to Detroit.

We were full of nervous laughter when the taxi dropped us off at the St Regis, an old-fashioned luxury hotel in the city center. We knew we were on the verge of something memorable. We'd followed them countless times, but for the first time there were no obstructions. Tam wasn't on the tour, while Pecker, who was, was keeping a low profile. Plus which, the sole security guard, Bob, was actually friendly. After two years, things finally seemed to be looking up.

Bob was in the lobby when we arrived, and seemed glad to see us, or rather, to see Kim. Sue and I checked into a room on the fifth floor, next door to Barbarino and Kim. Barbarino was dispatched to find beer, and when he returned with two six-packs of Bud, all of us including Bob assembled in Sue's and my room. Barbarino, bless him, immediately suggested, 'Why don't you get some of the guys up here for a party'. Bob, double bless him, picked up the phone, dialed a room and said, 'Les – five-one-four, immediately.'

Less than a minute later there was a knock. I answered, and there he was. Leslie. He was standing in the corridor waiting to be let in, casually smoking a cigarette. He was wearing a brown-and-white Starsky & Hutch cardigan and lounging with a feline languor that took my breath away.

This was the moment I'd hoped for since I'd first laid eyes on him, and it was so stupendous that my mind went – well, numb is the only way to describe it. I absorbed the fact of his presence, showed him into the room and shut the door, but an impenetrable membrane slipped into place to block my emotions. Where was the exuberance I'd been saving up for this precise moment? What was this sudden queer emptiness?

McKeown greeted the room with a half-nod, and with one graceful movement sank to the floor next to Bobby. Absently accepting a beer from Barbarino, he fixed his attention on the TV, which was showing a horror movie. Barbarino got busy rolling a joint from the stash he'd brought for this very eventuality, and we girls chit-chatted with Bob, who was a good deal more voluble than his charge. *He* had yet to ask our names, or anything else, for that matter, and only spoke his first words when Barbarino handed him the joint for his approval.

'Thanks,' he said, taking a luxurious drag that ended in a coughing fit. When he'd recovered, he told Barbarino, 'You should use more tobacco.' Barbarino, puzzled, replied, 'Whaddaya mean? I didn't use any tobacco.' There followed a long exchange about the differences between British and American joint-rolling. Then Leslie offered it to Bob, who declined. He then passed it to me.

'I didn't know *you* got high,' Kim said, addressing me. 'Well, uh, yeah, sometimes,' I mumbled. How embarrassing – and typical – of her to point it out in front of Leslie. The last time I'd smoked pot had been three or four years ago at some Millburn party, and I'd long since decided not to bother again because of its lack of effect. I'd never actually been what you'd call high, unless you counted the time I tried a couple of David's diet pills. But I was willing to give it another crack because Leslie was doing it. (And no, still had no effect.)

I did have a full-fledged cigarette addiction, however, something I shared with Leslie. No one else smoked, so he accepted one of my pack of Benson & Hedges, grumbling, as he did, about 'this menthol shit'. We were bonding!

Then something occurred to him. 'I'm gonna call a friend of mine,' he announced, reaching for the phone and dialing three digits.

'D'ya wanna come up here and get stoned?' he asked the person on the other end. Ooh! Who was he talking to? Obviously, Kim and Sue were praying it was Eric, while I thought it would be rather amusing to have Derek up here, wheezing on Barbarino's tobaccoless joint.

A minute later there was a discreet tap on the door. I opened it and saw two figures, one of whom was Woody, and the other Lauren, a rival New York fan. What was *she* doing in Detroit? She was a few feet down the hall, watching to see whose door Woody was knocking on. She spotted me, watched me take Woody by the arm and pull him inside, and looked utterly stricken as I shut the door.

My mild triumph was forgotten as I got a load of Woody, who'd obviously had a couple of beers even before he took the can Barbarino waved in his face. He was wearing a thin black anoraky thing with no shirt underneath and hugely flared jeans. Despite the flares, his clothes were much more becoming than what he'd worn onstage that afternoon, a striped vest-top with ballooning white 'harem' pants.

Woody mumbled something, took a head-clearing swig of Budweiser, and dropped down next to Leslie. Sue passed him a pillow, and as he half-rose to take it he knocked over a chair. Still completely detached, joy and excitement trapped behind this curious pane of emotional glass, I watched Woody right the chair and mutter impenetrably to Leslie, who grinned and nodded. How the hell did they understand each other?

That was when I began fumbling in my bag for my tape recorder, because I had to have some proof that this wasn't all a bizarre dream. I finally found it and pressed Record, casually leaving the bag open on the edge of the bed so it could pick up the whole proceedings.

Woody's presence seemed to spur Leslie to greater heights of surliness toward us. What a strange thing he was, sprawled there, eating Barbarino's emergency M&Ms ration and resisting all attempts to draw him into the conversation. He'd occasionally make some indecipherable remark to Woody, and once in a while addressed the rest of us in a manner both imperious and vulgar. Like this: the ash dropped off the tip of my cigarette into my lap, and Les, the old suavester, advised,

'Don't burn your fucking cunt.' He swore with relish, as if making up for lost time.

Like, what was his problem? Was it so important to him to keep his distance from lowly fans (not that it stopped him from partaking of our booze and dope)? Was he drunk and/or stoned? Or was he just always like this?

After an hour or so of this awkward sparring, Kim got bored and her resolve not to mention Eric disappeared. 'I wish he was here,' she stage-whispered to Sue and me. 'I brought my stockings and suspenders.'

'Stockings and suspenders?' Leslie said, ears suddenly pricking up. 'Who's got stockings and suspenders?'

'I do.' She looked at him hopefully, as if they would persuade him to ring Eric. But he didn't; after a few mildly interested moments, he settled back and resumed popping M&Ms.

And then, another little while later, he decided he'd had enough, and rose, hauling Woody by an arm (not hard; according to the 1977 Annual, Woody weighed 126 pounds). Bob got up too, politely thanked us for our hospitality and they were gone. They were simply gone.

But at least I had my taped souvenir. 'I've been recording this,' I told the others, who yelped 'What?' and 'Ya shittin' me!' (that was Barbarino). But the excitement was short-lived. We gathered round, I pressed Play and . . . nothing. Nothing intelligible, that is. Mumbles, giggles, and a few Leslie-Woody exchanges which none of us could make out because of their accents. We could just perceive Leslie telling me not to burn my effing C-word, and that was it.

Fantastic.

Very, very deflated, I dropped down on to one of the beds. All four of us felt oddly disoriented, revellers blinking at the sun after an all-night party. Barbarino and Kim bid Sue and me a dispirited good-night and went to their room. Sue went to the bathroom and I lay back on my bed, taking in the view of beer cans and overflowing ashtrays. The strange numbness had disappeared when the Rollers had left the room, and I was desolate. Having finally got this close, it was intolerable to see them fading back into the distance. By morning, I knew, it would feel like a dream, the edges blurring until none of it seemed real.

I thought about it as Sue washed her face and began brushing her teeth, and then picked up the phone and dialed three digits. It was answered almost immediately. 'Hello?' said the quiet voice. 'It's Caroline,' I told him. 'Just wanted to say goodnight.' There was a short silence. Then he said, 'Why don't you come round?'

I went round.

20

'YOU'LL NEVER BELIEVE what happened last night,' I told David. It was ten the next morning. I'd just returned to my room and rung him because, inexplicably, he was the only person I wanted to talk to. After I told him everything, whispering so as not to wake Sue in the next bed, he was quiet. 'Well,' he said. 'Well, well.'

'Yeah.'

Much later, he told me that afterwards, he'd sat and stared into space for a long time. 'You sounded so euphoric that I couldn't help being happy for you,' he said. 'Even though I didn't want to be.'

Considering I'd been awake for around forty-eight hours, I was amazingly chipper. The events of last night had been so remarkable that adrenaline was coursing around like I'd mainlined caffeine. I couldn't tell whether I was madly happy or just shellshocked, but the morning-after comedown I was anticipating didn't materialise. I felt buoyant and alluring.

He had been as sweet as I could have hoped, and cute and funny. He'd been everything. And it had all been focused on me, during the long, luxurious hours in which neither of us had slept. I felt I'd never be able to sleep again.

I decided to work off some of the energy by taking a walk. The tape recorder provided an excuse, as the batteries were almost flat and I didn't want to risk it not working if I had another chance to tape Leslie being rude. Leaving Sue semi-conscious – she woke for long enough to grunt, 'Well, congratulations' – I went downstairs. I was about to go out into what looked like a scorchingly hot Friday afternoon when I spotted Lauren in the hotel coffee shop and decided to ask if she felt like a walk.

A word about Lauren. Only Barbarino and Kim knew her well; to the Tacky Tartan Tarts she was simply a rival who occasionally turned up outside hotels and had an irritating habit of referring to the band as 'the boys'. I'd been surprised to see her in the corridor last night, as it suggested someone (presumably not Bob) had told her where they'd be staying.

I wasn't best pleased to see her for one simple, petty reason: she was extremely pretty, in a delicate, English-rosey way, and that kind of competition I could do without. The rest of us were passable, but Lauren was in another league altogether – such a different league, in fact, that I'd often wondered why she bothered hanging around hotels and stage doors.

And it was obvious, I realised as I entered the coffee shop, that her charms had not gone unnoticed by at least one Roller. For there was Leslie sitting at her table, accompanied by the faithful Bob. And it was plain that it had been Leslie who'd asked if he could join her, not the other way around. The three of them noticed me simultaneously, but with wildly differing reactions. Bob gave me a cheery smile, McKeown looked blank, like he'd never seen me before, and Lauren shrieked, 'For Christ's sake, Sullivan, get lost!' She didn't actually say it aloud, but that was exactly what she was thinking.

To her great chagrin, Bob invited me to sit down, which I did. So what if I was butting in? I wasn't about to pass up the chance to be near Leslie. And even though he was clearly intent on talking to Lauren, who had begun eating a plate of veal scaloppini with barely repressed hostility, I was just as intent on talking to him. I did, using the tape recorder as an excuse. 'Do you have any idea what kind of batteries I should get?' I asked, playing the helpless woman card. He did know, told me, and resumed his conversation with Lauren.

Bob was politer – after all, he *had* asked me to sit – and inquired how we'd be getting to the gig, which started at 5.00 at the State Fairgrounds on the other side of Detroit. But after a few minutes of stilted chat, I finally decided to heed Lauren's tacit signals to go away. It had nothing to do with being nice to her. In fact, I'd started to dislike her a fair bit, partly because of her looks, which remained cool and radiant in embarrassing contrast to my own hot sweatiness, and partly because of her highly un-American reticence. The latter bugged me a lot. She was almost English in her reserve, which was rich considering she came from The Bronx. I hated this poised act she seemed to be putting on for Leslie's benefit. It wasn't till a good while later I realised that was simply the way she was, which was even worse.

No, I left the coffee shop because some benign neurotransmitter in my brain was flashing madly that if I wanted Leslie to like me (getting him to love me now seemed out of the question) I'd better make myself scarce or he'd have me down as an incorrigible pain in the ass. It seemed best to leave while I still had a modicum of dignity, so I joined Sue, Kim and Barbarino in the lobby.

Chastened, albeit only temporarily, by the experience, I resisted their entreaties to reveal what had gone on the night before, when I had left our room. I had a whole audience by this point, because there were other New York fans in the hotel, and word had spread. So there we were, me sitting regally in the middle of a sofa, surrounded by half a dozen girls and Barbarino, all desperate for me to dish. Normally I reveled in being the center of attention, but this time instinct told me not to blab for fear of it getting back to the one person I didn't want it to get back to.

We hit the Michigan State Fairground early to size up the terrain. It was the sort of fair you only find in the Midwest, with a midway and rides, exhibitions of prize-winning turnips and Guess Your Age booths. I challenged the guy to guess my age, and was stung to find I looked twenty. Because he was wrong I won a mirror with a picture of Deep Purple on it.

The place was huge, with the arena where the Rollers would be playing plonked in the middle, away from the main road. That meant we wouldn't be able to follow them when they left, but for once it didn't matter. We already knew where they were staying, and all we'd have to do after the show was make our leisurely way back to the St Regis and drape ourselves in the lobby.

The gig finally kicked off. Barbarino was gone for half of it, unsuccessfully trying to wangle a backstage pass. He eventually joined us up in the bleachers, petulant at having to be in the audience instead of where the action was. He was hard to figure, the old Barbster. His real name was Howie; Kim had christened him Barbarino because he swaggered like John Travolta in the TV sitcom 'Welcome Back Kotter'. None of us was ever sure what his real interest was in the Rollers. He was one of the few males who liked them, and practically the only adult male we knew of. We accused him of having the hots for them, but he always denied it, and he was probably telling the truth, as his interest in girls was both constant and rapacious.

Conversely, he wasn't hanging around them in order to meet girls, because he rarely talked to females other than ourselves. It appeared that he simply wanted to become friends with the band, and bask in the minimal reflected glory. To that end, he did everything possible to ingratiate himself with the Rollers and their management, running errands, getting to know the staff at Arista, anything he could think of.

Unfortunately, all the effort never really paid off. Although he became friendly with people around the band, who rewarded him with tidbits of gossip and advance copies of records, he didn't penetrate the inner circle, the Rollers themselves. It was understandable; why would the Rollers – who were a professional pop group, after all – want to hang around with a kid from Queens?

They would have the odd conversation with him, which he would repeat to us embellished out of all proportion, and they obviously had no qualms about smoking his pot. But as for being buddies, it didn't happen. He never transcended the boundaries between fandom and friendship, and stayed always a fan – one of us, never one of them.

For all Barbarino's annoying qualities, we liked him. His annoying qualities *were* supremely annoying, one of his favorite stunts being to tell you that one or another of the Rollers thought you were really hideous, and you'd never be quite sure whether he was lying. But he also had his sweet side. If you were feeling down, he'd come over and whisper, 'Les was telling me he likes your hair that way' – and, of course, you'd always choose to believe him. I'm not sure what he got out of being around us because we teased him mercilessly, but he was always there. After a while, he became our first and only male Tacky Tartan Tart.

And this time we really owed him. By the simple expedient of bringing along five bucks' worth of pot, he had lured the Rollers our way and helped us make the connection we had longed for.

Meanwhile, the gig was turning out to be interesting. Leslie must have been feeling his oats, for he was changing lyrics into extremely unsubtle single entendres. On 'Don't Stop The Music', the Faulkner/Wood line 'How can I tell her that I really love her?' became 'How can I tell her that I wanna get right into her?', while Eric went even further. 'Hot tramp, fuck me so,' he rasped, at which Kim flung herself back into her seat and clutched her heart.

Then, between numbers, Leslie casually remarked, 'Woody wants to tell you all something about last night.' We waited, stunned. Woody merely stepped up to his microphone and sang 'Eagles Fly', the one number on which he was allowed to do lead vocals. (It was a little ditty by Faulkner and Wood about the joys of getting on a motorcycle – that was the 'eagle' – and hitting the open road: 'Ride on the highway/Hear their engines scream/Eagles in motion/A thousand CC dream'. Even if one of them owned a motorcycle, it was extremely improbable he would have the courage to scream down any highway. Just another example of BCR wishful thinking.)

The gig ended, as ever, with 'Saturday Night', after which we made our way out and back to the hotel. It was 6.00, and we had the choice of either going back to the venue for the second show at nine or hanging around the hotel till they got back for the night. The matter was decided when Barbarino spoke to the sound engineer, who let it slip that the band were flying to the next city, Charlotte, straight after the second show.

By the time we'd collected our stuff at the hotel and got a cab to the airport, we'd acquired Lauren as a traveling companion. She wanted to get to Charlotte, too, presumably to finish the conversation she'd had with 'Les', as she insisted on calling him (real fans knew he preferred Leslie), in the coffee shop that afternoon. At Detroit Metro we discovered to our chagrin that the only direct flight to Charlotte was full. The only way to get there that night would be to go on standby for a flight to Atlanta, then on standby again for a connection to Charlotte.

We just made the first leg, which made us feel terribly smug. Boy, did I regret the smugness when we ran into a storm somewhere over northern Tennessee. The plane rocked terrifyingly as it lumbered through an electrical field, its wingtips a conductor for the lightning flashing all around us. Across the aisle, a woman began to cry, scrabbling in her bag for a string of rosary beads, which she held tremblingly. The plane jolted and seemed to lose altitude. What a way to go, and even if we made it to Atlanta we'd have to go through it all over again on the second flight.

But we did make it, and at 2.30 in the morning finally reached Charlotte, to be greeted by a couple of dozen fans who expected the Rollers to be on our flight. What were their mothers thinking, letting them out in the middle of the night like that?

The hot dampness, even at that hour, was overwhelming. As soon as we left the air-conditioned terminal we were enveloped in Southern summer heat, which was a different thing altogether from New York heat. This heat lay heavily in the atmosphere, filling every nook and cranny and sticking to you like a second skin. 'I ain't gonna like it here,' Kim complained, already worried about her hair, which she spent hours blow-drying straight every morning. 'Why can't these suckers just play New York?'

That night's hotel, the Radisson Plaza, was by far the nicest place the Rollers had stayed this tour. It was modern and plant-filled, the furniture was soothingly cushiony and security was such that there was little chance of any local fans getting inside. Excellent. We walked in, and there in the lobby, to our shock, were two New York fans, Susie and Robyn, whom we'd last seen eight hours before at the Fairground. Seems they'd gotten the last two seats on the direct Detroit-Charlotte flight, the one we couldn't get on, and had arrived hours before. Bitchstresses.

And there, on an overstuffed sofa and not looking at all happy, was Cathy, who'd gotten in from New York shortly after Susie and Robyn arrived from Detroit. 'You won't believe what happened,' she told us, or rather, told Sue, Kim and Barbarino. Me she studiously ignored. Susie and Robyn began to laugh. 'The police were waiting for her when she arrived,' Robyn said, smiling hugely at the memory, 'because of what she said to Sue on the phone this afternoon.'

It transpired that Sue had called Cathy to tell her what had gone on the night before. Of course, she mentioned that I hadn't slept in our room, and Cathy – shocked, flabbergasted, whatever – spluttered, 'I'm gonna kill Caroline.' Sue had laughingly mentioned this to Robyn at the gig, and Robyn had repeated it to Susie as they checked into the Radisson Plaza.

Sorry if this is getting complicated. Anyway, Robyn made the mistake of phrasing it as, 'Cathy said she's going to kill Caroline when she gets here', which was overheard by the desk clerk, who took it to mean someone was literally coming to kill someone else. When Cathy turned up an hour or so later, a couple of cops greeted her in reception. Apparently, it took quite a while to convince them she wasn't a contract killer.

So she wasn't at all pleased to see me, and ignored me as Sue and I checked in and took the elevator up to the room we were sharing with her. She was really upset, because actual contact with a Roller such as I had experienced wasn't in the rulebook. You could get close up to a point but no closer. We'd fantasised about going all the way hundreds of times, but Tacky Tartan law ruled that the band had to remain at a safe shadowy distance. Despite all our lurid boasts of what we'd do were we ever alone with them, we knew it would probably never happen, and that was how we wanted it. They had to be fantasy figures, inviolate, for fear of ruining the magic. That was why their successively raunchier antics over the last few months – from Debbie Bottom in Pittsburgh to Kim's dalliance with Eric in Louisville – both tantalised and upset us. And now, as far as Cathy was concerned, I'd betrayed all of us by exposing them to daylight too close to home. Debbie Bottom and Kim she could deal with, but a sister Tart – it was too much.

'Yo,' Barbarino shouted through the door, startling us – we were sitting on the floor next to the bathroom, drinking Tab and trying to patch things up. We let him in, and he helped himself to a Tab before announcing portentously, 'The guys just checked in.' We automatically began to rise. 'Don't bother, they've already gone to their rooms,' crowed the little monster, repulsive in his triumph. 'They looked really tired.' Hardly surprising – it was 3.00 in the morning.

We were on the same floor as Kim and Barbarino, Susie and Robyn, and Lauren, who had a room to herself. With the Rollers securely tucked in bed three floors below, we didn't have anything better to do than visit each other's rooms and loudly hang out, making frequent trips to the soda machine. Lauren, meanwhile, slipped downstairs, murmuring that she was going to read a book in the lobby. Typical – she was probably embarrassed to be around us.

But she had an ulterior motive, as we found when Sue returned from a reconaissance trip to the lobby half an hour later. Lauren was still down there, she reported, but she wasn't alone with her book – Leslie was there, and the two were deep in conversation. 'Bitch, bitch, bitch,' Cathy moaned softly.

This I had to see. Grabbing a handful of change for the cigarette machine, I went downstairs. Lauren glanced at me for the barest millisecond – was she gloating, the slag? – then returned her full attention to Leslie, who was describing something with small, abrupt hand movements. He was sitting next to her on a chubby beige couch, and the body language was unmistakably intimate.

From the cigarette machine, where they couldn't see me, I studied them. Sick with envy, I compared Lauren's looks with my own. She won hands down in almost every respect, except perhaps height. But what good was being five foot nine if I also had plumply curly hair that laughed off any attempt to style it? And why, if Mother Nature had allowed me a slim top half, did she have to compensate so much in the bottom half – which, despite my weight loss, was still way too girthy? For that matter – I was working up a righteous head of self-pity – I could have done without the obviously Jewish nose, and wasn't it a bit unfair, with all that going against me, that I was also practically blind without my contact lenses?

Lauren, on the other hand, looked like Jean Shrimpton circa 1964. She had straight blonde hair with bangs, large blue eyes and, though she was Jewish too, she'd been spared the nose. No wonder Leslie was attracted to her, I told myself in an ecstasy of jealousy. He was probably intrigued with her aloofness, too. Except in absolute crises, she always kept herself separate from the rest of us, as if to say, 'I'm not with them, I'm not like them'. Going off to read while we partied upstairs was very Lauren. She made herself quietly available (but how did she know he'd come downstairs??) and he took the bait.

Was that how you got a Roller, I wondered. Just hung back and waited for one to notice you? It hadn't worked for me – I'd had to make all the running the night before. I watched them a while longer, wallowing in misery.

Back upstairs, Cathy was close to apoplexy. 'Were they touching or holding hands or anything?' she demanded. No, no, just talking, I assured her. 'I'm still gonna kill her,' she seethed. Lucky there were no cops around to hear her. After brooding for a few minutes, she decided it was necessary to witness it herself. But she was back moments later, declaring, 'They're not there.'

'Well, we'd have heard her come back,' someone pointed out. 'She must be in Leslie's room.'

'I'm gonna kill her, I'm gonna kill her,' Cathy mooed, sucking fiercely at her Tab. We were still discussing Lauren's perfidy when we finally fell asleep, well after the sun had come up.

21

S OME INTERNAL ALARM CLOCK roused Sue, Cathy
and me about three hours later. It was 10.00 Saturday
morning, and since waking up Wednesday morning,
the day before the tour, I'd had about five hours' sleep. But
who had time to sleep when there was so much Roller business
to be done?

Sleep is for wimps, I told myself, and, strangely enough, I
did feel pretty good. I even hummed a little tune in the shower
as I washed my hair with Gee, Your Hair Smells Terrific
shampoo, which did actually make your hair smell terrific.

Cathy shuffled into the bathroom next, and Sue went to the
drink machine down the hall to buy our breakfast Tabs. While
they were thus engaged, I had a sudden strong urge to call the
Roller I was beginning to think of as 'mine'. I was in a good
mood – my hair was freshly laundered and I was high on sleep
deprivation. It just seemed like the right thing to do. I was sure
he'd enjoy the spontaneity.

Quickly, before Cathy finished her shower, I dialed the hotel
operator and asked for the pseudonym he was registered
under. Barbarino had used one of his contacts to discover
the band's 'tour names', which included Rikki Fender for Eric,
Johnny Noname for Derek and S Pine for Woody.

A pause, then one ring. Two rings, three, six, and I was about
to hang up – was he asleep? In the bath? – when he answered.
He sounded groggy – God, I *had* woken him – and I considered
putting the phone down, then decided to plow ahead.

'Hi, it's me,' I said, pitching my voice somewhere between perky, moody and suggestive to try to match whatever frame of mind he might be in. The only sound was that of the receiver quietly being replaced.

He'd hung up on me. I was horrorstruck. Had he not recognised my voice and thought I was a fan? Had he *recognised* my voice (the implication of which was infinitely worse)? I hadn't been prepared for this, and sat there on the bed, frozen with mortification. He must have known it was me, I told myself, furious and appalled. He must think I'm completely pathetic if he won't even say hello to me.

I would have gone on kicking myself a good deal longer if Sue hadn't returned with the Tabs. Tab was an official Tart beverage because it contained all the caffeine of Coke but none of the calories. It was good for whatever ailed you, and we drank crates of it.

It worked that morning – after a can-and-a-half I was less ravaged by wretchedness, and even felt a dart of pleasure when I saw myself in my silver-star T-shirt and zip-pocket bell-bottoms. So what if He didn't want to speak to me? There were plenty of guys who would. We were in the South, last redoubt of chivalry – some drawling Romeo would probably be bewitched and ply me with Goo Goo Clusters, a legendary marshmallow-and-chocolate delicacy found only below the Mason-Dixon line. Then little Mr Roller would be very sorry he'd been so rude.

The problem, though, was that it was Mr Roller I wanted. I moped all the way through breakfast, which was the hotel coffee shop's blue-plate special: waffles, hash browns, grits and red-eye gravy – scrumptious. I could understand why Elvis had weighed nearly 250 pounds when he died. Then, to get my mind off things, I decided to find some Goo Goo Clusters and look around Charlotte.

As I left the coffee shop I passed Leslie and Big Bobby waiting for a table. I managed to restrain myself from greeting

Leslie, and just as well, because his thin lips were set and there was a pugnacious air about him.

The heat changed my mind about walking before I'd gone 100 yards, and I trudged back, dripping. Cathy and Sue were in the lobby, as was Lauren, who was sitting as far as possible from everyone else, reading her book. 'So what did you *say*?' Cathy was asking Sue as I approached. 'What *could* I say? I just walked out,' said Sue, rolling her eyes.

It transpired that while I'd been out, Sue had gone to the coffee shop to eat, seen Leslie and gone over to say hello. His response had been a crisp 'Piss off'.

'God, what's eating him?' Cathy wondered, shaking her head in bewilderment.

'I just think he's tired of this whole thing,' Sue ventured, and she had probably hit the nail on the head. McKeown's behavior for the entire two days we'd been around the Rollers suggested he *was* sick of it all – sick of the gigs, the fans, the restrictions, the not being able to walk down the street, not that he'd want to in Charlotte . . .

Even finally being allowed off the leash a bit, being able to quietly drink, smoke and schtup, didn't seem to help. If anything, the new freedom seemed to be engendering a bitterness and contempt that increased by the day. This was a man who was fed up.

The only time he seemed to come close to enjoying himself was when Lauren was around. It pained me to admit it, but she loosened him up – she even made him laugh. Her quiet presence answered some need in him, even if it was only for the companionship of a woman who didn't treat him like a pop star. I had it on good authority from Barbarino and Kim that Lauren could be as fannish as the rest of us – she even had the scrapbooks and photo albums – but she radiated a calm that must have been irresistible to someone in chaos. As I've said before, I didn't have the slightest idea how to radiate calm. I was unspeakably jealous.

My jealousy was temporarily assuaged by the fact that Leslie was in the coffee shop and Lauren was out here in the lobby. If he liked her that much, wouldn't he have invited her to his table? I said as much to the others, and we snickered spitefully, just loudly enough so Lauren would know we were talking about her. Her response was to squint at her book. We were such brats.

When we had glared at her to our satisfaction, we left for the venue. It was an amusement park called Carowinds, ten miles away on the South Carolina border. The group were doing two shows again, which was par for the course at the sort of places they were playing.

Going through their paces twice in the same day must have been tiring for them, not to mention a galling reminder of their lowly status in the rock pecking order. Two shows a night used to be the norm for many bands up until the early seventies, with places like New York's Academy of Music expecting groups to follow the usual 9 p.m. set with one at midnight, so the band wouldn't get out of there till the small hours. My greatest dream at fourteen was to move to Manhattan so I could go to the late show, which was impossible when you had to catch the last train back to Millburn.

But by 1977, such labor-intensive tours were a thing of the past – except for bands like the Rollers, who were not only doing two shows a day but doing them at woefully un-cred fairgrounds and family parks. You wouldn't catch even Peter Frampton at a place like Carowinds, which was pristine and kiddie-oriented, a South Carolina Disneyland without the talking mice. Another reason, no doubt, for Leslie's grouchiness.

The poor old Rollers were playing the park's Paladium amphitheatre, which consisted of rows of benches fanning out from a big white stage decorated with crisp white curtains, an ornate roof and two glitter balls suspended from the ceiling. It had been conceived for country acts, and sure enough, a banner outside the arena advertised a show the very next day by the Starland Vocal Band, a hideously twee Nashville-style girl/boy quartet who'd scored a freak hit the year before with something called 'Afternoon Delight'. The Rollers must have been overjoyed to be keeping the stage warm for them.

When we got there, an hour before the first show, Barbarino disappeared, grunting something about tracking down Bobby. We didn't see him for nearly an hour, during which we conserved our strength with a great deal of fruit punch and hot dogs in thick batter, known as corn dogs. If nothing else, I was coming to love Southern cooking.

He finally reappeared with two backstage passes, one of which was already stuck to the chest pocket of the tartan jumpsuit he always wore at gigs. He handed the other to Kim, smiling an apology to the rest of us. 'I couldn't get no more, I'm sorry,' he said, not sounding at all sorry. We were annoyed, but not half as annoyed as we were a bit later, when we spotted Lauren sitting in the front with her own backstage pass. 'Now, who could have given her that?' Cathy asked sourly.

This was the last day of the tour, and once they'd got through their two sets, they'd be on holiday for the better part of a month. They were in correspondingly high spirits at the show, Leslie altering lyrics with the *joie de vivre* of someone who sensed freedom just around the corner. 'I only wanna do it to you,' he cried on 'I Only Wanna Be With You', while Eric did the customary 'Hot tramp, suck my toe!' his croak echoing around the Paladium. Even old Derek was merry, battering his drums with atypical zest.

It was a rousing finale, and we beeped and hooted along to every word of every chorus. Just as well we gave them a good send-off, because, though we obviously couldn't have known it then, they wouldn't tour again for two years.

When the set finished, Barbarino and Kim slipped off, presumably to use their accursed backstage passes, and Cathy,

Sue and I were left standing around like the girls no one wanted to dance with at the party. Ushers began clearing the place for the second show, which we didn't have tickets for, and there was no choice but to return to the hotel.

Daylight was fading pinkly when we got back. The second show wouldn't be over, we knew, till around ten, which meant the band wouldn't be back at the hotel till elevenish. We parked ourselves in the lobby to consider our options. There was a hairdressers' convention at the Radisson, and it had just finished for the day. The lobby was full of beehived women who looked like they'd answer to the names Arlene and Mary Beth.

'We could always get our hair done,' Cathy suggested.

'Hey, where can I get one of those outfits?' Sue interrupted, pointing at a clothing rail being wheeled in by a bellboy. It was jammed with half a dozen identical white suits, their collars and cuffs spangled with red sequins. Maybe they were having a bad-taste convention, too. As the rail went by, I asked the bellboy who the suits belonged to. 'The Commodores, ma'am. You know, the soul group?' Indeed we did know. The Commodores were in the chart at that very moment with the slushy ballad 'Easy'. How mildly amusing that one of my current least-favorite bands were staying in our hotel.

We discussed going out for dinner, counted our money and found we were collectively down to less than $40. So our choices boiled down to hanging around in the lobby or hanging around in our room. We voted for the latter so we could indulge in some primping before the band got back.

When we got to our floor, it seemed as if nearly every door had a food tray outside waiting to be collected by room service. Some of them contained a lot of stuff – barely touched hamburgers and the like. Which gave me an idea. I was starving, and it would be immoral to see it go to waste. I shamelessly picked up a plate containing an intact hamburger and salad, then prowled down the hall, looking for something to go with it. Five or six doors along, someone had left a buttery baked potato, so I knelt down to shovel it onto my plate, and as I did the door opened. A tall black guy in enormous red bellbottoms and I looked at each other, he in astonishment, me in roiling embarrassment.

'Can I help you?' he asked.

'No, it's all right,' I muttered.

He grinned and opened the door wider. 'If you're hungry, girl, you just have that potato,' he encouraged, kneeling to help me transfer it to my plate. 'In fact, I can order you another from room service. A nice hot one.'

'Really, it's all right,' I repeated, rising and casually strolling back to our room, where Cathy and Sue were rolling on the floor.

'That was one of the Commodores,' Cathy woofed. 'You should've let him order you a potato.'

'Never mind the potato, he could afford to get her a steak,' Sue burbled, nearly insane with hilarity. Yeah, yeah, how very funny. I ate my hamburger with dignity, refusing to share it with the sluts.

Barbarino and Kim finally got back a couple of hours later, bursting into our room all a-twitter. Barbarino was a-twitter, at least, because the band were coming to our room for a party when they returned.

'Bob said he'd bring them up,' he bubbled, and he actually sounded convincing. Convincing enough, anyway, for each of us to pony up five bucks for booze. He hauled back a couple of six-packs of Bud, two bottles of Wild Irish Rose strawberry wine and a bottle of vodka, all of which we put in the bathroom sink to chill.

An hour and most of a bottle of wine later, we were getting itchy. 'So where the fuck are they?' Kim inquired from the floor, where she was sprawled. She'd changed into stockings, suspenders and a lacy blue off-the-shoulder dress with a full skirt, and one of the stockings had run when she'd fallen over Barbarino on her way to the bathroom for a beer.

'Where the fuck are they, Howie?' she repeated, one foot twitching menacingly. Barbarino looked apprehensive. She only called him by his real name when she was on the verge of losing control, and she was on the verge of it now.

'Bob said they were coming . . .' he whimpered. The rest of us watched blearily, curious to see if she'd hit him. There was a tense moment when it seemed like she was about to seize him by the lapels of his jumpsuit, but it passed. 'Fuck this,' she suddenly said. Pulling herself up effortfully, she left the room. Seconds later, he followed her, whining and protesting.

It didn't look like we were going to see much of the band that night, so we concentrated on finishing the wine. Within half an hour we were completely blotto, and Cathy and Sue decided they needed to go down to the lobby and sit there till they saw a Roller – 'or a Commodore,' Cathy added. When they'd gone, I called Big Bob to say that if he saw Barbarino, who I assumed was lurking somewhere on the Rollers' floor, to tell him I hated him. 'He's right here,' Bob laughed. 'Why don't you come down and tell him yourself?'

I didn't need to be asked twice. Swiping a lipstick at the bottom half of my face in case I encountered a Roller, I marched off to the BCRs' floor. An unappetising sight greeted me. Eric, a hotel security guard and a lady policeman were sitting on the floor of the corridor, drinking paper cups of sangria, Kim was lying half on and half off a folding chair, holding a can of beer, and Barbarino was trying, unsuccessfully, to prop her up. He was too sorry to waste my stream of expletives on, so I halted and woozily leaned against the wall. Eric suddenly saw me, and, with a look of alarm, wobbled to his feet and disappeared into his room. What was he afraid of, that I was gonna ask for his autograph, the big putz?

But I forgot about him, because Bob had suddenly appeared

and was speaking to me. I listened fuzzily, and caught the end of a sentence.

'. . . and he was asking where you were, so I told him if I saw you I'd send you round.'

What? *Who* was asking where I was? Who wanted me sent round? Bob caught a whiff of my Wild Irish Rose breath and winced. 'You've had a few, haven't you, love?' he remarked, shifting so he was upwind. 'Just hang on a sec.'

He went down the hall, knocked at a door and had a brief exchange with the person who opened it. 'Go on, he wants to see you.' He smiled encouragingly.

I approached the door, which was half-open, the room beyond in cool darkness. He was waiting for me, young and smooth-skinned and heartachingly beautiful. 'Hi again,' he said, and I knew with absolute and complete certainty I would never again be as happy as I was at that second. 'I'm sure I've met you before,' I replied feebly, decanting myself through the door and shutting it behind me.

22

THREE SECONDS LATER it was morning and Bob was knocking and telling him to get a move on because they were leaving in an hour.

My Roller ordered coffee, which I drank even though I didn't feel like it, and I wondered whether to give him my phone number. Instinct said no. I knew he wouldn't call.

I didn't know if he had a girlfriend, because there had been an unspoken understanding that there would be no mention of personal things. Not that he hadn't talked about himself, which I'd encouraged by asking questions as discreetly as possible, knowing this was the best chance I'd ever get to clear up things I'd always wanted to know. (Were they sick of being a teen band? Yes. Did they get on with Tam? Reasonably.)

He'd also spoken of his family and of a weekend he'd recently spent with friends in the Highlands. I was dying to hear more – wanted to know every tiny thing about him – but managed to restrain myself. He knew I was a fan, but there was a difference between being one and acting like one. It was important that he saw me as an equal, which meant repressing the urge to tell him, 'I can't believe you're three feet away, talking to me, smiling at me.'

Funnily enough, it was easy to make ordinary conversation. Actually being with a Roller was so ludicrously improbable that there was nothing for it but to treat him like a normal person. So I was able to talk casually, as if we were two people who'd met in, say, a club. We could have been – he was only a few years older, we appeared to find the same things funny, we even liked the same band, which he happened to play in . . .

For his part, he was content to not know much about me. In Detroit he'd asked how old I was – in case I'd turned out to be fourteen, I suppose – and he'd politely asked what I did. That was it – he simply bypassed the getting-to-know-you stage. But I couldn't care less if he was interested in who I was as long as he was there talking to me.

He padded into the bathroom to have a shower and I was alone for a few minutes, looking at his things scattered around. It was typical boy stuff – T-shirts, jeans, rank-looking bloomers – all spilling out of a huge metal suitcase. One of the socks he'd been wearing the night before had made its way under the dressing table, where it lay balled up, the athletic stripes on the cuff just visible. It wasn't much, but it was something. I slipped it into my bag just as the shower was turned off.

'Ten minutes!' Bob bellowed through the door, like we were waiting to go onstage at the London Palladium. A peck on the cheek and I left, knowing a post-passion depression was just around the corner but feeling too high to worry about it right then.

In our room, Sue and Cathy had already broken out the Tabs. 'So?' they asked. So I told them.

'What happened to Kim?' I asked as an afterthought. 'She was sitting in the hallway, really smashed, when I last saw her.'

'Oh, Barbarino said she sat out there and got even drunker, cos Eric was ignoring her,' said Cathy.

'And Lauren?'

'Never saw her.'

'And Leslie?'

'Him either.'

'Hmm.'

The band were leaving at eleven, and we trooped down to

watch them go. For once I tried to be inconspicuous, as I didn't want Him to see me acting like a fan, which was exactly what I was doing by hanging around, looking at them get into a limousine.

Our own flight wasn't till late afternoon, and we'd planned to spend the remaining hours checking out Charlotte. That was until Robyn came puffing up from outside.

'I think Kim and Barbarino have pulled a fast one – they just got into a cab with their luggage.' We instantly knew what that meant – the treacherous scumlets were going to try to get on to the Rollers' flight to New York. (We discovered later that Kim made the flight, but it did her no good, because none of the Rollers spoke to her. Barbarino, who couldn't get a seat, took the next flight back on his own.)

With the rest of the afternoon ahead of us and our desire to sightsee extinguished by Kim and Barbarino's deceitfulness, we trudged off to the airport to wait out the hours till our flight. Lauren joined us. With 'the boys' gone, she was suddenly friendly again.

Turned out she'd been with Leslie again the night before. Just talking, she claimed. 'He's a really nice person, very deep and thoughtful,' she insisted.

We looked at her incredulously. If there was one thing he hadn't been in the past seventy-two hours, it was nice. Or thoughtful. Deep I could just about buy. There were obviously things going on beneath that truculent surface. Maybe he was great when you got to know him.

Perversely, we were full of hilarity and dirty jokes on the flight to JFK, and the six of us – Cathy, Sue, Lauren, Robyn, Susie and me – parted at Kennedy amid hysterical laughter.

An hour later I was trudging into my mother's apartment – my apartment, too, I reminded myself with great gloom. 'Did you have a good time?' asked Ma from the kitchen, where she was futzing around with a salad. 'It was all right,' I replied, suddenly struck by the tininess of the apartment. It hadn't been so evident when I'd moved in because I'd been too busy anticipating the tour.

'Where did you go?' she persisted. Her curiosity was justified, because I'd left without warning four days before, simply announcing that I was going away for the weekend.

'Oh . . . Detroit and stuff . . . a couple of Roller shows with Cathy and Sue,' I mumbled, settling on to the couch that was also, I glumly recalled, my bed. I lit a Benson & Hedges – the cigarettes Leslie had scoffed at because they were menthol – and turned on the radio.

'. . . Stevie Wonder's new single,' the DJ was saying. A patter of drums followed, then a buoyant female choir trilling, 'La-la-la-la-la-la-la', then Wonder's voice came in. It was a love song to a girl whose thoughts were elsewhere – fixed on 'another star' – while his own remained with her.

I'd been thinking something similar, in a deepening depression, all the way back from the airport, and to hear my feelings summed up so exactly was a shock. The misery hit me then, and I snuffled as quietly as possible so Ma wouldn't hear me from the kitchen. It was half an hour and another two cigarettes before I could even begin to think about unpacking.

23

' I CAN'T EVEN PUT MY feelings into words,' I wrote on September 2.'I feel sort of empty, and I guess the illusion disappeared the minute Leslie walked into our room in Detroit.'

It was four days later, and I'd spent the whole time morosely sitting around the house. As I saw it, I had a lot to be morose about. The focus of my whole summer, the tour, was over. I was desperately in love with my Roller, but knew I'd probably never see him again.

It was a set of circumstances I'd never expected to encounter. How could I have anticipated this melancholy and regret? Regret not for what had happened but for a connection too briefly made – for everything I had ever wanted, it seemed, had gone with him when they drove away from the hotel in Charlotte.

In the cool neutrality of his room I'd bridged the gap between fantasy and reality. It bestowed a different sense not just of him but of me, because my feelings about myself had suddenly become less self-critical. If he had wanted me, I must be more wantable than I'd ever allowed myself to believe. He was, in my eyes, so desirable himself that, by desiring me, he validated me, endowed me with worth. It might sound achingly lacking in self-esteem, but that was how I felt. To me, the bond was real and permanent, which provided some comfort against the painful knowledge that he probably hadn't spared me a thought since flying back to Scotland on Sunday.

It was just about the only comfort I had just then. Sue J, who hadn't been able to get time off work to go on the tour, was jealous she'd missed it all, and going out of her way to be bitchy to me. Autumn was in the air, and I had to get a job. Life stank.

I said as much to Sue P and Barbarino on Saturday, when the three of us got together at my place over a couple of bottles of Wild Irish Rose, which I'd bought because it reminded me of Charlotte. 'I'll never be happy again,' I declared, or words to that effect, because six glasses of rotgut had taken me to the verge of incoherence.

'Yes you will,' Barbarino said comfortingly, leaning across Sue on my sofa-bed to pat my shoulder. 'I can probably get you a job at Radio City.' Radio City Music Hall, the famous Art Deco movie theatre, was where he'd worked since finishing school in June. He was only a popcorn seller, but apparently you could quickly rise to become the candy-counter manager, which was certainly something to strive for.

'You're so sweet,' I sniveled, and threw up on my pillow. Turning it over, I fell into a sodden sleep, only waking sometime in the middle of the night when I felt Barbarino trying to get into bed beside me. 'Don't be ridiculous,' I mumbled, swiping his cheek with the nails I'd stopped biting specially for the tour. I fell asleep with his cry ringing in my ears.

24

B ARBARINO WAS AS GOOD as his word. Three days later I found myself beside him at the popcorn counter, explaining to my first customer that the reason he couldn't detect any butter on his 'buttered popcorn' was that it was 'pre-buttered'. That was what we were instructed to say when they asked, and they all did.

His boss had offered me the job practically as soon as I'd arrived for the interview, and I soon realised why. Blue polyester uniform, minimum wage, seven-hour shift with a mere half-hour break – this wasn't exactly the most desirable position in New York. It suited me, though, because it was undemanding, you could stuff your face with candy all day, and mope about the Rollers without anyone noticing.

I liked most of my co-popcorn-mongers, most of whom were too bright to be there. The only one I didn't get on with was Griffin, a young Cary Grant whose looks were only slightly diminished by the polyester tunic. He was an aspiring actor, and had a condescending way of implying that he was going to be famous while the rest of us were destined to work at Radio City forever. He was half-right. He did become moderately famous – I well recall my dismay when I first saw a movie poster with the name Griffin Dunne on it – but none of us stayed at Radio City very long. It was just too tedious.

Just after I started, Emma returned from a summer with relatives in Buckinghamshire. Among the Roller paraphernalia she brought back was a copy of a British tabloid with a report of the band's supposed plans to move to Los Angeles. This was the first we'd heard of it, and we thought it was a terrible idea. LA was a revolting, cultureless den of coke-addled iniquity, and the thought of them living there and changing even more than they'd already changed was impossible to accept. (They did go, but not till the summer of '78.)

But a career revamp was definitely in order. That was brought home by the October issue of 16, which had just hit the newsstands. The front cover, which had been dominated by the Rollers for the last two years, had a large picture of David Cassidy's younger half-brother, Shaun. And the Rollers? Nothing but a small picture at the bottom, which didn't bode well, considering they'd just finished a tour that fans would presumably want to read about.

A couple of days later, one of the teen idols the Rollers had supplanted, Marc Bolan, died in a car crash. Remembering my 'interview' with him in London eighteen months earlier, I was mildly sad. Among other things, his death confirmed that the relative innocence of early seventies music was gone for good, unseated by punk and, in America, by disco.

Disco had spawned a hard-edged nightclub scene epitomised by Studio 54, the most famous club in Manhattan, which apparently allowed only celebrities to enter. It was peopled by the likes of Bianca Jagger and Andy Warhol every night, and the amount of cocaine reputedly consumed on the premises was legendary. It made me loathe disco music all the more – if repellent socialites like Warhol danced to it, it had to be crap.

Nor did I think much of Marvin Gaye, who at that point could definitely be described as disco. He did a three-night, six-show run at Radio City that week, and I heard all six dishing up the popcorn. I mention it because Gaye has become so iconic since his death in 1984 that people are usually impressed when I say I've seen him, and not once but six times.

'He wore a white suit, and whenever he so much as raised his hand the girls got hysterical. It was cute, esp. during "What's Going On",' I wrote after the first night. It took me years to recognise 'What's Going On' for the work of genius it is.

A few days after Gaye, David Soul came in for a couple of shows. Soul was, of course, Hutch from Starsky & Hutch, the definitive cool-rocking seventies cop show. Along the way, he'd ill-advisedly taken a shot at singing, and now had three hits to show for it, including 'Silver Lady'.

I couldn't abide his drippy romanticism, and since I wasn't working the nights he was on there was no reason for me to see him. But I went to one show anyway, to get my mind off the Rollers, who, I wrote in late September, 'fill my every thought'. Soul was grim. His charmless balladeering made me long to surgically attach a pair of headphones to his ears and plug him into a Clash album turned up to maximum volume.

Barbarino was working that night, and in between stuffing hot dogs into buns and pouring Cokes said there was something he had to tell me. So I hung around till the end of the show and then he confided, crazed with pride, that he'd lost his virginity a couple of days ago. It had happened with an older woman of twenty-one in the bedroom he shared with his brother. How he convinced her I'll never know.

The grisly news made me reflect yet again how much things were changing. The Roller tour had been a watershed, creating a schism in our feelings. Getting close up, witnessing their boredom and frustration first-hand, was a sad and lonely thing for us. Our fantasies had always been predicated on the belief that the Rollers were happy with their lot – those constant smiles! – in their sunny world where the growing-up process was permanently suspended. If they no longer believed in it, how could we?

'Seems like nothing's been the same since the tour. All the familiar things are changing,' I lamented in my diary. That was how it was starting to feel. We were, in small ways, starting to go our own ways. Cathy, Emma and Sue P had new jobs, and Sue had also just landed her first boyfriend, a rotund Brooklynite called Mike.

I couldn't say I was thrilled. I sensed a threat in these new diversions, every one of which put a rent in the fabric of our friendship. A real-life boyfriend was bound to replace Eric in Sue's affections, and sure enough, within weeks of meeting Mike, Sue was seeing him most nights, and pronouncing herself 'really bored with the Rollers'. And Cathy's new job, as a receptionist at a jewelry company, kept her too busy for two-hour Tart phone calls.

I may have been the only one of us to buy the new single released in early October. It was an *It's a Game* track called 'The Way I Feel Tonight'. Not their finest hour – in fact, this lifeless ballad ranked as one of their weakest songs in years. It wasn't as if Arista Records had much choice, though. The last single, 'You Made Me Believe in Magic', had been catchy and uptempo, but fared poorly in the chart. A ballad seemed the safest option, as a good, solid slowie almost always sells (witness the success of slop like Whitney Houston's 'I Will Always Love You' and Bryan Adams's 'Everything I Do' in the nineties).

Also, *It's a Game* didn't leave Arista with many viable alternatives. Take the song 'Sweet Virginia' – it was catchy, but America just wasn't ready for ditties about ambiguous sexuality. As for woolly concept numbers like the title track, with its chorus of 'There are faces all around me, they were running everywhere/But everywhere is nowhere, and nowhere isn't there', forget about it. That left little else but 'The Way I Feel Tonight'. And guess what? It ended up bombing, selling less than any other single they'd released in America.

Faced with mass defection in the Tart ranks, I made an effort to fill the Roller-sized gap. One night Robyn invited me on a double date. Our swains were Al, a DJ from the local pop radio station WXLO, and his friend Paulie. 'We picked Al up at the station, then drove to the Fulton Fish Market to pick up Paulie, and went to Paulie's in Flatbush. The place was beautifully decorated for someone who works at the fish market,' I wrote. Paulie, my date, was nice enough, but I was more interested in talking to Al, who'd once interviewed the Rollers on the air. 'His impressions of them were hilarious. He seems to have a particular dislike for Woody.'

Poor Al, forced to spend his hot date discussing the Bay City Rollers. It was becoming obvious I was never going to get over them.

It was also around this time I began to miss Millburn. I'd only been back a few times in the year since I'd moved to New York – a whole year of staying out as late as I liked, blissfully free of worries about missing the last train. I'd certainly taken advantage of living in the very center of Manhattan. It was like being at a perpetual party, opportunities for glorious, high-cholesterol fun everywhere. I absolutely loved it.

And then, out of nowhere, Millburn began to come back to me. The quiet streets and trees started to steal into my thoughts, exerting a pull which gradually got stronger. After a while, the need to see it became undeniable, and David and I – friends again – took the train there after work one Friday.

It was mid-October, leaf season, and South Mountain was vibrant, the maples and hickories crisp with red and amber foliage. We had dinner at the Pancake House on Millburn Avenue – the top place for post-date refreshment for couples from Millburn High – and I realised how much I'd missed homely food and nature and the constancy of suburbia.

From the Pancake House we phoned our friend Marcy, who still lived in Millburn, to see if there was anything going on that night. 'You can come to a Folk Society singalong,' she suggested. I rolled my eyes and made gagging noises. She was a member of the Folk Music Society of Northern New Jersey, which held regular jam sessions at members' houses. I'd been to a number of them, so I knew their bearded, natural-fibered like.

We went anyway, and it was just as I knew it would be. Marcy brought her guitar and was soon the centre of attention, playing nineteenth-century Appalachian work songs to a foot-stompingly appreciative crowd. We were there till two in the morning, David gustily singing along, me sulking in a side bedroom, engrossed in a magazine I'd brought for that purpose.

Back in New York I wrote: 'All the girls there were beastly – for the most part, they were fat; none of them wore makeup or bothered to tweeze their eyebrows; and to a woman, they all had long, stringy hair. It was depressing to be in their midst. I got to talking to this girl who lived on a farm somewhere. She was depressed cos one of her piglets had just died. Ha!'

I only relate this to atone for being so smug and mean. It would be a long time before I appreciated that the piglet girl might be a nicer person than the teenaged brat who sneered at her with all the contempt she could muster. I still wish I hadn't laughed. I'm glad the piglet's life didn't pass unmourned.

Still collecting punk bands, I was excited when The Jam came to town the next week to play NYC's premier punk venue, CBGB's. I'd been unconvinced by the one single of theirs I owned, 'In The City'. It sounded a lot like tuneless thrashing to me, but they were an English punk band, so I was compelled to see them.

'They're all about my age and very pretty, but Paul Weller, the singer, jumps up and down to little effect,' was my assessment. 'The music was quite average. The Jam are the English critics' darlings (along with The Clash) and it's very difficult to see why. I had more fun reading the graffiti in the ladies' room than I did watching them.'

And I started as I meant to go on, Weller-wise. Didn't like

him in The Jam, didn't much like him in the post-Jam Style Council, don't like him now that he's one of Britain's biggest solo turns. But then, he doesn't like me, either, as I discovered years later, after I'd become a rock journalist.

He's renowned for both hating critics and bearing grudges against them, and in 1986 he took exception to a review I wrote about his wife-to-be, the pop singer Dee C. Lee. A few months after the review appeared, he and I happened to be in the same bar in London. Someone told him I was there, and seconds later I was confronted by a furious, fulminating Weller, who told me, loudly and at length, what he thought of the review. Lucky he never saw what I said about him in my diary back in '77.

25

'IS THAT JOHN LENNON?' I whispered to my friend Andy. He looked up from the bronze bowl he was examining, and peered myopically across the room. 'It must be', he decided, 'because there's Yoko.' How impressive to see a Beatle at an exhibit of Irish religious relics at the Metropolitan Museum.

Andy, a fellow popcorn-slinger, and I were at the museum this November day as part of my campaign to develop new, non-Roller interests. It wasn't going well so far. We'd started with museums, and so far had visited the Met, the Whitney, the Museum of Modern Art and the Frick collection, but all that kulcher just seemed to make me hungry. At any rate, every time we did a museum I ended up wolfing down hamburgers afterward, maybe to reward myself for making the effort. I figured it was a reaction against Ma, an opera buff who'd banned pop in the house till I was a teenager.

So what was Lennon doing here, I wondered, covertly watching him inspect chalices and illuminated manuscripts. He was looking very English-gent in tweeds and his little glasses, very much the antithesis of the rock superhero. He and Yoko appeared to be genuinely captivated by the display, which perplexed me. I found the exhibition dry and unmoving, and wondered what Lennon saw in it that made him take Yoko by the arm and lead her over to admire a gold urn.

Lately I'd been wondering if I should have gone to college after all. I was dimly coming to realise that my aesthetic development in all areas except pop music was profoundly stunted. It was worrying.

But the museum phase didn't last long; nor did an abortive attempt to acquaint myself with French literature through Ma's collection of Colette. I was soon back to pop-gluttony, gorging myself on rock music to the exclusion of all else. Even my increasing Roller-ambivalence didn't stop me buying a copy of their *Greatest Hits* when it appeared in November. 'Woody's zits have been skillfully airbrushed out,' I noted.

I shared that thought with my new penpal, Tracy, with whom I was developing a rewarding relationship. I'd been given her address by Kim, who met her when the Rollers played her home town, Columbus, Ohio. I was drawn to her because, according to Kim, she, too, had had a fling with a Roller.

Tracy confirmed it in her first letter to me – heck, she went into graphic detail. 'He didn't take his shirt or socks off 'cause he said he was cold,' she wrote, spending three pages describing their act of congress from start to finish. She might have been too open for her own good, but she had a warmth that was very appealing, especially at this melancholy time when the Tarts seemed to be drifting apart.

A week or so later I had an interview for a job that would have changed my life if I'd got it. It was for the post of trainee publicist at Howard Bloom, one of the major music PR companies. I wanted it a great deal because I would be in the music biz properly, with a real career and no more hanging around on the fringes, forlornly buying the Brit music papers every week. I didn't get it because they found someone who was 'better qualified'. I was irate. What better qualification could you have than knowing practically everything about pop music, which I did? It sucked.

So was getting mugged that weekend on the way to a Ramones gig in Passaic, New Jersey. David, Marcy-from-Millburn and I had just parked in a dimly lit back street and were walking the three blocks to the venue. As we went along, Marcy, the folk fan, was instructing us how to sing our fave Ramones song, 'Beat on the Brat', as a madrigal. We'd just reached the chorus, 'Beat on the brat, beat on the brat, beat on the brat with a baseball bat,' Marcy's voice soaring angelically, when we were shoved from behind.

Suddenly four guys surrounded us, pushing and grabbing. One of them ripped Marcy's pocketbook out of her hands, while another began roughing David up, trying to snatch his wallet. They ignored my own bag, because instead of a proper one I was carrying a plastic supermarket bag, which I thought looked punk. The muggers probably thought it was full of cornflakes.

While they were busy with Marcy and David, I did the noble thing and fled for my life. A couple of blocks away I ran into two cops – sometimes they *are* there when you need them – and we rushed back to find my friends standing where I'd left them, shakily pulling themselves together. The muggers were gone, of course. The cops had a glance down the side streets but, predictably, the bastards had hauled ass out of there. Just so it wouldn't be a complete waste they made an arrest anyway, pulling in a kid who happened to be ambling down the other side of the street carrying a police nightstick. He wasn't one of our muggers, but arresting him cheered up the cops.

None of us was in the mood for the Ramones after that, so after dropping Marcy off we returned to the city. It hadn't been the most auspicious start to the weekend, and the next day wasn't the most auspicious end. It was Cathy's birthday, and to celebrate she'd booked a table at Maxwell's Plum, the East Side singles bar where the Rollers had gone last May on the first night of their tour. The entire Tart membership was invited, but only Emma, Barbarino and I turned up.

'Well, at least you know who your friends are,' Emma pointed out to an exceedingly disappointed Cathy. 'At least you've got your health,' I added. 'I'm trying to see it that way,' she said tersely.

That night was typical, really, of the whole autumn. The high expectations of earlier that year were fading, supplanted by a sense of regret and loss that hung heavily, refusing to lift. I'd never known such a lonely time. Later, I saw it as a portent, because a few days after Cathy's party, life as I had known it changed forever.

26

O N THE LAST TUESDAY of November, I went to CBGB's to see a reggae band. I didn't know much about reggae – wasn't even sure how to pronounce it – but my non-Roller friends Brian and Karen assured me it was the hippest possible music. So we went, watched a band who slipped my mind as soon as they'd entered it, and when we were ejected at 3 a.m., we headed up to Brian's pad on 8th Avenue. It was only a few blocks from Radio City, and I figured I'd get a few hours' sleep, then walk to work.

Once home, Brian and Karen fell on each other, voraciously sucking face not six feet from the single bed where I was queasily lying. They appeared to be on the verge of consummating their new relationship (their very new relationship; they hadn't actually met before that night, when matchmaking me had brought them together).

Oh, God, they *were* going all the way, with much slobbering and oozing. Then a few minutes of squishing sounds and a rutting-stag groan from Brian, and they were done. Within moments both were asleep, Brian's fleshy behind protruding from the blanket like cookie dough.

Their performance had succeeded in so grossing me out that I couldn't get to sleep. Not that it really mattered, because it was now half past four, and I had to be up in only two hours to be at work by seven. Yep, seven – we were into the Christmas season, Radio City's busiest time of year. We had a film playing, and the popcorn crew had to be in at the crack of dawn, ready for a 9 a.m. onslaught. You've never wanted to go to the movies at nine in the morning? You'd be amazed how many people did.

So, after lying there for two hours, longing to bite Brian's fat ass to see if it would stop him snoring, I dragged myself out of bed. I felt wretched, but managed to plod to Radio City, where the first thing I did was pour black coffee down my gullet. I followed that with another coffee and then, when that failed to rouse me, a No-Doz caffeine tablet. Just before we opened I had a last cup of coffee and, just to be sure, two more No-Doz. They were the closest I came to recreational drugs – the Tarts occasionally used No-Doz in all-night-vigil situations because it gave you a mild buzz while keeping you alert.

The three No-Dozes were the equivalent of about ten cups of coffee, plus I'd had three cups of the real thing. You might have thought I'd expect some sort of reaction. But when I started to feel a bit odd about an hour later, it didn't occur to me to link it to all that caffeine. I just thought I was losing my mind.

This is what happened: I was working at the downstairs counter, in the gilded Art Deco lounge (which I suggest you visit next time you're in New York), dishing up the usual sodas and pre-buttered popcorn in a fuzzy daze. Then I began feeling less fuzzy, a queer detachment displacing it. The feeling wasn't like anything I'd experienced before. It was a sort of severing of mind from body; I automatically continued to ring up Cokes and Milk Duds, but I seemed to be observing from outside myself.

As if that weren't bad enough, I began to have the idea that every third or fourth person I served was strange in some way. One guy was so short he could barely see over the counter, another regarded me with his mouth hanging open like it had been welded that way, a woman twitched continuously while waiting for her popcorn. Fellini wasn't filming in the lounge, as far as I knew, so I couldn't understand where all these people had come from. And they were interspersed with normal people. So I'd serve three ordinary people, then someone who rattled his teeth at me furiously, then four normal ones, then an old woman wearing a kid's plastic necklace who could hardly stop giggling long enough to ask for a Hershey bar.

If they'd all lined up together I'd have realised what they actually were, a group of patients on an outing from Willowbrook, the local psychiatric hospital. But turning up in dribs and drabs, they made me wonder if I was imagining things. It compounded the weirdness I was already feeling from the coffee. So I panicked.

Years later, someone asked, 'But why did you think you were losing your mind?' to which I replied that he'd obviously never been confronted by a dozen mentally handicapped people while whizzing along on a mega-dose of caffeine. (Yep – I went nutso on caffeine. How sexy is that? Not acid, which ruined Syd Barrett of Pink Floyd, not booze, which did for Ernest Hemingway, but caffeine, 'a white crystalline bitter alkaloid responsible for the stimulant action of tea, coffee and cocoa'.)

But I didn't know what was going on, and simply assumed I was going crazy, which I didn't like one bit. All I knew was that I had to get home, where I could pack some clothes before checking into the nearest hospital. I told my counter partner, Marty, I was sick and had to leave. One look at my white face convinced him.

Home – it was all I could think of, and the quickest way there was the subway. Bad mistake, I realised, as soon as the doors had shut and we lumbered off into the tunnel at 50th Street. A panic attack, which was what I was having – though I didn't know it and wouldn't have recognized the term – and a subway jammed with commuters is the worst combination I could have contrived.

Omigawd, I'm going crazy and I'm stuck on this train with millions of people, I thought hysterically, and would have screamed the place down if the train hadn't arrived at my station right then. I loped up the stairs to 14th Street, restraining myself from running because I knew giving way to the panic would have made me lose it right there and then.

By the time I'd walked the five blocks home I was ready to forget about packing clothes; I'd have gone in what I stood up in. Finally, after an interminable elevator ride to the eleventh floor, I was in my apartment.

David, I thought. He'll know what to do. Maybe he can get me into a decent hospital on his father's Blue Cross.

'You're not going nuts, you schmuck, you've had too much coffee,' he sighed, when I finally got through to him.

'What?'

'You just told me you had three cups of coffee and three No-Dozes. Think about it. You're having a bad reaction to all the caffeine.'

'I am?'

'Yup.'

'I'm not going crazy?'

'Nope.'

'Oh.'

With that I started to feel better. By evening I was fine. I had a pre-arranged day off the next day, so when I returned to work on Friday I was in robust fettle, my unsettling experience behind me.

I was perky till mid-day, when the theatre began to fill for the 1.00 show. Then slowly, delicately, tendrils of anxiety unfurled somewhere far back in my mind. Naturally, I hadn't drunk any coffee this time around, so I didn't understand what was wrong. I managed to ward off the unpleasant sensations by concentrating on pouring drinks, but I was uneasy.

A few days later, I became uneasier still. David had invited me to dinner with him and a client, the plan being to eat at an Italian joint near Madison Square Garden, then see a basketball game at the Garden.

But I didn't get to the game, because midway through dinner in the big, busy restaurant I was suddenly swept with fear. I'd been edgy from the start of the meal, feeling exposed and uncomfortable at our large center table, but thought I could manage the odd feelings. Suddenly the small, niggling sensations combusted into full-fledged panic. It was as bad as that first day at work. And like the first day, all I could think of was getting home. I excused myself as best I could, pleading a migraine – more socially acceptable than saying, 'Sorry, but I seem to be besieged by uncontrollable fear, and I'd better leave before I start screaming.'

One of my greatest regrets is that I didn't know then what was wrong with me. If I had, it would have made the following months so much easier.

A first attack usually requires a catalyst, e.g., coffee, drugs or plain old stress, but subsequent attacks can occur for no 'reason'. The first time primes the mind for the next, which often occurs in the same place, the surroundings recreating that initial scary buzz. After this happens a couple of times, panic becomes a pattern, and happens in all sorts of places that have no connection with the original setting. Unless something is done to break the cycle, it can end up ruling your life. It ruled mine.

As the days passed and the anxiety continued (mostly in a less ferocious way that I could just about tolerate unless I was on a subway or in a crowded shop), I was sure I was having a nervous breakdown. I didn't tell any of my friends because I knew none of them had experienced anything like this, and they wouldn't be able to help. The only people who knew were David and Marty at work. Both were compassion personified, never once less than kind and reassuring. It was a considerable strain for them to be my friends during the month of December 1977, because most of my conversation was limited to 'Do you think I'm going crazy? What's wrong with me? I'm so scared.'

And I was scared, hugely, because I seemed to have no

control over the anxiety, which could turn from a small black cloud into a hurricane within minutes. I never knew how I was going to feel from one hour to the next. It seemed like the first episode had turned on a tap I couldn't turn off. I'd never realised that you could feel so much fear – where was it all coming from?

'But what are you afraid of?' David asked patiently.

If only I knew. I wasn't afraid of any particular thing, like losing my job or being single; I was just afraid of going crazy. I dreaded the panics for fear of what they might presage, namely madness. I couldn't imagine anything worse than going mad. Nor could I imagine quite what it must feel like to be mad, but I thought it would probably involve talking to myself on the street, rummaging through garbage cans and having un-controllable screaming fits. The idea of it made me sick with horror. I just wanted to wake up and be my normal fearless self. That self was swiftly receding, and I was appalled at the timorous thing I was becoming.

It was also becoming impossible to relate to my friends. Their problems seemed so . . . well . . . normal compared to this. Cathy had recently met and fallen for a guy named Mark, and called most nights to report on her progress, or lack of. Listening to her made me feel worse, as her troubles seemed so trivial. What I'd have given for this Mark to be my biggest problem – at least he was a concrete problem with, presum-ably, a concrete solution.

But even in the midst of all this, the Rollers were still on my mind. The first week of December, Barbarino reported they were to play some big one-off extravaganza at the Boston Garden on the 17th, headlining a bill that also featured Andy Gibb, the Bee Gees' younger brother, who'd had a huge hit over the summer with 'I Just Want to Be Your Everything' (or 'Your Hairy Thing', as the Tarts called it).

The show was only two weeks away, and I was in a quandary. The only person other than Barbarino who was

interested in going was Lauren, who viewed it as an opportunity to see 'Les', something she urgently wanted to do. She'd
spent the last couple of months sighing, 'I've just got to talk to
him', and was even reading a book about ESP to try and
contact him telepathically. She perked up when she heard
about Boston and immediately agreed to come.

So I'd at least have company, but I didn't know whether
schlepping 250 miles to Boston in my state of mind was a good
idea. What if I went bananas in a strange city? I also knew
there'd be almost no chance of repeating August's romantic
encounters. In fact, I told myself, I probably wouldn't even get
to talk to My Roller. Then Lauren pulled out because of a
family thing, and Barbarino said he wouldn't be able to travel
up with me because he mysteriously 'had' to go the day before.
To top it off, I had no idea how I'd track down the band.

None of it augured well. I went anyway, taking a Trailways
bus by myself to Boston on an icy Saturday a week before
Christmas. When we rolled into Boston early in the afternoon,
I was struck by the folly of being there. The gig was sold out, I
didn't know where the band were staying, I didn't even know
where Barbarino was. It was a challenge.

Out of long habit, I found a phone booth, consulted the
Yellow Pages and copied the addresses of likely hotels, i.e., the
better chain places. Then I methodically walked to each and
checked it out. By the time I'd got through most of my list it
was nearly dusk. The last place, the Sonesta, was a long way
from where I was then, so I decided to leave it for the moment
and get to the Garden in the hope of buying a ticket from a
scalper. To my relief, the box office still had a few singles, and
I went in, thankful to get out of the cold, lowering afternoon.

To our mutual astonishment, I was in the row behind
Barbarino, Kim and Diane, a fan we'd met in Charlotte. I
was particularly surprised to see Kim. As far as I knew, she
was on her semi-annual tanning trip to Florida, where she
worked on baking her hide an even darker mahogany than it

already was. (These were, of course, the days before anyone knew about sun damage, and I've not infrequently wondered what Kim's skin must have been like by the time she was thirty.) She must have flown back especially for this show. Anyway, to say she was displeased to see me is an under-statement. She looked like a Mafia godfather who's just lost the Brooklyn waterfront. If we hadn't been friends, I'd have been afraid of her.

I hadn't done anything to upset her, that was just what she was like. If you caught her on a good day she was pleasant enough, as long as you didn't try to lead the conversation around to yourself or interrupt one of her monologues about Eric. On a bad day, and there were a lot of those, she treated you like a nasty smell. So it didn't surprise me that she wasn't thrilled to see me – why should she? Another girl just meant more competition. But I was having such a dreary day that a friendly face would have made a big difference.

Over the next few hours she slowly thawed, and by the time the Rollers finally traipsed on to close the show we were exchanging cautiously friendly comments, mostly about how bad our seats were. We were so far from the stage we were in a different zip code from the Rollers, but it was immaterial, as the band were putting on one of the most dispirited shows we'd ever seen them do. Why? Probably for the same reasons that we were feeling grumpy and blue – it was freezing and they didn't really want to be there.

I watched them with a lack of interest that would have amazed me a couple of months before. Even the sight of my personal Roller left me unmoved, though if I'd analysed my feelings more closely I'd have detected longing and sadness in there somewhere, and anguish that I would never be as close to him again as on those two nights in August.

At the end we shuffled into the parking lot. Diane had a car, and from the conversation it appeared the three of them knew where the Rollers were staying and were going there. We reached the car and there was an awkward moment when everyone climbed in except me. They hadn't actually invited me along, but they weren't just going to leave me there, were they? Thankfully, they weren't, though I'll bet they would have if it had been up to Kim. 'Get in,' she ordered impatiently, and I did, squashing into the back seat as the other three discussed the show.

They essentially ignored me, laughing and singing along to that month's Queen hit, 'We Are The Champions', as it blared from the radio. I felt rather miserable. I had quite a few thoughts about the show I'd have liked to share – why was Woody wearing a plaid tie over a bare chest, for one – but no one asked for my comments, so I sat huddled as close to the window as possible until we pulled into the parking lot of the Sonesta. It was the one hotel I hadn't checked in the afternoon. Typical.

We got into the elevator, me trying to avoid Kim's Why-don't-you-piss-off-Caroline? stare. The three of them had a room on the tenth floor, five stories above the band. In fact, the entire tenth floor looked like a Roller-fan campsite, with at least eight rooms occupied by people I recognised from New York, New Jersey, Philadelphia and Ohio. It was a sort of end-of-term bash, with people noisily visiting from room to room, parading back and forth with ice buckets and loudly debating how to get to the band.

The answer to that was that it was impossible. There was a guard on their floor – not Bob, unfortunately – and all we could do was hang out in the lobby to see if any of them came down. Leslie did, accompanied by some road crew, at about midnight. Barbarino darted over to one of the roadies as they got into a taxi and came back grinning importantly. 'They're going to a club, but that roadie-guy says they're gonna come to our room for a party when they get back.'

I'd heard that one before, in Charlotte, so I didn't take him seriously, but for once he was right. At about three in the morning, when we were sitting around the room, smoking and watching TV (Kim seemed to be allowing me to stay – at least, she wasn't actively kicking me out), the roadie, Greg, came a-calling with a crew member called Jake. No Leslie, sadly – he'd gone to bed, the lightweight. But roadies were better than nothing, and we welcomed them with the remains of a take-out pizza.

Other fans appeared, having scented the spoor of BCR, and the room filled until there was no space on either beds or floor. All fifteen or so of us chatted about nothing much for half an hour, trying to seem coolly indifferent in front of our guests. Then, without so much as a by-your-leave, Greg threw a lamp across the room. Kim's precious rabbit-fur chubby would have followed, but she clung to it ferociously as Jake hauled his suddenly crazed friend away and out of the room, apologising over his shoulder as they left.

'God, what was with *him*?' someone asked. 'Road fever,' Barbarino said knowledgably. A discussion of 'road fever' ensued, and I bleakly wondered if and when I'd get any sleep. Then I noticed Jake's jacket scrunched up in the corner of the bed, forgotten in all the fuss. Ha! An excuse to go down to the Rollers' floor. Slipping it under my arm I quietly left the room.

The guard rose to challenge me when I stepped out of the elevator on the fifth floor, but I waved the jacket and ex-plained. He directed me to a room at the end of the corridor and Jake answered the door. I handed over the jacket and he looked at me for a moment, unsure of how hospitable to be. 'Do you want a quick drink?' he said at last. Just what I was hoping he'd say. No, what I was really hoping he'd say was, 'Your personal Roller misses you – I'll let him know you're here', but a drink with a roadie was better than nothing.

Actually, Jake was more than just a roadie. The only Scottish member of the crew, he'd worked with the Rollers for years and was their right-hand man. So it was a tiny coup to be sitting in his room with a glass of tap water, as he lounged in an armchair, silently inspecting me. I was hoping he'd dish lots of gossip about the band, and tried to maneuver the conversation in that direction.

'They've got a lot more freedom now, don't they?' I asked. 'They must go pretty wild sometimes, huh?' It was 3.30 in the morning, I didn't care how unsubtle I was being.

He just looked at me, trying to remember where he'd seen me before tonight. 'I thought I recognised you,' he said after a while. 'You got very close to one of the band. In Ohio or somewhere.' I smiled with faint pride at his gentlemanly euphemism before my brain kicked in and I began to wonder how he knew. Had my Roller, in a moment of laddish bonhomie, told him? Surely not.

'That was you, wasn't it?' His tone wasn't especially pleasant, and he continued to look at me with . . . was it contempt? Before the conversation entered even less fruitful waters I decided it was time to go back to my own room. 'Well, thanks for the drink,' I said.

'Stay out of trouble,' was his reply.

I rang for the elevator in the early stages of berating myself for my foolishness. I was wishing I'd never gone to his room. He was bound to mention me to Him, and I could just imagine the two of them having a manly chuckle the next morning. The idea was terrible. Worse than terrible, because it ruined the sanctity of our two lovely nights. One of the things that had sustained me during the whole autumn was the belief, however unlikely, that our time together had meant something to him. The possibility of him discussing it with the rest of the group – with the roadies, too, for God's sake – simply hadn't occurred to me.

But what did I expect, I thought miserably as the elevator arrived. They're a bunch of guys on the road together in a foreign country. Of course they talk about girls. But still . . .

Back on the tenth floor people were settling down for what remained of the night. The beds in our room were full, so I pulled two armchairs together and arranged myself across them. I wasn't a good sleeper at the best of times, and this wasn't the best of times, so I sighed deeply and lit a cigarette. It was the last one in the pack, and the pack had been my third of the day, meaning I'd gone through sixty cigarettes in less than twenty-four hours. I'd also eaten nothing since leaving New York except two slices of pizza, and I hadn't slept. I added all this up and suddenly felt agitated. Not in a panicky way, but in a Gawd-what-am-I-doing sort of fashion. All things considered, this was turning out to be my worst Roller expedition ever.

We knew from Jake that they were leaving to go to Los Angeles at noon, so we were already waiting in taxis, ready to race them to the airport. Why we bothered after such a downer of a night I don't know – probably ingrained habit. When we hopped out of our cab at Logan Airport, I hung back as Barbarino and the others pounded after the band, who were whisked into the VIP lounge before the Barbster could even get a photograph. All I saw of my Roller was his skinny denim backside as he scurried away. Their flight duly took off for Los Angeles, and that was that.

And then we were alone in the terminal. Bleak gray Sunday morning, nothing to do, and on the spur of the moment we decided to fly back to New York. I'd planned to take the bus, but the idea of five hours of jouncing along the highways of New England was suddenly too much to contemplate.

Once we were airborne, Kim was suddenly my buddy again, apologising for her coldness of the previous twelve hours. 'I'm just really bummed out about Eric,' she sighed. 'I really like him and I'm never gonna talk to him again at this rate.' She passed a sun-baked hand over her eyes and her shoulders quivered under her rabbit fur. She hadn't been this upset since the last night in Charlotte, when she'd got so plastered she'd practically passed out in the hall in front of Faulkner's room.

I knew how she felt. The closest I'd got to Him – my Roller –

on this little jaunt had been at the airport, and he hadn't even seen me. He'd looked utterly beautiful, of course, his desirability having increased in direct proportion to his remoteness.

The forlornness of that glimpse stayed with me all the way to La Guardia Airport and home on the subway. He was as unavailable as if we'd never met, and I was half-convinced we never had. The soft intimacy of those two summer nights, the effortless sweetness, were no longer a clear memory but softening around the edges, like a dream. I could no longer remember everything he'd said, every nuance in his voice, the contours of his accent. Little sensory snapshots like the smell of his skin, which he perfumed with lime-flavored Yves St Laurent for Men, and the silkiness of his hair were fading. I had recently taken to re-reading my diary entries for the last days of August (the seventy-two hours we'd been away on the tour had taken eight pages to describe), and it was only when I did that I was able to bring the sensations alive again for the merest few seconds.

27

WORK CONTINUED TO BE TERRIBLE. The anxiety thing was settling in for the long term, becoming something I could rely on as surely as I could rely on Barbarino to come up with his quota of lies about the Rollers (his latest was that they were planning a coast-to-coast tour for March, which they weren't).

It became a pattern: wake up, orange juice, cigarette, anxiety. The first daily stirrings of panic would occur as my nerves woke and yawned and prepared themselves for another day of wild fluctuation.

I'd arrive at Radio City, set up my counter and try to relax. No use. The increasingly familiar flutterings of fear would make themselves felt, occasionally accompanied by strange tricks of perception.

Really scary, that last. Things would look freakishly big, or as tiny as if I were looking through the wrong end of a telescope. My hands, resting on the counter, seemed miles away. Or they'd hang numbly at my sides, and I'd be cognisant of them but feel weirdly separate from them. People take drugs to achieve exactly these effects, and here I was, getting it all for free.

The worst thing was that I never knew when anxiety would happen. I was beginning to recognise triggers – Radio City, obviously, and big shops, and basically anywhere large and crowded where I couldn't easily get out. But sometimes there was no apparent cause. Sometimes I'd just wake up in the morning and immediately feel uneasy.

I'd still never heard the term 'anxiety attack', and simply thought, with a sense of daily increasing despair, that my mind was unhinging itself. So after a month I did what any middle-class Jewish girl does when she thinks she's going nuts. I went to a shrink.

Dr Kalman was an old Jewish guy whose Upper West Side office window faced the airshaft of another building. The only ornament in the room was his diploma from New York University, from which he'd graduated sometime in the eighteenth century. He discouraged smoking, and only with great reluctance would search his desk for an ashtray when I arrived.

The only good thing about him was that he didn't have your typical shrink's couch – thank God, because lying on one would have made me feel like I really was sick. But that meant I had to sit and face him, feeling abashed as I tried to direct the cigarette smoke away from him.

I'd babble about how lousy I was feeling and he'd take notes, but he was selective about what he wrote down. I'd watch him and wonder why he'd scribble something about the Rollers, say, but not about how I'd had to get off the subway four stops early that day because I'd been so choked with fright.

I could see, though, how the Rollers might possibly be implicated in all this. If I was losing my mind, it had to be for a reason, and what better reason than my intense relationship with them? They'd been the biggest thing in my life for two years, I'd gotten closer to them than I'd ever dared hope and as soon as I did I went into a decline. The decline had lasted all autumn and, now that I thought about it, had seemed to portend this thing that was happening to me now. The initial anxiety attack, I was starting to believe, had been just a catalyst, and what was spilling out was pent-up Roller-madness. That was my theory, anyway, and Kalman agreed, inasmuch as he ever expressed any kind of opinion.

Okay, so the anxiety was Roller-related, Kalman and I finally decided, and then he wanted to know why I developed such an attachment to them in the first place. This necessitated many dreary sessions about my childhood, parents, school, blah-de-blah. Kalman encouraged me to go into endless detail about what I saw as trivia – like, yeah, I'd have preferred to have been born with straight hair, but it didn't mean I had a problem with my 'Jewish identity', as he suggested. It just meant I'd have been able to get a comb through it.

The panics didn't improve. If anything, they got worse, and so did my state of mind, because everything in life that had seemed stable and predictable was now unstable and chaotic. The panics were coming from a mental region I'd never realised existed – and if it was possible for a mind to conjure up such fear, what else was it capable of doing? All my assumptions about the sort of person I was were completely awry. I felt rudderless, at the mercy of any panic signal that came crackling along my synapses.

And if I couldn't trust my own mind, how could I trust the outside world, which till then had been a safe, comprehensible place? In fact, I asked myself one particularly dismal winter evening, how did I know that the whole world wasn't just a figment of my imagination? I was literally having an existential crisis. David, who'd done philosophy at college, told me about them. 'How do I know *you're* real?' I inquired miserably. 'You sound like everybody in my class,' he grinned.

I couldn't shut off the panics, and I couldn't shut off my imagination, and they fed on each other to angstful effect. The worst thing of all was feeling totally alone with it all.

It wasn't till about eight months later that Kalman casually remarked that the anxiety itself could be controlled with tranquilizers. What?? I gasped. You mean I don't actually have to go through all this terror all the time? I can actually take a pill to stop it? Thanks for fucking telling me!!

He wrote me a prescription. I filled it. It was September of 1978 and I'd been enduring the emotional disintegration for nearly a year. Within a couple of weeks I was on my way to recovery, pissed off that he hadn't nipped it all in the bud months before. He explained he'd wanted the panic to run its course naturally, which would reveal all sorts of insights about 'the inner psychodrama' (his words) that had made me love the Rollers. Well, it didn't, assface.

But back to the end of '77, which I celebrated by quitting my job. Radio City had become unendurable, and unemployment seemed preferable to having to go there every day. I couldn't tolerate being uptown, overwhelmed by the looming skyscrapers and dizzied by the ceaseless flow of people around me on sidewalks that felt sickeningly wide and exposed.

'You did the right thing,' Cathy comforted me the next afternoon, which was New Year's Day. We were at the movie theater near her place in Brooklyn, watching a new John Travolta flick called *Saturday Night Fever*. We'd wanted to see it because it was set in Brooklyn – had, in fact, actually been filmed in Cathy's neighborhood, Bay Ridge.

'I hope you're right,' I whispered as Travolta, or Tony Manero as he was in the film, strutted into the local nightclub, 2001 Odyssey, which in real life was only six or seven blocks from where we were sitting. He was dancing to some thudding disco track – God, you can't get away from disco even in the movies, I thought disgustedly – when suddenly he saw a girl across the floor and did a double-take. The rest of the movie was about his pursuit of her, an ambitious little cookie named Stephanie who had moved to Manhattan and considered herself too sophisticated for the likes of Travolta.

Despite its disco soundtrack, which included contributions from some of my most detested groups, including the Bee Gees and K.C. & The Sunshine Band, the movie was uplifting.

When it ended with Tony and Stephanie hugging in soft focus as dawn broke over Manhattan, I felt rejuvenated and hopeful. I was gonna deal with this panic business, I told myself spiritedly. I knew I could. It would just take a bit of effort.

I left the theatre jollily humming the film's closing song, 'How Deep is Your Love'. Maybe I could even get to like disco.

28

1978

First UK #1 of the year: 'Mull of Kintyre'/Wings
Biggest Roller hit US/UK: none

YEAH. My high spirits lasted precisely five days, till my next panic. Actually, it wasn't a panic *per se*, more a queasiness that oozed blackly into my mind as Cathy, Lauren and I were watching the Rollers on 'The Midnight Special', the music show they'd last appeared on over the summer. The queasiness seemed to be linked to Leslie, who was wearing a black shirt trimmed with chains, black jeans and high black boots. He looked tragic – a cross between a fetishist and a stormtrooper – but there was something disturbing about the flirtation with taboo imagery. He was a Bay City Roller, ferchrissake. What did he think he was doing?

I was taking everything about them very personally these days, and as I watched him on the TV I had a sudden vivid memory of his crudeness back in August. That memory dovetailed with this cut-rate S&M look, and he suddenly struck me as deeply creepy. Wishing I didn't, I remembered chasing him into the Youngstown pizzeria, and his contemptuous rejection ('You can do whatever the fuck you like').

How could I have been so desperate? I thought, swamped with anger at both him and myself. It really ruined the rest of the week.

But I could never keep my distance for long. I took on board Leslie's new look with the same inevitability that I'd taken on things like Debbie Bottom and Kim's fling with Eric. You simply adjusted your perception of them each time. It was all you could do unless you were willing to sever the connection completely, and I wasn't ready for that.

But despite slowly accepting each small change, at heart I wanted them to return to their early smiling innocence. In the two-and-a-half years I'd been following them, my needs had never changed. Neither had most fans', I'd guess. All we asked of them was to stop us from growing up.

The Rollers' whole career was thus a constant struggle between the fans' expectations and their own. Ours never kept pace with theirs, and as theirs grew, we had the choice of either accepting each new version of the band or jumping ship. I couldn't jump, not then. Life was too painful because of the anxiety attacks to cope without the Rollers. I'd rather have them in stormtrooper boots than not have them at all.

My misgivings temporarily faded a week later when Emma gave me an early birthday gift – a bottle of my Roller's perfume, Yves St Laurent for Men. The lime scent brought back the cool darkness of our liaisons in Detroit and Charlotte. I knew that whatever they did, I'd never stop adoring them. I doused myself in the scent.

Finding a new job quickly became imperative, not just for the money but so that I wouldn't have time to sit around letting the anxiety spiral out of control. The beginning of 1978 wasn't a bad time to be looking for work. There were plenty of entry-level secretarial and reception jobs going in glossy Midtown offices, and despite my lack of qualifications and abysmal typing I found one within a week.

I was never entirely sure what the International Council of Shopping Centers did, or what my duties were as one of its employees. In the interview, the chic head of personnel had explained it was a trade organisation representing the interests of shopping centers across the country, and that I'd be in the membership department, processing new applications. But even as I accepted the job over the phone a few days later, I didn't know what I was saying yes to.

In the whole three months I was there, I was never able to figure out what any of us in the chrome-and-glass building on East 54th Street (which we shared with a major record company, Elektra, a great source of excitement to me) actually did. I sat at my desk, bewilderedly answering calls from the owners of Midwestern malls, trying to grasp the point.

Which pretty much echoed my state of mind. What was the point of anything? All I could do was try to distract myself from the perpetual tension inside. I went out as much as possible, to see soul stars Al Green ('He didn't put a damn bit of effort into it,' I noted sniffily) and Barry White ('Funny as hell – all fat and glittery'). I checked out David Cassidy's wussy brother Shaun, who filled the huge Nassau Coliseum – something the Rollers certainly never managed – and ranting Scottish comedian Billy Connolly, who was as bemused by his audiences as they were by him.

One weekend in February, desperate for something to take my mind off my anxing – I had even invented a verb for it, 'to anx' – I flew to Columbus, Ohio, to visit my penpal, Tracy. She met me at the airport with her husband – she had a *husband*? – who apparently knew nothing of her one-night-stand with Eric. The hubby hung around with us for most of my visit, so Tracy and I could only discuss Eric when she took me shopping at the mall on Saturday after-noon.

She had it really bad for Faulkner, and you could under-stand why. He must have seemed like an incredibly glamorous alternative to life in a one-story house in Columbus, especially now that she and her husband were expecting a baby. She'd confided that news on the way back from the airport, adding in a forlorn whisper, 'I wish it was Eric's.' She'd have been surprised to know that the uneventfulness of her life was highly attractive to me, besieged as I was by unpredictable eruptions of fear. I'd have given a lot to swap places and live in her placid suburban street forever.

29

T HE SEX PISTOLS SPLIT UP. They arrived in America for their first tour, played a handful of gigs to belligerent audiences and called it a day after the last gig, in San Francisco. Then, on his way back to London, Sid Vicious collapsed on the plane after a drug mishap, the sort of thing that was always happening to him. I read about all this with a sense of detachment, as I was an ex-punk fan by then. The genre's nihilism and aggression were too upsetting to me in my state, so I turned to comfortingly stolid Americana for my musical needs.

After years of cordially loathing them, I could suddenly see the point of acts like Meat Loaf, the arena-rockin' Styx and Dickey Betts, a hairy Southern bubba who used to play guitar with the Allman Brothers. They might not have been sexy, they might not have been pushing back the barriers, but they were solid and reassuring. You knew where you were with the 'Loaf.

It was lucky I could suddenly appreciate Meat Loaf and friends, because I'd have had a very thin time of it otherwise. In the late seventies, American rock was at an all-time nadir. The overblown Mr Loaf, Styx and the rest were just the tip of the blandberg, and if I tell you that the US music industry's great new hopes for 1978 were prog-rock beardos Boston, you'll have some idea of what I mean.

There was no relief from the pop sphere, either, which was dominated by lightweights like Shaun Cassidy and David

Soul. The only area where US music was really happening was disco, but I was still convinced it was made exclusively for the brain-dead, who might be able to dance but couldn't appreciate proper middle-eights. *Saturday Night Fever* had confirmed all my prejudices about disco – not only was it intellectually negligible, it compelled men to wear white suits. Plus which, all disco fans seemed to live in the outer boroughs, and had terrible Bronx accents. If only I could have foreseen that twenty years later I'd write a long newspaper piece about *Saturday Night Fever*, which in the interim had become my favorite movie of all time.

No, I couldn't get into disco and I couldn't listen to punk, so it had to be straight rock all the way. I even bought the Boston LP.

The next step in my attempt to stabilise myself was landing a boyfriend – a proper one, which I'd never really had. If I couldn't divorce myself from the Rollers I wanted to at least scale them down, which meant I needed a new love interest. For the first time ever, I tried dating. I wasn't fussy, I decided to just go out with the first person who asked me, as long as he was hygienic and spoke at least some English.

A cab driver named Scott was the first who met the criteria. He picked me up outside Dr Kalman's one night, and by the time he dropped me off on 9th Street he'd asked for my number.

He was from Brooklyn – land of *Saturday Night Fever* – but I was trying to be open-minded. So one date led to another and then another, not because we had anything in common, but because he was so comfortingly solid. He lived with his parents in blue-collar Bensonhurst, loved the Jets and the Knicks and knew himself with calm certainty. He didn't lie awake at night wondering if he was going insane. His stability was deeply appealing, and I automatically accepted each time he asked me out.

It ended on the fourth or fifth meeting, as we were cruising along in his taxi, which he brought on dates because he got a kick out of zooming past people who hailed him. 'I thought maybe next week we could go over to my brother's place,' he said, craning his neck to scream, 'Fuck you, buddy!' at a delivery van. 'He's on vacation, so we'd have the place to ourselves.' He grinned in happy expectation. 'We've known each other a month, and we've never been, y'know, intimate.'

I briefly pictured being 'intimate' with him. 'Yeah,' I agreed, feeling faint. When he called a few days later to arrange this meeting of bodies I took the chicken's way out – I got Ma to say I'd gone upstate to stay with friends for a few weeks. He didn't call again. Despite my relief I was a bit irked.

Then there was Farrell, a professional golfer I met on the subway, and Mark, a lawyer who lived in my building. There was Clark, who worked at the big newsstand on 6th Avenue and 8th Street – he stood me up – and Ronnie, a partner in a shopping mall in Nyack, New York.

Ron and I met over the phone when I processed his application to join the International Council of Shopping Centers, and ended up talking several times a week. When he invited me to visit his mall and have dinner, adding, 'And you can stay over if it's too late to get back to the city,' it sounded pleasant.

The moral of that little adventure was: Always ask their age. I hadn't because he'd sounded young, and he turned out to be fifty if he was a day. A thirty-odd-year age gap was just too much even for the sake of a 15 per cent discount at the mall. We slept in separate rooms – it *was* too late to get back to the city – and the next day he drove me to the train in rigid silence. Thereafter, he spoke to the other girl in Membership when he called.

Most uncomfortable of all these encounters, though, was Steve from San Francisco. He was the roommate of my Brit friend Michael. Remember Michael, the one who flew to New York to visit me, but I was too hung up on the Rollers to notice? Michael's office had since transferred him to San Francisco, where he'd moved into the spare room of a guy called Steve.

He called me to say hello, and we began chatting every few weeks. One night I telephoned and got this Steve, who was so witty and loquacious that we were on the phone for nearly an hour. He called me the next night, and within a week we were talking about our 'relationship', as if we really had one. (I asked his age. He was twenty-six.)

They were terribly exciting, those nightly calls, which got confessional and not a little steamy. 'I'm in the middle of some peanut butter on toast,' I said one night, to which he replied, 'I'd like to have you on toast,' and I wince to recall that I melted. It was so easy to whisper into the phone for hours, and wishful thinking ignited the calls into a full-blown romance. We exchanged photos, and while his beard was a bit unsettling, I figured I could handle it. All we needed to make this complete was to actually meet.

So in July I went to San Francisco. He was there to meet me at the airport. We took one look at each other, and even as we hugged hello, we knew that it wasn't there, whatever 'it' was. All those phone calls were as nothing in the face of something we hadn't anticipated – a complete absence of attraction. The instantaneous cooling of ardor made the ride back to his place stiff and uncomfortable, and what was even worse was that we were both thinking (I certainly was) that I was going to be there for five days.

Thankfully, Michael had arranged time off work. He hung out with Steve and me as we did tourist stuff – the Golden Gate Bridge, Haight-Ashbury and the hippie trail – and his presence acted as a buffer between two people who were by now deeply embarrassed about all those giggly phone intimacies.

But it actually wasn't a bad little vacation, once I'd gotten over the disappointment that Steve wasn't going to be my one-and-only. So the trip wouldn't be a total loss, I tentatively

broached rekindling our own romance with Michael, but he
was in love with some girl in England. Even so, I had fun, and
when Steve dropped me off at the airport we cheerfully
promised to stay in touch, knowing we wouldn't.

The sum total of my lovelife, then. By the middle of 1978, I
was still boyfriendless, and grumpy about it. With resignation
I decided to renew my interest in the Rollers, who were
spending the summer in Los Angeles, filming a thirteen-part
TV series for broadcast in the fall.

Just before they went to California, Alan rejoined, his two-
year solo career having produced a total of one flop single.
They were back to the classic five-piece lineup, but a bit
belatedly, since their fans were by then defecting at an alarming rate. But obviously not alarming enough to worry the
producers of their TV show, which was titled 'The Krofft
Superstar Hour'. It was due to be shown on Saturday morn-
ings, prime teenybopper viewing time, so someone clearly had
faith in their ability to still pull in the kids. But we ground
troops could have told them that times were changing, and
changing fast.

It had been three years since the band had been launched in
America, which is a lifetime in teen-band terms. The original
1975 fans were now sixteen or seventeen, and had boyfriends
and lives of their own, while younger kids had a whole array
of new idols to choose from, from Leif Garrett to Andy Gibb
to John Travolta. The Rollers were decidedly old-hat next to
Garrett's vapid blond charms, and their new, more adult
image hadn't won over the older audience they coveted, either.
So they were at an impasse, stuck with a diminishing cluster of
fans that was rapidly leaving them behind.

And that was just in America. In Britain they were completely over, bumped off by poppier punksters like Blondie,
and by Travolta, who followed up *Saturday Night Fever* with
the immensely popular *Grease*. His duet with Olivia Newton-
John, 'You're The One That I Want', topped the chart for no

fewer than nine weeks in the summer of 1978. By contrast, the Rollers' final UK hit, 'You Made Me Believe in Magic', had barely scraped into the Top 40 a year before. No surprise, then, that they were focusing all their energies on America, correctly perceiving that it was their last chance.

A Los Angeles-based friend of Barbarino's named Jan managed to get into one of the 'Krofft Superstar Hour' tapings, and wrote to us about it. 'It's a kiddie show . . . the guys do a couple of skits, like they pretend they're lost in a haunted house or something, and then they do a couple of songs. There's a character called Witchipoo (you got it, a witch!) who keeps cropping up to keep things moving along.'

It sounded desperate. But there was more. 'They did a new song called "All of the World is Falling in Love", which is the worst thing they've ever done,' Jan added, ending her letter with, 'Christ, I hope the rest of the new album is better.'

I hadn't even known they were making a new album, but inquiries to Arista elicited the information that they had recorded one in the spring, and were putting the final touches to it for a September release, to coincide with the TV launch.

Jan wrote again a couple of weeks later. 'The wrap party was Friday, and Leslie got hit in the face with a cream pie! The crew decided to teach him a lesson for being a big shot. Everybody here thinks he's a dork. He went back to Scotland right after the party. People are taking bets on him quitting the group.'

Well, this *was* something. When I finished her letter, I called the Rollers' new US publicists, a big New York firm called Levinson Associates, and, posing as a journalist, asked if it was true McKeown was on the way out.

'Pat, the girl who answered the phone, got quite chatty,' I wrote on August 28, 'and told me he was sent back to Scotland by the others cos he was getting unbearably big-headed, and at the moment the others are rehearsing for a Japanese tour without him. If he doesn't come off his high horse, they'll go without him. Seems he wanted things like a separate dressing room and separate press photos. Jerk!'

During his LA sojourn he'd found a celebrity girlfriend. At least, he was seen out a few times with Britt Ekland, then Rod Stewart's recent ex. Whatever went on between them – and McKeown unchivalrously hinted in a tabloid interview that quite a lot did – their liaison was another signal that he'd had enough of the Rollers. His petulance implied that his BCR days were numbered, and the mantra 'solo career' must have been continually playing in his mind.

I wrote long letters to Jan – who was around twenty-five and did some ambiguous job that allowed her a lot of time off – speculating about the situation. I called her, too, whenever my new boss wasn't looking. For I'd found another job, having quit the shopping center place after three months. I left because I still couldn't figure out what I was supposed to be doing, and because my anxometer went off the scale each morning as I arrived. Having to traipse up to the very heart of midtown Manhattan every day was hard enough, but the tenth-floor offices were so unforgivingly corporate, from the beige carpet to the ergonomically designed swivel chairs, that I could hardly stand it. I longed for a quiet, dark corner, away from the fluorescent lights that made me quail, and from the rest of the terrifyingly efficient staff. I'd have sat under my desk if I could. At lunchtimes, I took to going to the Fifth Avenue Presbyterian Church across the street where I'd sit in a back pew, trying to breathe slowly and pull myself together to face the afternoon.

One morning I simply decided to quit, and did. I offered the standard two weeks' notice, and was told I could leave then and there. Charmed, I'm sure, but I wasted no time in clearing my desk, which mostly consisted of throwing out company memos I'd been too perplexed to read.

I was looking forward to an idle idyll, but only a couple of days later Ma said, 'I think I've got a job for you.'

'Yeah?' I responded warily.

'My new friend Eddie says he might have something for you. Go talk to him.'

Out of curiosity rather than a desire to work, I met her friend Eddie. A middle-aged, ruddy type, he was waiting in a coffee shop on the ground floor of the Empire State Building, and over a seltzer told me he owned a mid-market fashion company on Seventh Avenue in the garment district. He needed a liaison to work with his New York office, where the clothes were designed, and the factory in California, where they were made.

'You'd go to California four times a year and just keep an eye on things, make sure everything's running smoothly. Do you think you could do it?' He waited for my answer.

Could I? Well, let's see. I had no experience, either in the fashion industry or in any kind of responsible job, and I was barely old enough to vote.

'Sure!' I beamed.

'Come on up to the office tomorrow and let's get you started,' he said heartily, writing down an address and phone number on a piece of paper torn from a small spiral notebook. It seemed curious he didn't have a business card, but hey . . . fashion people. Cards were probably so yesterday.

Later that afternoon, after I'd got home and endured Ma's crowing about having landed me a job, I realised I'd forgotten to ask what time Eddie wanted me up there. I dialed the number he'd written down.

'Empire State Building,' came the reply – odd, because he'd said his office was on Seventh Avenue and 39th Street, which was nowhere near the Empire State Building. Nevertheless, I asked for Extension 33. 'There's no Extension 33 here, ma'am,' the operator replied.

How very peculiar. Starting to smell a fat rat, the next morning I went to the address he'd given me. It was definitely a fashiony building, with at least three dozen design houses sharing its twenty-five stories, but his company wasn't one of them. Still, I took the elevator up to the eighteenth floor, where he'd said his office was – and wasn't at all surprised to find that no one there knew anyone called Eddie.

Neither Ma nor I ever heard from Eddie again, and I have no idea what was behind it all. 'But he seemed so nice!' Ma protested, devastated at losing her chance with a single Jewish male.

Improbably, something similar happened about a month later. Another boyfriend of Ma's, this time called Nat. One night after they'd been dating a few weeks, he took both her and me to dinner. He asked me what I did. Unemployed, I said. He asked what I'd like to do. Be a journalist, I said, which was the first thing that came to mind.

'Now, how 'bout that?' he chuckled expansively. 'I own a weekly paper in Philadelphia.'

'You do?' I sat up straighter. 'Need any writers?'

'This could be your lucky day, honey, because two of my staff quit on me last week.' He chuckled again, showing Depression-era teeth.

'Really?' I squeaked.

'You got any experience?' he encouraged.

'Well, I've written for a music magazine,' I offered – not entirely a lie, as I considered *The Tartan Pervert* a music magazine, of sorts.

His smile grew even broader. 'I think you could be what I'm looking for.'

'Really?' I breathed.

'Really,' he nodded. 'How does editor sound?'

I had to restrain myself from flinging myself across the table to hug him as I squealed, 'It sounds great!' But as I spluttered my thanks, I knew there was something fishy. Even I knew that editing a paper required experience, contacts, years of slog, and that putting out ten issues of *The Tartan Pervert* didn't count.

But I didn't tell him that, because I instinctively grasped that his fantastical offer (and that's what it turned out to be, a fantasy; he didn't own a paper, or have anything to do with one) was a ploy to impress my mother. To her credit, she saw through him, and didn't go out with him again. But I sometimes wondered what he'd have done if they'd continued dating, and he'd been forced to admit he'd lied.

A little while later I got a job that wasn't nearly as glamorous as the two I'd been offered by Ma's swains, but which did exist. Thus, for the next year I was the receptionist at a small metallurgy laboratory way downtown, in Tribeca. That the job was wickedly dull was due to no fault of the other employees, who were the nicest bunch of chemists I'd ever met, forever joking about the clumps of dirt they had to analyse for their metal content. But at least the surroundings were quiet. The neighborhood was light-industrial – little factories that made paper clips, that kind of thing – and completely deserted after 5 p.m.. Which was exactly how I liked it. No crowds to contend with as I gingerly made my way home.

Sometimes the other typist, a lugubrious Italian girl from Jersey City called Theresa, walked with me to the subway. She was easily as neurotic as me, and prone to monologues about how wretched her life was. She was forever doing things like losing her glasses down sewers and getting into fights with her landlord, who'd retaliate by cutting off her heat. One day, on the way to the Chambers Street stop of the B train, she stopped in the middle of one of her soliloquies and eyed me soberly, preparing to make an important announcement.

'I've told you how much I hate my job, right?' she inquired, to which I could have responded 'Only about a million times', but simply nodded.

'I've been thinking about quitting for a long time now, but I've finally made up my mind.'

'So are you going to quit?' I asked.

'No.'

'No?'

'No. I've decided I'm gonna work here till I die.'

'Till you die?'

'Yup. I was reading the company insurance policy last night, and it says that if I'm still here when I die, they'll pay for the funeral.'

I laughed as I hadn't in months. I was unable to stop; every time I tried, the sight of her enraged face started me off again. I sank on to a bench to compose myself, then collapsed in another gale of hilarity, and might have gone on that way indefinitely if Theresa hadn't cried, 'Oh, just screw you, then,' and walked off. I ran after her, apologising, but she was standoffish for several days afterward. She was still working there when I left, and if she's still there now, I hope they haven't changed the company policy.

30

'ARE YOU IN THE MOOD for some juicy gossip?' Lauren asked one August Sunday. I was at her place in The Bronx for a mutual hair-frosting session, which consisted of pulling chunks of hair through holes in a plastic bonnet with a small knitting needle, then covering the exposed hair with bleach. The process was supposed to give you sun-kissed blonde highlights, and it worked perfectly on Lauren's smooth hair. But it turned my curls a wild orange that a circus clown would think twice before trying.

I was always in the mood for juicy gossip. Like she needed to ask.

She had an uncharacteristically ambivalent expression on her face, as if she was already regretting opening her mouth. Going into her bedroom, she returned with a red-bound book, a 1977 diary. She flipped to an April page and instructed, 'Read that.'

When I had, I asked, 'Are you putting me on?'

'No, I swear,' she said, and if she was lying she was incredibly convincing. According to the diary, she'd gone to Germany when the Rollers were playing a few shows there the year before – and I'd thought following them to Detroit was something – and in Munich had lost her virginity to one of them. 'He was so *romantic*,' she'd written, wistfulness flowing across the page in small, precise script.

I'd begun to think nothing about the Rollers could shock me any more, but the notion of one of them relieving a friend of her virginity did. Just as shocking was Lauren's ability to keep it secret for almost eighteen months. If it had been me, I'd have been straight on the phone to Cathy, Emma and Sue J, at the very least.

Not for the first time, I enviously wondered how you went about acquiring that sort of self-containment. Being described as 'a private person' would have been a great compliment in my book. Failing that, I'd have settled for simply toning down my mouthiness, which was great for tricking airline booking clerks into revealing flight details, but not so great for reducing men to jelly. And boy, did I want to.

I managed to not blab Lauren's secret two weeks later, when most of the Tarts convened at my pad on a Friday night to watch 'The Bay City Rollers Meet the Saturday Superstars'. This was a preview of their Saturday series, 'The Krofft Superstar Hour', which was starting the next day. The 'Saturday Superstars' of the title, who were created by the Hollywood production team of Sid and Marty Krofft, consisted of costumed characters including Witchipoo and H R Pufnstuf. The Rollers must have felt they'd hit a career low when they learned they'd be co-starring with something called Witchipoo.

The Tart opinion was mixed. 'It was a hoot. Eric is now being played up as the Casanova of the band,' I wrote, 'and, due to elocution lessons, all of them are actually intelligible. There was a medley of 50s songs for the finale, in which all of 'em wore gold lamé suits and greased-back hair (which made Eric's face look really fat). It was absurd, but hilarious.'

Poor Rollers! Not just Witchipoo, but corny set pieces with lamé suits! They really must have been desperate. We watched with sadistic glee, and the next day we all went to Cathy's for the debut proper of the show. Cathy set up a breakfast buffet next to the TV so we didn't have to leave the room, and we sat there with our bagels, utterly engrossed.

It was more of the same – the Rollers sang a few songs, bantered with Witchipoo and did a skit starring Leslie, sporting a stick-on mustache, as a film director. Lauren pronounced the show 'undignified', Cathy and Emma thought the band had potential as actors, Sue J and I enjoyed the foolishness of it all. We did agree on one thing – that 'The Krofft Superstar Hour' marked the start of their terminal decline.

But the worst was yet to come. It was called *Strangers in the Wind* – their sixth album, released a week after the TV show started. Gads, it was bad. The songs were terrible, the cover artwork was terrible, the 'concept' (the cray-zee life of a rock 'n' roll band on the road) was terrible.

The album sleeve delights me to this day, so indulge me by letting me describe it. It looks like this: in the background, a childlike sketch of an ice-covered mountain range rendered in an inadvertently Cubist style. In the foreground, five bubbles, with one badly drawn Roller's head per bubble. Ice crystals twinkle at the edges of the bubbles. The drawings were apparently done by someone working from blurry photos, and it's nearly impossible to tell who's who. The back cover finds the bubbles, little more than infantile doodlings by this point, drifting off toward a blue horizon. It's hard to believe that someone at Arista Records actually thought that this cover was going to hold its own in the racks next to Springsteen and Elvis Costello.

And the music is even better. In its defense, *Strangers in the Wind* was indisputably their most musically accomplished record yet. Fully employing the technology that was around then, the group and their producer, one Harry Maslin, achieved a lush sound far removed from the lite, brite early days. Even Leslie's thin voice, long one of the band's weakest points, was buoyed up by layers of strings, brass and electronic trickery. Meanwhile, Eric, the most serious musician of the group, expanded his range with state-of-the-art gadgets like 'synth-guitar'.

All told, each Roller did his job to the best of his ability, and their musicianship wasn't at issue. It was the actual tunes that

were so stinky. Even the titles were embarrassing. You can tell
a lot about what a song will sound like just from its title, and
never was that truer than with these. You didn't even need to
listen to 'All of the World is Falling in Love' to know it would
be a chinless wimpmeister of a ballad, or that 'Another Rainy
Day in New York City' would be built on a hundredweight of
sobbing violins. 'Back on the Street' was just what it sounded,
a stab at 'urban funk' that sounded as urban and funky as
Shaun Cassidy. The title track was a surprise, however –
instead of the romantic slop I'd expected, it was soft rock
that could have passed for the Doobie Brothers.

Then there were the lyrics. Now, don't forget that this was
intended to be a transitional album that would enable the band
to pick up older fans, so presumably Eric and Woody thought
long and hard before putting down a word. The lyrics would
have to tell the world that the Bay City Rollers were grown men,
no strangers to love and heartbreak. They'd need to incorpo-
rate the madness and lust of being in a rock band, and at the
same time weave in their experiences as cultural touchstones,
idols of a generation. This is what they came up with:

> What used to be an old apartment
> They've built a multi-colored jigsaw in the sky
> And where the children would play
> Well, they're not there any more
> But the rooms are nice, with numbers on the door.

Excuse me, but *what*? Multi-colored jigsaws in the sky, rooms
with numbers on the door . . . By the beaver-barbed buck
teeth of Stuart 'Woody' Wood, what in God's name were they
on about? It was terrible. It was preposterous. And before you
ask what right *I've* got to criticise, I appreciate that it must be
fiendishly difficult to compose song lyrics, and I'm sure Eric
and Woody sweated over every line. But this was really
something.

The great majority of pop lyrics are, as it happens, drivel. Dear old Led Zep, say, with their ruminations about stairways to heaven, were hardly world-class wordsmiths, and even Lennon and McCartney had their uninspired moments. But the Rollers' lyrics were more painful, because Faulkner and Wood were trying so hard to go against their teen-pop grain. They'd done the same on the previous album, *It's a Game*, but that one had at least had the benefit of some great melodies. *Strangers in the Wind* had none. When I played it a few months ago for the first time in fifteen years, I couldn't remember a single song.

Especially hard to take were their efforts to express the physical side of love. On 'If You Were My Woman' by Faulkner and Wood it came out as a confluence of soft-focus euphemisms like 'Oh, baby, when I feel your touch/ The magic in your fingers takes control of me'. Yech. There's much to be said for just coming out and saying it, as Robert Plant famously did with the immortal line about squeezing his lemon till the juice ran down his leg.

I played the album for David up at his place one day, and while we were debating its merits – he believed it didn't have any – Sue J turned up. 'Sorry I'm late,' she apologised, 'but I've just been watching Sid Vicious and his girlfriend staggering into the Chelsea.'

All Roller-thoughts temporarily ceased. Vicious and Nancy Spungen had moved into the Chelsea Hotel, next door to David's on 23rd Street, a month before. With Nancy acting as his manager, Vicious was trying to launch a solo career, which so far had consisted of two poorly received gigs at the punk club Max's Kansas City. Since then, the couple had reportedly spent most days asleep and most nights on the Lower East Side buying drugs. David had seen them blearily hailing taxis in front of the Chelsea, Vicious invariably decked out in crusting leather, his better half in something short and tight.

Because of the Sex Pistols connection, Vicious was considered cool by Manhattan nightlife types, and their second-floor room was a liggers' mecca. The hangers-on included the cream of the local drug dealers, who were happy to provide door-to-door service because the Vicious-Spungens were such good customers. The pair and their retinue quickly became local legends. Rumor had it Nancy had even been seen in our favorite pizza joint, Luv'n Oven, but that was probably apocryphal because they certainly didn't look like they ever ate.

I had yet to see them in the flesh, so when Sue announced they were right down the block at that precise moment, I was tempted to dash out for a quick look.

'Why don't you call him instead?' Sue suggested. We decided I'd phone and invite Vicious (and Nancy, too, if necessary) out for a drink. If they said yes, well, we'd go out for a drink. But when I rang, the phone was answered by an American guy, who said, 'Sid's in no condition to talk – I'm trying to bring him out of it right now.'

Cool! He'd obviously passed out or something. Highly impressed by this rock'n'roll drama being played out mere yards away, we gave it an hour, then called back. This time Sid himself answered. They'd managed to 'bring him out of it', and he sounded little the worse for wear. As instructed, I invited him for a drink.

'I dunno,' yawned the hero of the punk wars, jacket creaking audibly. 'Ask my girlfriend.'

'Who the fuck's this?' snapped Nancy, sounding less comatose than hubby. Less bravely now, I repeated my invitation. 'Hey, Sid, you wanna go for a drink with this chick?' she shouted, though he couldn't have been more than a foot away. 'Nah,' I heard him say. 'Ha-ha, ya stupid fool!' she cackled triumphantly, and slammed down the phone.

'Cool,' breathed Sue when I related the exchange. 'Assholes,' was David's judgement.

He turned out to be right. Less than two weeks later, of

course, Sid stabbed Nancy to death in that same hotel room in circumstances that have never been satisfactorily explained. David was just leaving his building when he saw the police car and ambulance stop in front of the Chelsea. 'If I'd known what it was I'd have stuck around,' he said. He missed seeing Nancy wheeled in a body bag, and a handcuffed, expressionless Vicious pushed into the back of the police car. He was wearing his leather jacket, and quietly swore at the TV crews as he got into the car.

The murder was viewed with a peculiar sang-froid by the city's downtown crowd. As the thinking went, the couple's self-destructiveness had made an outcome of this sort almost inevitable. In some circles, Sid won approval for having done something so interestingly punk. The *Village Voice* even ran a piece about 'Nauseating Nancy'. Out on bail, poor, stupid Vicious died of a heroin overdose a few months later.

And by then, Leslie had quit the Rollers, and their career gently slipped down another gear. All in all, a pretty bad time for pop stars.

31

I T WAS OBVIOUS Leslie wasn't long for the (Roller) world when the October '78 issue of a teen magazine called *Tiger Beat* ran a picture on the cover of him with a cream pie all over his face. You'll remember that Leslie had been hit with the pie at the wrap party for their TV show, a little memento from the crew for having acted like a star throughout shooting. The magazine would never have run the photo if McKeown hadn't been on his way out, and by November he had indeed quit.

It was the end of an era not just for the band but for the Tarts. A member like Alan could come and go as often as he pleased, but Leslie was the fulcrum, the axis, the one who encapsulated Rollerdom. We noted his departure with a pang, as much for us as for him. His resignation, which supposedly occurred amid much acrimony, severed, abruptly and forever, the link between the Tarts and the happy days of Roller-chasing.

No sooner had McKeown flounced off, muttering about solo records, than the Rollers replaced him with one Duncan Faure.

Blond and baby-faced, Faure looked like a teen idol all right, but he wasn't cut out to be a Roller. He was South African, of all things, and thus totally devoid of that malnourished Scottish quality. Worse, there was no personality niche for him. He wasn't a vulnerable Eric type, a sagacious Alan, a chipmunky Woody or a faithful old Derek. He was just blond and perky and generic. He rose without trace, slipping into

Leslie's place but never managing to impose his own character on the role.

I could attest to that because in December, just weeks after Faure joined, the Tarts got a close-up look at him. The band came to New York for the first time in over a year, and none of us could resist going to the airport to meet their plane.

Former Spice Girl Geri Halliwell once said something along the lines of, 'The Spice Girls are like heroin. Even if you don't like us, you're addicted.' It was the same with the Rollers. By December 1978, nearly all the Tarts had gone off them for reasons ranging from real boyfriends to simple boredom, but the emotional commitment wasn't that easy to eradicate. When our Los Angeles mole, Jan, told us that the band would be flying from LA to New York sometime around December 10 to do some TV shows, I didn't even think twice.

Borrowing my boss's Official Airline Guide, I copied down every flight for December 9, 10 and 11, then automatically checked for reservations on every one. I finally tracked them down to an American Airlines flight arriving on the evening of the tenth, a Sunday. I couldn't believe I was bothering, but it would have been unimaginable not to bother. They were the Rollers, part of my DNA, and as long as there was a single atom of pleasure to be wrung out of them – even if most of the pleasure was by then nostalgic – I would bother.

The other Tarts sheepishly concurred, and all of us crammed into a rented car to go to Kennedy Airport that Sunday. We assured each other it was just for the hell of it, but we were, all of us, more excited than we'd admit. The foolish thrill of an airport run even now was enough to get us out in our Sunday best.

I dressed carefully in the secretarial look I'd recently been cultivating – pleated tweed trousers and a fluffy mauve turtle-neck – and did the best I could with my orange hair. The others were similarly primped and laundered, and Sue P had made free with her new bottle of Charlie.

I'd also written an earnest letter to my personal Roller, which I intended to hand to him at the airport. Mercifully, I can't remember what it said. Hopefully nothing like 'I love you' or 'I've missed you', even though I did, and had. I was resigned to the probability that we'd never be together again, but a letter seemed a way of renewing the bond, however briefly. Maybe it would remind him there'd once *been* a bond.

We were surprised to see our old rivals Joey and company at the airport. So we weren't the only ones who still cared. The old rivalries dissolved as we came together, a pitifully over-aged bunch in our late teens, still transfixed by one small Scottish pop band. We laughed in recognition of it, and Sue J was even feeling generous enough to tell Joey that she'd just spotted Mick Jagger and his new girlfriend, Jerry Hall (tall, blonde, beautiful – what did she want with an old coot like 35-year-old Jagger?), checking in for a flight to London.

Jagger was forgotten as the Rollers suddenly appeared in the arrivals lounge. It was the first time in a year that we'd seen them at such close quarters, and we whipped out our cameras. Passers-by must have wondered about the commotion, because the band looked like such nonentities you'd never have believed they *were* a band. They'd tried a few rockish touches, Woody opting for aviator sunglasses, Alan for highlights in his hair, and Eric – who had developed noticeable jowls – a full-length fur coat. Otherwise there was nothing to distinguish them from any of the other passengers. No tartan, no bodyguards, no squealing fans unless you counted us.

I hurried to catch up with my Roller and thrust the letter at him, forcing him to focus on me for a moment. 'Thanks,' he said and tucked it into his jacket. Was there a flicker of recognition? Hard to tell, and there was no time to think about it because after the initial glance he didn't look at me again as he strode along. I was disappointed but stoically told myself that he probably just wanted to get to their car. I hadn't expected him to stop and chat. Had I?

And so we followed them into the city, watched them check into a hotel near Central Park and hung around outside in the dark for an hour, till it became obvious they were settled in for the night. 'See ya tomorrow?' suggested Joey and we agreed, no longer rivals but allies bound together by mutual sadness.

For the four days they were in New York, at least a few of us were never far away. When they taped a kids' TV show right in the middle of 58th Street on Monday morning, Kim and I were there, watching as the script girl rushed to drape Eric with his fur coat every time there was a break in taping.

When they went to an Italian restaurant Tuesday night, Barbarino and I were there, keeping vigil from a café on the other side of Mulberry Street. I'd been about to go to bed when Barbarino phoned; within ten minutes I was dressed and heading downtown in a cab, wondering if I were insane. But at least I didn't try to follow the band when they left the restaurant – Barbarino did, reporting that they all went back to the hotel except Eric, who took the script girl from the day before out for a drink and didn't get in till nearly four in the morning.

Sue J, Barbarino and I were there, too, when the entire band went to the Bottom Line to see the promising young country singer Tanya Tucker. We managed to get a table a few feet behind theirs so we could easily watch them while pretending to watch the stage (Miss Tucker acquitted herself well, by the way, and we'd have probably enjoyed it had any of us liked country music).

The band knew we were there, and resolutely ignored us. You could hardly blame them. In the last few days we'd been nearly everywhere they had, and it must have been a pain in the ass to see our faces every time they looked up. Having said that, though, we were always well-behaved, kept our distance and didn't try to talk to them when they were busy. Heck, we felt entitled to a bit of respect. Who else would have stuck with them for so long?

As they continued to pretend we weren't there, Sue, Barbarino and I got annoyed. All right, so they were having a night out and hadn't invited us to stalk them. And okay, we weren't their buddies, just fans. I had reconciled myself to that lowly status when my Roller hadn't acknowledged me at any of the places I'd seen him in the last few days. He'd been just a couple of yards away on a number of occasions, but was somehow always looking the other way when we passed. I had managed not to speak to him, but was stung by his indifference.

All we wanted was acknowledgement, and in four days they hadn't stopped to say so much as hello. We knew that the more we hung around the less likely they were to talk to us, but they were breaking their part of the fame transaction, the bit about being nice to fans – even ones like us, who were too old to be fans. As Tanya Tucker sang and the Rollers fixedly watched – who knew *they* were country fans? – I worked myself into a fine state. 'I'm gonna write him a note asking who the hell he thinks he is,' I whispered to Sue, nodding toward my Roller.

This I did, scribbling a plaintive little missive asking what I'd 'done to deserve' his coolness. Holding my breath, I tapped him on the shoulder and handed him the note. As strategies go, it was a flop. It was more than a flop, it was excruciatingly humiliating. He read it with two of the others peering over his shoulder, then passed it to the rest of the party. He didn't glance at me again the rest of the evening. At least I'd been clinging to a shred of pride before I wrote it – now I'd not only surrendered it but invited him to walk all over it. The moral: don't put anything in writing, especially if half a dozen of the recipient's friends are there.

Nevertheless, when they left New York the next day, to go God knew where, I was able to muster up a bit of sympathy for them. 'I was thinking about them today and suddenly felt more compassion than annoyance,' I wrote. 'The pressures they're under must be horrendous, and the lack of privacy must be crushing. No wonder they weren't exactly all smiles this week. I wonder if this Duncan kid knows what he's gotten himself into.'

I wonder indeed. Maybe Faure ('cute except for the bald spot') hadn't realised that he had joined the group when it was well past its peak. That said, a successful band past its peak must have looked a lot more attractive than a South African band that had never had a peak. Faure's previous musical endeavors, whatever they were, had not attracted the slightest attention outside South Africa, so he must have seen the Rollers as his big break. Sadly for him, it wasn't. He never even had the experience of singing on a hit single, because by the time he joined hits were a thing of the distant past. But as Robert De Niro says in the film *The King of Comedy*, 'Better king for a day than schmuck for a lifetime'. I'm sure that's relevant somehow.

32

1979

First UK #1 of the year: 'YMCA'/Village People
Biggest Roller hits of the year (UK/US): None

1978 ENDED AS IGNOMINIOUSLY as it had begun. New Year's Eve found two friends and me trying to get into Manhattan's most snobbish disco, Studio 54. It was now so notorious – rumor had it that celebrity habitués like Andy Warhol and Halston sexed and drugged right on the dancefloor – that we felt we should see it.

We knew you had to dress creatively to get past the doormen, who were so notoriously selective that when two naked girls once rode up on a horse, only the horse got in. So we did our version of creative: Ellen was head-to-toe sequins, Sandra wore farmers' overalls and carried a pitchfork, I wore nothing but a slip (pretty brave, considering it was December). We didn't get in; the doormen didn't even notice us in the milling crowd. And I'd thought the pitchfork was such a good touch.

After hanging around for a while to see if any celebs turned up, which they didn't, we ended up seeing in 1979 in a coffee shop down the block. 'I didn't want to go there anyway,' Ellen flounced, and we agreed vigorously.

My main goal for the first weeks of '79 was to stop seeing Dr Kalman. I'd been trudging up to his bleak office every week for a year, but the hours of talking and talking had done nothing to quell the anxiety. Only Valium, which he hadn't got around to suggesting for eight intensely painful, fear-wracked months, made any difference. Once I discovered that tranquilizers could bring it under control by smoothing the edges of the panic, I was able to wake up without feeling sick at the thought of facing another day. Within days of taking it, I was able to do things I'd avoided for months, like taking trains and entering big stores.

Kalman wrote me a prescription once a month, and I kept the bottle in my bag at all times. Just knowing it was there often stopped nervousness from becoming full-blown panic. Recklessly, Kalman didn't prescribe an exact dosage, just telling me to take as many as I needed when I needed them. It was practically an invitation to abuse them, but, curiously, it made me abstemious – maybe Kalman was counting on that – and I only dished them out when I really had to.

That turned out to be nearly every day at work, but never on weekends. The five-days-on-two-days-off schedule was both comforting and worrying – not needing them at weekends reassured me I wasn't addicted, but I quickly realised that hardly a weekday went by without my creeping up to the water-cooler and knocking a couple back after checking that no-one was around. Still, the improvement in the anxiety was so marked that semi-dependence seemed a small price to pay.

Anyway, several months on them had restored my confidence to the point that a break with Kalman seemed like the next step. No more sitting in his bare room, feeling his disapproval when I lit a cigarette (he was palpably thrilled when I finally quit toward the end of our time together). No more listening to the dry scratch of his pen as he noted down my thoughts, no more inadvertently overhearing other patients. One guy once cried, loudly enough to be audible in reception where I was waiting, 'When I had my breakdown I went as stiff as a board, but they should never have taken me to the hospital', which horrified me. Is that what happened

when you went crazy? You went as stiff as a board? I didn't
want to know.

And no more puzzling admonitions about not getting
pregnant while I was on the Valium. He warned me about
that every time he renewed the prescription, as if the pills
would make me forget myself to the point of bedding everything in sight.

He seemed happy enough to let me go, which I took as a
sign that I was better, and it was with great relief at the end of
January that I said goodbye to him and his receptionist, whose
name, if it wasn't already, should have been Ethel Frump. It
wasn't a complete parting of the ways, because he had agreed
to still give me a prescription every month, but basically he and
I were splitsville. Hooray.

I don't know if the Rollers visited any psychiatrists in early
1979, but it might have crossed their minds, because by then
they weren't happy boys. Shaken by the failure of *Strangers in
the Wind*, which hadn't even made the Top 100, they were
starting to write songs for their next album, but were beset by
doubts. Despite fresh blood in the shape of Duncan Faure,
they were thinking of packing it in.

I knew this because Leslie's brother, Hari, told me. I'd got
his home number in Edinburgh from my London penpal,
Brenda, who still wrote to me every couple of months. 'He's
quite friendly,' she said, which was all I needed to hear, and I'd
taken to calling him once a fortnight.

I'd have preferred to talk to Leslie, but his brother would do,
especially as he always seemed pleased to hear from me and
would usually chat for at least half an hour. He didn't think it
at all odd that a strange girl was calling him, because, as he put
it, 'I get calls and letters from all over the world, but you're the
first one I've really talked to because all the others just want to
know about Leslie.'

As it happened, I just wanted to know about Leslie, too, but
was sensible enough to never mention him, with the result that

Hari often talked about him anyway. But as we went along, I became fond of Hari himself, who'd had an unsuccessful crack at pop stardom under the name Jamie Wild. Now he was working as a DJ at some Edinburgh disco, and he seemed a poignant figure. After a couple of months, as a little friendship gesture I offered to send him some up-to-the-minute American dance records to play in his club.

Disco records. God, the lengths I'd go to to impress a guy. I had to consult an expert – the guy at the newsstand downstairs – and duly bought 'I'm Every Woman' by Chaka Khan, 'To Be Real' by Cheryl Lynn and a couple more I'd never heard of. I waited ten days after dispatching them, then called to see if they'd arrived. A girl – London accent, snooty – answered. She said Hari was out, and he was also out when I tried again the next day. I finally reached him at the end of the week, but the warmth in his voice was gone. Something to do with the chick who seemed to be living with him, I surmised.

I didn't call him again, but by then it didn't matter. Brenda had come up with the real deal – Leslie's home number. She had a lot of other beans to spill in the same letter, dated April 1979. For one thing, Leslie had a new pad in London, which he was sharing with a fellow Scot called Scobie, who was producing McKeown's first solo album. He hadn't wasted time since leaving the Rollers – not only was there a new LP in the works, there was a new group, whom he'd named Leslie McKeown's Ego Trip ('Bloody apt,' as Brenda said). The album was to be titled *All Washed Up*, and the cover illustration depicted Leslie climbing out of a plane that had crashed in the ocean. On the tail of the plane were the letters 1X-BCR. You had to admire McKeown for so thoroughly burning his bridges.

Its title turned out to be prophetic, because this piece of autobiographical synth-pop did virtually sink McKeown's career. He was out of the public eye for a year as he worked on it, and when it finally came out in the spring of 1980, it simply disappeared, despite being a reasonable success in Japan. You can't even find it at jumble sales.

But in April '79 he was feeling confident, according to this Scobie, who answered the phone when I worked up the nerve to call. Cathy was with me; we'd shared a bottle of Amaretto and goaded each other till I finally dialed the number. A Scottish voice wheezed 'H'lo?' and I announced, with a brisk confidence I didn't feel, 'Hi! You must be Scobie.'

'Who's this?' he asked, perking up at the sound of a female voice.

'Caroline,' I said, relieved that he sounded friendly.

A flirtatious note crept into his voice. 'And what can I do for you, Caroline?'

Put your paymaster on the phone, I wanted to reply, but instead said that my friend Cathy and I were fans who were curious about what Leslie was up to. That was all the introduction he needed. For the next twenty minutes he talked with barely a pause about the songs he and McKeown were writing and how they were going to make the next Rollers album sound as wimpy as Art Garfunkel, who was then in the singles chart with 'Bright Eyes'. That'll be tough, I thought.

At length I ever so casually asked, 'So, uh, is Leslie around?'

'He's out, kitten, but give us a ring tomorrow around this time and he should be in.'

I repeated the whole conversation to Cathy, including the 'kitten', and she was very impressed. 'We've got to call them tomorrow,' she decided. Hence, twenty-four hours later almost to the minute, we called again and this time, as promised, Leslie was there.

'Have we met?' he immediately demanded. I could have told him, Well, a couple of years ago you swore at my friends and me all night in Detroit.

'Oh, sort of,' I replied.

'Have we slept together?' Cathy, whose head was next to

mine, swooned when Loverboy said 'slept together' and began fanning herself like she had the vapors. 'No, we haven't slept together,' I told Leslie and put my hand over Cathy's mouth so she couldn't shout, 'I'll sleep with you!' as she was about to.

'Well, have we fucked together?' he persisted, young slobhood at its most endearing. Some embryonic feminist part of me told me to hang up, and if this had been anybody but McKeown I would have, but it *was* McKeown, and his magic still exerted its hold.

'No, no,' I giggled.

'Well, what did we do together, for fuck's sake?' he was saying.

'Oh, we met on your last tour . . . Detroit . . . you were in our room. I was with Barbarino and Kim and Lauren . . . remember?' As he thought it over, I could hear him chomping a wad of gum, and presently he lit a cigarette. Smoking and chewing simultaneously, he emitted a small moan of recognition. 'Oh, Lauren! Pretty girl from New York, right?'

Cathy, who'd never got over Lauren monopolising his attention on that tour, made throwing-up noises.

'Who's that?' he asked alertly. It was Cathy, I told him, not adding that she was gagging because she'd loved him for years and couldn't bear the idea that the only one of us he remembered was Lauren.

'Well, let's talk to Cathy,' he offered generously. She took the receiver and I checked to see that the tape recorder was getting all this down. We'd pooled our money that afternoon to buy a small suction-cup recording-device thing that stuck on to the phone so that we could re-live our conversation with Leslie over and over again.

The expression on Cathy's face gradually changed from ecstatic to ambivalent. 'Uh-huh . . . is that so? . . . I'll see what I can do . . . yeah, you too . . . bye.'

She rolled her eyes and shook herself like a cat emerging from a puddle. 'He was really nice at first, but then he started saying how he and "Scobe" were planning to come to New York soon, and could we arrange a party for them and invite lots of girls?'

'How many girls?' I asked.

'He just said lots. And then he goes, "Why don't you and your friend fly over here and entertain us?" '

And I'm sorry to say that we actually considered it. Instead of dismissing Leslie and 'Scobe' with the figurative kick in the behinds they deserved, we actually sat there and talked about whether it would be feasible to go to London. If we'd had more experience of men – non-Roller men – we'd never have contemplated it for an instant. But we didn't, so we gave serious thought to going to London at our own expense to be their concubines. We reluctantly concluded we couldn't afford it, but if we'd had a couple of hundred bucks to spare we'd have been over there faster than McKeown could say 'Your conjugal services are required, and get me a bacon sandwich on the way'.

We'd have undoubtedly loved every minute of it, too. In our minds, far from being servile, this would have been an incomparable chance to experience Leslie in his own habitat (we didn't discuss which of us would end up with Scobie, we'd cross that bridge when we came to it). We'd have a wild weekend, and then we'd come home. Sadly, our expectations were that modest. Even the most demeaning attention from McKeown was preferable to no attention; if anything, his charmlessness was queerly exciting.

Of course, we rang Chez McKeown again. Several times, in fact. The next time we spoke, he was huffing about a story that had run in that week's *Sunday People*. Headlined 'Living a Lie for Five Years', it was a kiss-and-tell job about the Rollers' supposed sex-and-drug escapades.

But the informant wasn't some disgruntled employee in search of quick tabloid money, it was the Rollers themselves. In a last-ditch attempt to change their image, they went the whole hog, Derek discussing his many lovers, Eric, the time he took acid and 'ate a giant box of cornflakes in one sitting' and suchlike. It was terrible that they were reduced to this, I told McKeown, who agreed. 'I've just written to the paper to disassociate myself from their moronic nonsense,' he sniffed.

Cathy and I would probably have continued the phone calls had the bill not intervened. It was $337 for just one month – they never called us, of course – and it was clear our little chats, which were mostly with Scobie anyway, couldn't continue. It was also clear, as I struggled to find money to pay the bill, that I couldn't support myself on my salary from the metallurgy lab.

Synchronicitously, another job came up – a typist thing at a rehearsal studio-cum-instrument-rental-company uptown. I applied, got it, and in one fell swoop was making $25 a week more and, more importantly, *working in the music industry*! Finally, after years of longing, I had a real, live music-biz job involving studios, contact with groups, everything.

The actual job, which consisted of billing clients for instruments and studio space, wasn't glamorous. Nor was the office, which was in the down-at-heel West Thirties. Nor were my new colleagues – a hard-bitten office manager called Don, the even harder-bitten owner, who was derisively known as Mama behind her back, a dour black bookkeeper and an aloof senior secretary who was Mama's favorite and got to use the only electric typewriter. None of them was really even a music fan. I'd imagined discussions about the records we'd bought and the gigs we'd been to, but quickly grasped that I was the only one with an active interest in such things.

Moreover, it was soon clear that the rehearsal studios were frequented not by coolski rock bands like, say, The Clash, who were just then launching their first American tour, but by middle-of-the-road crooners like Barry Manilow and Dionne Warwick.

The instrument-rental part of the business was more interesting. There was a brisk flow of guitars, amps and whatnot to top artists at recording studios and venues, and I got a kick out of typing names like David Bowie on invoices. But I began to wonder why they only hired one or two items at a time. That was when I discovered that our company, which I'll call Mama's, was very much number two in the rental biz – for most of their needs, nearly every group went to another company nearby, and only turned to us when the other people had run out of something.

But hey. I was in the music biz. I was an official insider. It was intoxicating.

And a couple of weeks after I started at Mama's, I finally landed a boyfriend. A proper one that lasted more than a couple of dates. He had an accent I mistook for English but turned out to be Australian, and was darkly brooding in an Anthony Perkins sort of way. Lush. His looks went a long way toward making up for the fact that he worked in computers and never shut up about them, and that his favorite derogatory expression was 'canine afterbirth'. The other Tarts were deeply respectful. Australian! It was practically Scottish.

So there I was, April '79, equipped with a boyfriend *and* a job in music. Finally, a compelling interest in something other than the Rollers. Life was grand, and it was a beautiful, soft springtime of strolls in the Village and dinners in Italian restaurants.

Despite interminable lectures in a flat Melbourne drawl about how computers talked to each other in languages called 'Basic' and 'Cobal', I was convinced it was love. Sadly, it wasn't love on my dashing swain's part, and after two months of canine afterbirths and software chat he dropped out of sight.

He bequeathed me an album by Skyhooks, then Australia's biggest band. They were a wretched comedy-rock ensemble who presumed that jester's hats and fake bosoms made up for their manifest lack of talent. The album's highlight, a skiffle number called 'You Just Like Me 'Cos I'm Good in Bed', was certainly an insight into contemporary Antipodean music.

'Think of me when you play that one,' he winked (those eyes, that hair . . .) from behind his computer. He was the only person I knew who had a computer in his apartment. Heck, at that point most offices didn't have them – Mama's sure didn't.

I did think of him. Though probably not in the way he'd have preferred.

33

B UT NEVER MIND THE BOYFRIEND. Even as he left me for his real love, the binary system, other interests were lining up to take his place. Mama's was going through a phase of renting equipment to punk and new wave bands, and every couple of days brought a new intake of droopy-jeaned roadies collecting guitars and drum kits. The bands themselves rarely deigned to visit our plywood-walled hovel, but just being around a Magazine, Iggy Pop or Damned technician-type made my week. It didn't take a lot to thrill me, as long as they were young and punk, for after a year of listening to Meat Loaf and company to calm my anxiety, I was back into punk.

Sadly, I was much more excited when The Damned, the crudest of Sex Pistols wannabes, rented a monitor than when Stevie Wonder himself – an awesome talent then at the height of his powers – came in to use a rehearsal room. Not that I saw much of Wonder. He was a briefly glimpsed tall figure encircled by minders, who tenderly led him down our narrow hallway. There was a muffled yelp as he thwacked his shoulder against the pay phone, and with that he disappeared into the elevator and was still upstairs when I left for the day.

Simultaneously, news of a Roller tour was surfacing. It was set for July and August '79 and, as in 1977, would consist of outdoor shows at agricultural fairs and amusement parks. As if that weren't enough of an admission of defeat, this time they weren't even hitting the big cities. No sir. Apart from one show in Philadelphia, they were booked into backwaters like Pensacola, Florida, Greenville, South Carolina and Portland, Maine.

The tour was a disaster. Gigs were cancelled due to poor sales, and in Pensacola a contractual mix-up nearly landed them with a lawsuit.

That's what we were told by a roadie we phoned in Greenville. Cathy and I hadn't been able to resist calling their hotel, where Cathy crisply requested that the hotel operator put her through to 'a member of the Bay City Rollers tour group'.

Ten seconds later some drowsy roadie was on the line, saying 'Huh?' as Cathy introduced herself with our usual, 'You don't know us, but we're fans and we just wanted to know how the tour was going.' Once he was awake, the guy was more than happy to gossip. He painted a dismal picture of trundling through the South on a bus – private planes were just a memory – bypassing cities where they'd once known triumph because they could no longer fill large venues and being reduced to chain motels or sometimes sleeping on the bus.

It was all such a comedown we knew we'd have to witness it for ourselves. There were still tickets left for the Philadelphia show just days before the gig. Barbarino, Kim and I prepared to go.

The day of the show, it was cancelled without explanation. That would have been that, had Barbarino not discovered that a replacement gig had been hastily slotted in at a New Jersey safari park called Great Adventure, the kind of place where you drive around with the windows up, urging wildebeests to snuffle around the engine. The gig wasn't till Monday, though, and this was Friday. The band were going to spend the weekend in a hamlet called Bordentown, just down the highway from the park, and there was nothing for it but to get into our car, which we'd already rented anyway, and go to Bordentown.

August 3 turned out to be the last time we travelled outside

New York to see the Rollers, because the tour turned out to be their last American one. In the future, they would play small club dates, but would never again attempt a full-scale US jaunt. Most of this was down to the failure of their new album, *Elevator*. The tour coincided with its release, and if the album did well in the chart, the band would have reason to continue their annual US tours. If not, bye bye baby.

It was a profound flop. Justifiably so, as it was their silliest yet. It was even more foolish than *Strangers in the Wind*. Heaven alone knows what they were thinking, but on *Elevator* they pulled out all the stops. They were grown-up, hairy-palmed rockers, by God, and they were gonna make people listen.

The first and most drastic thing they did was drop the 'Bay City'. This sacrilege was presumably committed in the hope people somehow wouldn't associate them with the tartan pantywaists who made twelve-year-olds pee. Ladies and gentlemen: 'The Rollers'.

It would have been instructive to have been a fly on the wall during the album planning session. I'd like to think it went something like this:

Alan, as oldest, calls meeting to order: 'All right, everyone, now sit down and listen up. We've got a lot to get through today. Let's deal with the album sleeve first. Any ideas?'

Eric [eyeing plateful of plump custard tarts on table]: 'The name change was a great idea. Long overdue. So we've got to come up with something just as rad for the cover, and I have an idea. At this point, no offense, guys, it would probably hurt more than help to have our picture on the front. [Chorus of 'Are you joking?' and 'But I've cut my hair for it!'] No, no, hear me out. Now, this is our most down and dirty album yet, and it needs a really striking image. So what about [deep breath] an elevator with its door open, and a giant red pill leaning against the wall. Y'know, pill as in "mood elevator". Get it?' [Cries of 'Genius!']

Woody: 'But aren't we going to have our pictures on it at all?'

Eric [popping whole tart into mouth]: 'I'm coming to that. So we turn over the cover and there's us on the back. But instead of the usual posed studio number, we're gonna use onstage shots. Y'know, show us really doing our thing on the road. The shots'll be a bit darker than usual to make us look hard. My mustache will be perfect.' [Strokes newly hatched mustache proudly as other Rollers watch with envy. All except one.]

Derek: 'You don't think your mustache makes you look like a pizza delivery boy?'

Alan: 'Oi, don't you start. Now, let's go on to lyrics. Eric, I hear you've been hard at work. What have you come up with so far?'

Eric [rising and riffling through sheaf of papers]: 'I'll read you this one. It's called "Instant Relay". I see it as a solid track in the middle of side two. Here we go. [Dramatic pause and clearing of throat; then he recites verse with references to transvestites and the Ayatollah. Murmurs of 'Beautiful' and 'Hey, suck on this, Rolling Stones!']

Duncan Faure [timidly rising]: 'Hey, guys . . . guys? Can I read you one of mine? I'm quite proud of this one.'

[Hubbub subsides as Faure reads, emphasising the words 'cocaine' and 'backstage pass' with a shy flourish.]

Faulkner [standing importantly, stepping in front of Faure, who stumbles backward]: 'Well, if it's drugs you want, check this out.'

[Strikes Churchillian pose and orates sonorously. When he comes to line about 'Ludes', twirls ends of mustache mischievously.]

Derek [looking troubled amid more cries of 'Too much!' and 'Brilliant!']: 'Uh . . . look, guys. "Cocaine"? "Ludes"? Who are we trying to kid? What *is* a bloody "lude"? [Sheepish glances. Faulkner pipes up, "Well, it's something to do with drugs, isn't it?"] And Eric, what's this ridiculous two-part song called "Stoned Houses #1 and #2"? What's that all about?'

Faulkner [by now blushing furiously]: 'Well, we all agreed when we started this album that we had to update, and this seemed a good way . . . I mean, drug songs are always hip – look at Lou Reed.'

Derek: 'But he's Lou Reed! We're the Bay City Rollers!'

Alan [sternly]: 'We've dropped the flipping "Bay City", remember?' [Debate rages into night. Band retire, exhausted, at dawn.]

Elevator's disappointing performance probably accounted for the group's mood when Barbarino, Kim and I got to Bordentown that Friday night. Once we'd checked into the only hotel in town, we went to the cocktail lounge and there they all were, bellied up against the bar, gloomily drinking double shots of spirits. Even the baby-faced Faure looked thoroughly out of sorts, scratching under his hair absently, as if searching for something.

To our great surprise, they brightened when we walked in. Eric even blew a little kiss at Kim. That had certainly never happened before. We settled in on the other side of the circular bar, and they began to talk to us across the expanse. Note: *they* talked to *us*. That had also never happened before. Always, always, they had treated us as, at best, fans; at worst, pains in the ass. Now we were suddenly shooting the breeze like old buddies.

After a few minutes, my personal Roller slipped out of his seat and ambled over to mine, clutching his drink. Leaning over, he quietly said, 'I really want to apologise for what happened at the Bottom Line.' Huh? What had happened at the Bottom Line? Then I remembered – the note I'd written him when they were last in New York, which he'd passed around to the others. But he was gazing at me with such spanielish earnestness that I knew he was mine to do with as I would.

'Oh, don't worry about it,' I told him charitably.

Apology accepted, he leaned closer. 'Are you doing anything later?'

Was I doing anything? Yeah, I'd come to Bordentown for the nightlife. I shook my head.

'We're going for a smoke. D'you fancy it?' I saw one of his colleagues walk toward the door and glance at us questioningly. I didn't want to smoke, but that wasn't going to stop me hanging out while they did. So we all went up to the other Roller's room, where the two of them flopped, prone, on to a twin bed apiece and passed a joint back and forth. Now, this was a thing – the last time I'd seen Bay City Rollers smoking dope, Barbarino had supplied it. Looked like they had their own stock now.

The two of them began giggling at the TV – Johnny Carson was shaking hands with a monkey in a bonnet, or something – and my Roller kept laughing until he choked. He gasped for air, kicking the headboard in a spasm of mirth. Boy, was I glad I was on ginger ale.

'Come on,' he wheezed, grabbing my hand, 'I need some air.'

We trotted outside the hotel and he sat on the curb, still cackling. I wondered what to do with him. Finally I asked if he wanted to go for a drive.

'Yeah, as long as I get to drive,' he giggled.

I shook my head. 'You're too out of it.'

That seemed to sober him up, and he deliberately got to his feet and met my eyes. 'I'm fine.'

I handed him the keys. Why? Because I *wanted* him to drive, so I could pretend he was my boyfriend and we were on a date. I'd never been in a car with him before – never been anywhere, in fact, but hotel bars and bedrooms, and the hermetic interior of the rented Chrysler would make it feel like we were on a real date, or near enough.

So, I let him drive – he was actually more together than he

sounded – and we ambled down Route 206 in search of Bordentown's hot spots. I hoped we'd find a bar or club so I could have the ecstasy of walking in as a couple, but 206 was little more than a country road, and everything was locked up for the night. After driving aimlessly for a while, he made a swerving U-turn, and soon we were back at the hotel.

I obediently trotted behind him to the elevator, seeing out of the corner of my eye Kim sitting at the bar with Jake Duncan, the former roadie who was now their manager. She had gotten hold of a couple of plastic Hawaiian leis from somewhere and was wearing them around her neck, and her shoes were gone.

Her eyes were red-rimmed from, I surmised, the usual bout of weeping, and it was easy enough to guess what had brought it on this time. Eric had been flirting with her earlier and now was nowhere in sight. He'd obviously raised her hopes, then disappeared. And now Kim, blotting her eyes with a cocktail napkin, was obviously telling Jake all about it. Going by his expression, he'd been listening for hours.

The mystery of Eric's whereabouts was solved as soon as my Roller and I got upstairs. As he searched for his key, another door opened across the corridor, and there was Faulkner, clutching the doorjamb like a drunk hanging on to a lamppost. As my Roller opened his door Eric followed us into the room, strode over to the gap between the two beds and planted himself there, feet wide apart, Captain Birdseye on the high seas. My Roller was rooting through the mini-bar, and Faulkner watched him for a while before focusing, with an effort, on me.

'You've been phoning my friend Sheryl,' he said by way of greeting.

'I've been phoning your friend Sheryl?'

'That's what I said.' His tone wasn't cordial.

'Sorry to disappoint you, but I don't know your friend Sheryl,' I replied. He took a step forward and I instinctively took one back. He craned his neck so his face was no more than eight or nine inches away, dewlaps flapping. He's still got such beautiful eyes, I thought automatically, as he screwed up his face and concentrated on enunciating his words. 'My friend Sheryl is a friend of mine,' he said with curious logic, 'and she's been getting phone calls from some girl who's been threatening her, and I know it's you.'

'You know it's me?' I'd read somewhere that repeating an incensed person's words back to him is supposed to calm him down. Not this one.

'Don't act so fucking innocent,' he snapped, his face pinched and nasty. 'I wanna know why you've been calling her and I wanna know when.'

'Oh, I usually call her on Tuesdays,' I riposted, hoping to shut him up. 'Sometimes Thursday, too, when I'm bored.'

He fumbled for the hotel notepad on the night table and, with exaggerated patience, wrote in block capitals, 'TUES- DAY AND THURSDAY'. Then he looked at me expectantly, waiting for the next part of my confession. He pointed the pencil at me, Perry Mason with a Latin-lover mustache.

I looked to my Roller for help in fending off his lunatic friend. He just shrugged and stuck his snout deeper into the can of Pepsi he'd found in the mini-bar.

'Look, I'm kidding, okay? I don't know your Sheryl, I've never called her, I don't wanna call her. Where would I have even gotten her number? Don't be silly, okay?'

But it wasn't okay. He continued to rant till my Roller led him out and forcefully pushed him into his own room. He slouched off, still clutching the scrap of paper bearing the words 'TUESDAY AND THURSDAY', wadded into a moist little ball. His face was forlorn, belligerence replaced by bewilderment. Ironically, his instincts weren't entirely wrong. I didn't know this Sheryl, but if I had I might not have been above giving her a prank call. But in this case, I was innocent.

Unfortunately, the contretemps had dispelled the romantic atmosphere. When my Roller and I were finally alone, his coolness was tangible. He was, I knew, wondering if there was any substance to Faulkner's accusations. You could hardly blame him – the whole incident hadn't exactly reflected well on me.

Switching on the television, he sat on the end of one of the beds, chin in hand, and quickly got absorbed in the 'I Love Lucy' rerun monochromatically flickering on the screen. His body language practically shouted 'Go away'. But I couldn't. This was my gorgeously nubile waif of a Roller, my crush-object, to whose warm skin clung the scent of lime aftershave. He smelled edible. He *was* edible. Go? Not unless he made me.

Which he didn't. It was two in the morning, an hour when men start thinking that if they're going to stay up any later, it might as well be in amiable female company. On the screen, Lucy and Ethel were working on a factory production line, stuffing chocolates down their blouses. It was one of my favorite episodes of all time, but I womanfully turned it off, and in the darkness there was just skin and the scent of lime, insidious and clinging.

34

H E WAS WEIRD IN THE MORNING. The closeness was gone, and the intimacy of six hours before might well have been a dream. It was Saturday and the band had a free day, but from the way he immediately flipped on the TV and devoted his energy to uproariously laughing at the cartoons, it was obvious he wasn't going to be spending it with me.

The phone rang. 'All right?' he greeted the caller, who spoke loudly enough for me to realize it was Faulkner. 'Are you watching Channel Two? Daffy Duck's on,' I could hear him saying. My Roller changed the channel and there indeed was Daffy Duck. I think Elmer Fudd was there, too. Faulkner continued, his voice rising, 'And you'll never fuckin' believe this, man, "The Prisoner" is on next!'

Please, not 'The Prisoner'. I knew about this tedious cult series from my Australian ex, who, in company with every male of British origin the world over, was absolutely addicted to it. The Australian loved quoting a reputedly famous bit of dialogue that went something like, 'Who are you?' 'You are number six.' 'No, I'm not, I'm a free man.' 'No, you're not, putzhead, you're number six', ad infinitum. I loathed it. Meanwhile, my Roller was writhing with glee because when Daffy Duck finished he was going to get to watch 'The Prisoner'. I knew when I was beaten.

'See you later, maybe,' I said, pulling on my tunic-sized Jam T-shirt. I'd bought it on impulse before leaving for Bordentown – I wasn't a Jam fan, but I'd wanted to impress the Rollers with my musical sophistication. Eric had been the only one who'd noticed. 'You're not into that punk shit, are you?' he'd sneered. 'That punk shit' – like it had only just been invented.

You only had to look at the Rollers to know they had a problem with that punk shit. They still wore their hair long, and a couple of them even sported flares, as if it were 1975. Their attitude was truly Luddite, considering that punk was now so entrenched that it had already spawned a second wave of bands like Magazine, Ultravox and Joy Division. And here the Rollers were treating it like a passing fad. No wonder they hadn't troubled the charts in two years.

My Roller managed to stop hooting at Daffy, who was having his feathers blow-dried in a beauty parlor, long enough to see me off with a wave. He seemed to have forgotten me even before I shut the door. Out in the hallway I could still hear him yipping at the TV. I pictured his little 'tuftie' haircut quivering with mirth. If ever there had been a meaningless one-night stand, this was it.

Barbarino, Kim and I reconvened in our room. He was chewing the last dripping morsels of room-service French toast, and she was sitting next to the window, cutting photographs of the Rollers into three-inch circles. This was one of Barbarino's scams – he'd recently invested in apparatus that turned photos into professional-looking laminated badges, which he planned to sell to kids at gigs. Kim was working on a stack of Alan pictures that Barbarino had taken himself.

The day stretched before us. So what was it gonna be? Back down Route 206 to go shopping at the local Kmart discount superstore? Hang out at the pool in the hope that a Roller might turn up and even join us? Call it quits and return to New York to see the first American gig by Magazine (about whom I knew nothing other than that they were led by a former Buzzcock and were getting raves in the Brit music press)?

Kmart, I decided, on the basis that I might find some fetching frock that would turn my one-night stand into two nights. As I drove I berated myself. Why was I still so transfixed by a guy who preferred a cartoon duck to me? The very fact that he found Daffy so fascinating should have condemned him in my eyes. It wasn't like I had any kind of claim on him. We'd spent a total of eighteen hours together in two years. He didn't know my last name, or where I worked. He'd never asked for my number or shown any interest in furthering our acquaintanceship. Face it, I told myself disconsolately, gliding into the Kmart parking lot, he's not my boyfriend, and I'm certainly not his girlfriend. It doesn't mean anything to him.

And even if it had, it didn't mean we were right for each other. He was acquiring dumb music-biz habits, like getting stoned and drunk, that were obliterating the boyishness I'd loved.

So what was I doing at Kmart, browsing through racks of polyester disco dresses? Why was I spending eighteen bucks on black spandex jeans that made me look like a habituée of a Bronx nightclub? And why did I go back to the hotel and immediately change into my new gladrags, then head for the pool to look for Rollers?

They were out there, Woody, Eric and Alan, prostrate on deck chairs, airing their white-boy pigeon chests. As protocol dictated, our bunch was a discreet distance away on the other side of the pool. We'd been joined by our California friend Jan – yep, some people would still fly 3,000 miles to see them – and when I arrived we huddled and discussed tactics. Basically, would it be really uncool to saunter over and just talk to them, the way we did in the bar last night?

Then Barbarino, who was dabbling his toes in the pool, came up with a way of getting their attention. 'Yo, Caroline, check this out,' he brayed, pointing at something in the water.

I came over to inspect, and with an agility I'd have never suspected of him, he leapt to his feet and pushed me in.

Ma had always nagged me to learn to swim. Now I wished I'd listened. Flailing wildly, I hit the bottom with a thunk, tried to look up and realised that the stupid shit had pushed me into the deep end.

I'm drowning, I thought, or would have thought if I hadn't been too busy trying to shriek for help. After about thirty seconds of hysterical thrashing, I somehow bobbed to the surface and was fished out by California Jan, probably as thanks for once sending her a really cute picture of Leslie. As I lay there, gasping like a salmon, I glanced over at the Rollers. They were convulsed with laughter. So were Barbarino and Kim. Really nice of you, dudes.

With very bad grace, I managed to join in the merriment. It wouldn't do to look like someone who couldn't take a joke. And, within minutes, the whole little scenario had its desired effect – a Roller hauled himself out of his deck chair and came to visit our table. Fabulous!

Not so fabulous was the fact that it was Alan, the one nobody fancied. There were reasons: at thirty-one, he was practically an old man, he enjoyed old-man hobbies like fishing, and he'd come snivelling back to the band when his solo career hadn't taken off. Still, a dull Roller was better than no Roller, and we welcomed him, Barbarino even vacating his chair so he could rest his old-man tush.

I'll give old Al this much, he was actually interested in us. He asked our names, where we lived and worked, what we thought of the new Roller album. 'Great!' we lied. Maybe he was nicer than his chums, maybe he was just less accustomed to seeing us around, but he sat there for an hour and shot the breeze, unfeignedly enjoying our company. He even found Barbarino's home-made badges amusing. Typically, Barbarino couldn't resist asking him to autograph a couple to increase their value. When he eventually lumbered off to rejoin the others, whose pallid skin was crisping nicely across the pool, we marveled at his un-Rollerish cordialness.

His behavior was so out of character that I did something out of character, too. Although it was only Saturday afternoon and the band were going to be hanging around till Monday, I decided to go home.

Seriously. I, Caroline Sullivan, voluntarily relinquished the opportunity to spend two whole days around the Rollers. I don't know what got into me – maybe it was no more than the sight of scrawny Scottish backsides failing to fill out clinging Speedo swimming trunks. But suddenly I'd had a surfeit of Roller. It was, in fact, starting to feel like a lifetime surfeit of Roller. I wrang another cup of water out of my spandex pants, told Barbarino and Kim I'd see their sorry asses later and drove back to New York.

35

1980

First UK #1 of the year: 'Another Brick in the Wall' Pink
Floyd
Biggest Roller hits of the year (UK/US): None

I WISH I COULD SAY that was the end of my love affair
with the Bay City Rollers. But it wasn't, though the long
gap until my next encounter with them weakened their
grip substantially.

In the meantime, the 1980s arrived, and with them the
desire for change. To Ma's undisguised relief, I finally moved
out of her apartment, and into a big loft apartment on 26th
Street with three other girls.

It seemed a good time to stop the Valium, too, and rather to
my surprise, I did. One day I got to work and simply decided
to cope without one at least until lunchtime. Lunch came, and
with it a cautious pride that I'd resisted the urge to slink out to
the water cooler with my stash. By the time I left at five, I'd had
my first tranquilizer-free work day in eighteen months. It was
like quitting cigarettes, and, as with cigarettes, the second day
was easier, and by the third I was beginning to envisage an
existence free of mother's little helper. It seemed amazingly
simple. But then, I was getting off lightly, mostly because I'd
never been a seven-day-a-week trankhead.

If I had, stopping wouldn't have been a matter of simply

deciding to stop, then doing it. A book out at the time called *I'm Dancing as Fast as I Can* contained a scary description of a hallucinatory slow withdrawal that stayed with me for a long time. In it, a young female Valium user – just like me! – decides to quit, flushes her pills down the toilet and ends up hospitalised.

'Do you think that could happen to me?' I asked Dr Kalman, whom I still saw once a month to renew my prescription. He shrugged – typical! – and made a few notes in my file – probably some old-bastard comment like 'Patient neurotically seeking reassurance'. Then, grudgingly, he told me that what with my relatively low dosage and the fact I'd always had a couple of un-sedated days each week, I'd probably be all right. He sounded disappointed.

One thing about Valium and other old-school tranquilizers is that, unlike new drugs like Prozac, they have no 'half-life' quality that prolongs their effect after the drug is last taken. In other words, while Prozac can keep working for up to a week after the last pill, Valium is only active for the couple of hours it's in the bloodstream. So there's no grace period to gently ease you out of your fuzziness back into the real world. The minute it wears off, everything is as bright and jagged as it was before.

The first post-Valium thing I noticed was how grim Mama's was. It wasn't just the primitive office equipment and cardboard-effect walls, nor Mama herself, a gray-mustached apparition who hovered over my desk to make sure I wasn't enjoying myself. It was also the drabness of the area – our nearest neighbor was Penn Station, home of every pimp and bum in Midtown – and the second-rateness of our clientele.

The latter was especially disheartening. The third day off the Valium, I was excited to hear the office manager instruct the stock guys to bring down two Fender Stratocaster guitars, a Precision bass and a drumkit – stuff obviously meant for a rock band. I was further inflamed when Mama remarked, 'Oh, that's for that English group, isn't it?' I flapped through the Village Voice to see who was playing that week. The Pretenders were doing the Palladium, Squeeze were at the Bottom Line . . . or could the equipment possibly be for Joy Division, the much-fancied young Manchester doommongers who were making their American debut the following week?

I was in a flurry of anticipation all morning, till a small van pulled up in the rutted street. Three weaselly-looking characters and a fat one trundled out, accompanied by a nondescript type who was obviously the manager. One of the weaselly ones, who was wearing black spandex pants much like the ones I'd bought in Bordentown, hawked several times, eventually bringing up a pod of mucus that he deposited on one of the glass door panels. This, it transpired, was our English band – The Lurkers, second-wave punk wannabes who'd never progressed beyond small club gigs back home. I didn't know how they could afford to come to America, but there they were, about to avail themselves of our finest Stratocasters. The lack of Valium made the disappointment that much sharper.

Days later, I quit my job at Mama's. I'm not saying it wasn't a tough decision – I'd lose all the music-biz contacts I'd made in my year there, plus the possibility of maybe marrying a rock star. Maybe even a Lurker. But the balance was tipped by the dullness of the work and the fact that Mama was, to use one of her own favorite catchphrases, a bitch on rollerskates.

Our final confrontation came the day she asked if I was wearing drawers.

'Of course I'm wearing drawers,' I said huffily.

'I can see through your skirt, and you're not wearing any,' she insisted. Like it was her business, anyway. But I was so indignant I pulled my bloomers up over my waistband to prove they were there. Pissed off at being out-foxed, later that afternoon she ordered pizza for the office and pointedly didn't offer me a slice. The woman was an arthritic ten-year-old. It seemed a good time to leave.

Quitting had its down side, of course. It meant goodbye to the occasional sightings of Barry Manilow making his way gingerly around the bums asleep on the sidewalk outside the office. It also meant goodbye to the odd free record and gig ticket, and admiring glances from hairy-backed roadies as they wrestled equipment past my desk.

It was a small price to pay for not seeing Mama every day. To celebrate, I bought a ticket for the upcoming Joy Division gig at Hurrah's, a New Wave disco on Central Park West. Their arrival was hotly anticipated by New York's downtown scenesters, who were impressed less by their angstful music, so redolent of singer Ian Curtis's internal psychodramas (as Dr Kalman would have put it), than by the fact the Brit pop press were going ga-ga over them. The *NME*'s approval was enough for us New Yorkers. The show sold out almost as soon as it went on sale.

Of course, it never happened. The day before they were due to fly to New York, Curtis committed suicide. Guess all that angst had been 4 Real. The English press took it badly, one writer going so far as to claim, 'This man died for you.' Joy Division went on to release one more single, the admittedly classic 'Love Will Tear Us Apart', then split up (before – ker-ching! – resurfacing as the much better New Order a couple of years down the line).

Curtis's death was a shame for more than the obvious reasons. In 1980, American music was nowhere, caught between the tail end of disco and the beginnings of rap. A new direction had yet to assert itself, and in the meantime there was none of the innovation of the Brit scene, which had begat not just Joy Division but electro-rock weirdsters like Gary Numan and the Human League. Which was why I'd been so keen to see Joy Division, who were the vanguard of everything new and interesting.

If poor Ian Curtis had made it to America, he'd have been unimpressed by what passed for the local alternative scene. It was dismal, and history has borne out this judgement by consigning most of the bands to obscurity.

I recognize almost none of the names on the long list of gigs I went to in 1980. Who, for God's sake, were Kongress, The Reactors, Brenda & The Realtones, Ballistic Kisses, B-Girls, Willie Nile, Joey Balin (saw him twice, apparently), Mofungo? Why can I remember nothing about The Nothing? Where is my recollection of trekking to the Ritz on October 21 to see Blue Angel, whose singer, Cyndi Lauper, went on to better things? It's all a blank.

That said, nondescript as American indie-rock was, it still had the edge over . . . ooh, just to pick a British act at random . . . Leslie McKeown. For his long-awaited opus, *All Washed Up*, finally appeared in the spring of '80, and failed to establish him as a solo star. It wasn't even released in America.

His former BCR buds might have indulged in a quiet chuckle as *All Washed Up* died the death. But it's probable they were too conscious of their own precarious position to engage in *schadenfreude*. As spring turned into summer, they were undoubtedly more worried about their next album, which was going to be recorded in, of all places, New Jersey.

And not just New Jersey, but my very own former patch of it, West Orange, not four miles from Millburn. Now, why the porking pork couldn't they have done that while I was still there? But more to the point, what were they *doing* there, at House of Music studios in West Orange, when presumably they could have recorded anywhere in the world they fancied? Even I, Jersey partisan that I was, had to admit that West Orange's attractions were limited to a diner called Pals Cabin and the Turtleback children's zoo. Maybe the Rollers were into miniature railroads – the Turtleback had a great one.

'It's because they've just signed a new deal with Epic Records and Epic probably ain't gonna pay for no expensive studio,' Barbarino guessed. So that was it – no longer a priority act, the hapless things were being packed off to Jersey to come up with something that would turn their career around. Well, West Orange would focus their attention, all right. It was the embodiment of quiet, well-heeled suburbia, bordered on the south by the wilderness of South Mountain Reservation. Maybe the band would find inspiration for songs while strolling in the woods. Perhaps they'd round off their days with a hot fudge sundae at Gruning's up there on the hill, which had been an unimaginably divine treat for me when I was eleven.

To simplify things, Epic rented them accommodation near the studio. It was a one-story brick ranch house on a small, affluent crescent, the kind of place where a fading Scottish pop group would stick out like sore thumbs. For wheels they had an unglamorous station wagon, which also stood out from the sparkling new Caddies and Lincolns in the street.

I knew all this because, in a moment of madness, I'd called Barbarino and proposed going out there. That August evening I'd come home exhausted from my new post-Mama's job as a cocktail waitress at a bar uptown (great tips; shame about the Olivia Newton-John records on the jukebox). I was in need of a diversion from the realisation that if I'd been an indifferent secretary, I was an even worse waitress. I didn't mind the work, it was the dress code of high heels and miniskirt. I had no ideological objection, I just couldn't walk in heels, and kept taking them off, only to have to put them back on whenever the boss noticed. When I got home that night I was in low spirits, gloomily envisaging a future of higher and higher heels. I needed a laugh.

The Rollers, I thought. And now Barbarino and I were sitting in a limousine in front of the house. It was 3.00 in the morning. We'd been there for half an hour, wondering what the hell we thought we were doing.

The limo, which was costing us $80 an hour, wasn't an affectation but a necessity. By the time I'd called Barbarino it was nearly midnight, and public transport had long since packed up. The only way to get there was to hire a limousine, complete with disgusted-looking driver, for eighty smackeroos an hour, four hours minimum. Barbarino had acquired the address through the simple ploy of ringing House of Music studios, claiming he had to deliver a parcel. Voilà – we were now parked next to the Rollers' station wagon, in front of their house, where the lights were still on despite the hour.

We were arguing about whether to knock on the door. I voted in favor because Barbarino had been insisting he'd chatted with various Rollers on the phone at the studio, and they'd been 'glad' to hear from him. In fact, these alleged chats had been my incentive to go to West Orange.

'Well, if they were glad to hear from you, they won't mind us dropping by, then, will they?' I pointed out. 'And they're obviously still up.' Indeed, we could hear heavy metal music (their new direction?) emanating from one of the front rooms. 'I dunno,' mumbled Barbarino. 'Maybe it's too late.'

'C'mon,' I coaxed. 'They're probably having a party in there. With booze and chicks and stuff,' I added, appealing to his basest instincts. He wavered for a millisecond, then chickened out. 'I don't want to.'

'But why?' I leaned in close. 'Barbarino, you did talk to them, didn't you?'

He shrank back, or would have if he hadn't already been huddled into the furthest recesses of the back seat.

'This isn't one of your stories, is it? Did you talk to them or not?' The driver was starting to look interested, shifting a little in his seat to get a better earful. I slammed the glass partition shut.

'You haven't talked to them at all, have you? We're sitting out here at three in the morning because you said you talked to them and they were glad to hear from you, you stupid shit.'

He did what he always did when caught in a lie and began to cry. My dander was up and I was completely unimpressed.

'Now listen, you little creep, I am not wasting a trip out

here. Go knock on that door.' I must have sounded menacing – I certainly felt it – because he gulped, sat up and got out of the car.

With a reproachful glance, he sidled across the lawn and, after long hesitation during which I hissed from the safety of my seat, 'Ring the doorbell!', he diffidently tapped on the door. No answer. He tapped louder. No answer.

I joined him on the doorstep. The music stopped and we could make out the murmur of conversation, but there was no sign they'd heard the knocks. 'Call through the mailbox,' I suggested. 'Tell 'em it's you.'

He wasn't at all happy about that, but dutifully bent down and muttered, 'Hey, you guys, it's me, Barbarino.' He looked at me pleadingly. I prodded him in the arm. He pushed the mailbox flap completely open and called again. 'Guys! It's Barbarino! We've come all the way from the city!'

That stopped them in their tracks. Conversation inside ceased, and the house became absolutely silent, as they pretended not to be home. 'Eric? Woody?' Barbarino pleaded. We heard a hysterical giggle, swiftly muffled. The Barbster gave the mailbox one final rattle and stood up. There was no room at the inn.

The chauffeur had been watching this performance with an unfathomable expression. He was a seen-it-all Brooklyn type, but he hadn't seen anything like this before. He probably couldn't wait to tell the guys at the depot about skinny runt-face Barbarino yelping through the door as bigmouth-broad Caroline literally twisted his arm. The humiliation was compounded by the fact that our driver used to drive the Rollers in the days when they used limos. He'd mentioned it on our way to West Orange, after Barbarino had confidently told him we were going to a party at the Rollers'. Now there was the embarrassment of having to go all the way back to the city with him. Not to mention the pain, when we got there, of signing a credit card receipt for $320, plus thirty-buck tip.

'It wouldn'a hurt them to open the door, you know,' Barbarino mused as we walked down 26th Street to my apartment, where I'd sullenly agreed he could spend what remained of the night. 'It's not like they've got a million fans these days.'

'It couldn't be anything to do with us standing on their lawn and shouting at them at three in the morning, could it?' I suggested. We thought it over in the five o'clock stillness and agreed it couldn't have had anything to do with that.

36

D IARY, September 30, 1980: 'The Rollers entered my life five years ago! They mean less than zero to me now, but at the height of it I was obsessed to a degree I can't imagine now.'

Oh, yeah? If they meant 'less than zero', why did I write on the next line, 'Barbarino has an up-to-date phone number, though I haven't called it yet.'

No, I hadn't called it yet, but of course I soon did. When I said 'less than zero', what I meant was 'less than zero as long as they're not in the immediate vicinity'. When they were, I simply couldn't help myself. Although I no longer listened to their records or searched magazines for articles, I was still drawn to them as vestiges of a less complicated time. And this time they really were in the immediate vicinity. They'd left the West Orange house and moved to Maplewood, the next town from Millburn. The suckers were living a scant mile from my teenage home.

There was no way around it. Where the Rollers were concerned, there was never any way around it. I just had to investigate.

Diary, October 4: 'Sue J and I went to see [small-time New Wavers] the Mo-Dettes at the Ritz. Not bad. At 2 a.m. after the set, Sue phoned up the Rollers for a laugh. She got Fatboy [Eric], who immediately asked us to come out there. We talked to him for about 40 minutes, and I even told him it was me (and he didn't hang up!). He kept insisting we get a cab out there and he'd pay for it. So we did, and he did – the fare was $60! He's gotten ever so fat, but he's much nicer than he used to be, and we sat around talking till all hours. He was really sweet and chatty. So unexpected. Then he went to sleep in his little room off the kitchen and Sue and I sat around the living room by ourselves for hours.'

'So unexpected' is right. After the embarrassment of being refused entry to their other house, I certainly hadn't expected a Roller to pay $60 so I could drop by. And remember, this was Eric, who'd spent our last meeting accusing me of harassing one of his girlfriends.

Weirder still, he wasn't even lecherous. He appeared happy just to sit and talk to us, and when he got tired he toddled off to bed, with no pervy hints about us coming with him (though I suspect Sue wouldn't have been unwilling). Maybe the old dog was lonely. Despite having a new record deal, the Bay City Rollers – sorry, The Rollers – were a long way down the pecking order on their new label. Being packed off to the Jersey suburbs must have been as plain an indication of that as anything. Maybe, for the first time, they were grateful to have fans.

As Faulkner had slouched off to bed, plump and cherubic, he'd suggested, 'Why don't you girls come to the studio with us tomorrow?' Then he'd shut the door and audibly collapsed into bed, which was a mattress on the floor. Sue and I looked at each other dubiously. Did he really mean it? This meant there was no way we were leaving before he woke up, whenever that was. The studio? *With* them? Of course we'd go to the studio. If he was serious, that is.

While we passed the long hours waiting for them to wake up, we had a poke around downstairs. We were too nervous to go upstairs, where the rest of them were asleep, but downstairs was interesting enough. There were guitars lying around, some besweated T-shirts, a copy of *Penthouse* hidden under the *TV Guide* on the sofa. In the kitchen was a stack of Polaroids of the band at rehearsal, including an oddly moving one of Woody, cigarette in mouth, brandishing his bass guitar like the proper rock star he presumably wished he was.

Most intriguing was the refrigerator. It was full, which was unusual for a household of five bachelors, but the contents were pure fast food. There was a near-complete range of Sara Lee cakes, pack upon pack of frozen hamburgers, family-sized bottles of Coke, and someone had a taste for kiddie luncheon meat, the kind with a teddy-bear face etched into it. If this was how they ate, no wonder Eric had chubbed out.

Knowing they'd never miss it, I put a Sara Lee pecan danish in the oven so we'd have some sustenance. Then, as morning broke and Maplewood came to life, we dozed on the couch as we waited for them to appear. The first one down the stairs, at about noon, snuffling and sighing, was my personal Roller. I'd braced myself, and thus wasn't completely crushed when he froze, mumbled something that sounded like 'Oh, hi', and vanished back upstairs, not to be seen again till they left for the studio.

And then I suddenly thought, So much for that. I looked around, taking in as if for the first time the matronly floral sofas and grubby crockery stacked in the sink. The Polaroids of them playing at being a real band were on the kitchen table, and I flicked through them again, then put them down with an emotion close to pity. I felt like a voyeur at this scene of their abasement. This was what my Roller had been reduced to. In that instant, I was free of the burden of three years of dejectedly loving him. His loss.

Eric hadn't been kidding about going to the studio. The entire band, who reacted to our presence with varying degrees of indifference, mustered in the living room at 1.00, and trooped out to the station wagon. As Eric gestured for Sue and me to get in, I could just make out my Roller whispering, 'Are *they* coming?'

'You bet,' I smiled, deliciously impervious to what he thought.

We not only went, but sat in the control room for two hours as the band struggled through a song. It was punctuated by many cigarette breaks and long periods of conferral about whether Derek's snare drum was too loud. It was touching that they concerned themselves with such things. They were having a lot of trouble with this song, an anonymous mid-tempo rocker. As far as I could make out, the first line was, 'She gets it off against the wall with her hand and she cries.' Duncan Faure proudly told us that he'd written it. A surefire Number One, I didn't think.

Just as we were considering whether to leave John, Paul, George and Derek to their labors, Eric slid over to me. He was pale save for vivid dots of crimson in the middle of his cheeks, and he'd begun to perspire. He looked sick. 'Did you put anything in my drink last night?' he asked urgently. I'd poured him a vodka and tonic in the living room, but that had been nearly twelve hours ago, and of course I hadn't 'put anything' in it.

'I feel weird,' he whispered, pulling his knees up to his chest. 'Like when you're starting on acid.'

Faure overheard him and joked, 'Then just go with it, man.' Faulkner wasn't comforted by this. Biting his lip, he repeated that he felt edgy. I realised he was displaying all the symptoms of an anxiety attack, and, from his reaction, it was his first.

As he continued to hug his knees, panic increasing, I found the bottle of Valium I still carried around in my bag. My own anxiety thing was in remission, but I kept the bottle with me anyway, for occasions like this.

'Look, you're not on drugs, you're having an anxiety attack,' I told him as the others began to gather round. 'Take this and it'll calm you down.' He refused – understandably, as he was hardly likely to accept an anonymous pill from someone he suspected of spiking his drink. Luckily, one of the studio engineers also had a tranquilizer stash, and forced one down Faulkner's gullet. Ten minutes later, he began to relax, panic ebbing. The other Rollers, who'd been watching worriedly, clapped him on the shoulder, guy-to-guy style. It seemed like an opportune moment to leave. Eric managed a weak smile as we went.

He was in better spirits when Sue J and I ran into him and the rest of the band a couple of weeks later at a venue in Manhattan. Electro-pop pioneers Ultravox were playing The Ritz, and the Rollers had come all the way into the city to see them. Who'd've thought they liked electronic music? Maybe they were thinking of trying it themselves.

We didn't spot them till the end of Ultravox's show. 'That's not the Rollers, is it?' Sue laughed disbelievingly. It was. They were sprawled around a large table in the balcony, the five of them and some record company types. Before I could stop her, she'd marched up to them. Trailing a good six inches behind, I heard her say, 'So you guys are into Ultravox?'

'Yeah,' Woody unconvincingly claimed. 'Just wanted to see how Midge is doing,' Eric added.

It was understandable they'd be interested in Ultravox singer Midge Ure, as he had once been in the rival Scottish boy-band Slik. I was curious myself, as I'd been a Slik fan since meeting their publicist on my 1976 trip to London. When Slik split, Ure had progressed to ex-Sex Pistol Glen Matlock's band, The Rich Kids, before signing up with Ultravox. By a remarkable stroke of luck, he'd managed to divest himself of the teeny-band stigma, and was now a respected musicianly type. The Rollers must have burned with envy as they watched him onstage, playing to the adult audience they believed they deserved.

'Okay,' one of the record company guys broke in, 'we're going backstage.' The group rose and trooped toward the stage door. How funny, they were going to meet Ultravox. Keen to witness the summit meeting of the Rollers and their erstwhile rival, Sue and I insinuated ourselves into the 'Bay City Rollers party' – that was how they were introduced at the stage door, 'The Bay City Rollers party is here'.

Ure's startled face revealed he hadn't been expecting them, but he smiled gamely enough. They all exchanged greetings and someone took a picture of Midge and Eric shaking hands. Then Ure turned away to talk to some friends, and the Rollers, sensing the moment was over, drifted out of the room.

All except Eric – having made contact, he wasn't ready to say good-night. He tapped the smaller man on the shoulder, and when he had Ure's attention, said, 'Fancy a drink when you're done here?'

Embarrassed, Ure explained Ultravox were going on to a party arranged by their record label. 'Great,' Eric replied eagerly. 'Um,' mumbled Ure, inspecting his shoes, 'I think it's a bit of a private do, actually.'

'They're not going to mind you bringing a couple of mates, are they?' Faulkner persisted. 'Just for a swift half?'

Ure covertly glanced around for help. 'I don't really think we can. They said the guest list is full. You know what New York is like, full of liggers.'

'Let me talk to them,' Eric insisted stoutly, but the light was dawning. A gentle blush began to creep from his hairline to the collar of his seen-better-days T-shirt. He shifted from foot to foot. He was a lumbering bear of a figure next to the diminutive, well-groomed Ure, who wore an expression combining pity and mortification.

Faulkner dredged up what was meant to be a hearty grin. 'I know the feeling. All the parties on our last tour were heaving. Arista were always tearing us off a strip for going over budget.' He laughed a small, pitiable laugh. His abjection was bad to watch.

Somehow he offered a dignified handshake, and Ure was kind enough to pretend the exchange had never occurred. He turned back to his friends as Eric gathered the remnants of his pride and made his way outside, where his bandmates were waiting to return to Maplewood.

'Midge invited us for a drink, but I told him we had to go to fucking New Jersey,' he informed them. 'Fucking drag,' commiserated Duncan.

37

1981

First UK #1 of the year: 'There's No One Quite Like
Grandma'/St Winifred's School Choir
Biggest Roller hits of the year (UK/US): None

THE ROLLERS STAYED in Maplewood for the rest of
the autumn and into the spring of 1981. Word of their
presence got around among the local high school kids,
and the place became a sort of 24-hour party. There was
always a handful of sixteen- and seventeen-year-olds around,
using the Rollers' phone, eating their food and drinking their
beer. They weren't fans, just kids who thought it was neat that
a rock group was living in the neighborhood, even if it was just
the Rollers.

Eric had invited me to drop by whenever I felt like it, and I
took him up on it four or five times. The house became a
tourist attraction and I was the tour guide, escorting small
groups of Tacky Tartan Tarts there on weekends. By the time
the band moved out, everyone who'd ever been a fan had spent
an afternoon in the Maplewood kitchen, dining on Twinkies
and listening to tapes of the new album, which was in its final
stages.

The local kids were invariably there, too, and glared con-
frontationally at us city sophisticates. One of them was a
younger version of Barbarino, full of stories about how close

he was to 'the guys'. He and the real Barbarino hated each other on sight, baring their teeth and growling from a wary distance.

The album, titled *Richochet*, was completed by June of '81 and the group booked a few low-key New York club dates to 'get a feel' for playing live after two years off the road. That, anyway, was their excuse for playing venues like Malibu on Long Island and Beggar's Opera in Middle Village, Queens – places I'd never heard of, in the most unglamorous areas imaginable. A few years before, when they were filling big, prestigious halls, they couldn't have envisaged being reduced to Thursday night in Queens.

All the Tacky Tartan Tarts convened at Beggar's Opera, a medium-sized disco in the middle of a parade of shops. The Rollers were by far the biggest name that had ever played there, but the joint was still half empty. The Middle Village youth who did venture into the club were of the New Wave persuasion, all leopard-skin tops and skinny ties. To them, it was plainly a joke. They twitched their heads to the old hits and smirked through the new stuff, much to the despair of Duncan Faure, who repeatedly exhorted them, 'Put your hands together – wooh!'

The Tarts felt just as lukewarm about the new songs. Much as we wanted to like them, we couldn't, and after watching in disbelief for a minute (why was Eric doing a Led Zeppish guitar solo? Why was Duncan tossing the mike from hand to hand like a cut-rate Rod Stewart?) our attention wandered. It was the first time we'd all been together in many months, and there was a lot of catching-up to do.

For one thing, two Tarts were leaving the fold. Sue P had just become the first married Tart, and her husband had celebrated by joining the Navy directly after the honeymoon. The newlyweds were being posted to Virginia, which Sue was none too happy about.

And my own faithful David was being transferred to his

company's head office in Louisville, which I was none too happy about. His imminent departure was forcing me to recognise that his quiet loyalty had been my respite and my refuge, and that I couldn't imagine life without his friendship. I wanted to write him a reference for Louisville's female population, something along the lines of 'Snap him up – he's a hell of a gent'.

'What are you going to miss about New York?' I asked him, flushed with affection.

'Not them,' he said, with a derisory glance at the Rollers, who were still begging us to put our hands together.

'Yeah, but' – shameless ploy for reassurance – 'will you miss me?'

'I might,' he replied lightly, 'but I probably won't.'

And he didn't. After he moved we exchanged a few letters, till he met the Kentucky girl he eventually married; then he told me, in a phone call he'd probably wanted to make for a long time, not to contact him again. I didn't try to defend myself. He was absolutely right – I'd abused his generosity, tested his kindness to breaking point, been, as Mama would have put it, a bitch on rollerskates.

Anyway, the whole gang was there at Beggar's Opera: both Sues, Emma, Cathy, Lauren, Barbarino, Kim, David, even Emma's sister, who'd been a Derek fan for about fifteen minutes in 1975. We were six years older, adults now, with jobs and headaches and rent to pay. The Rollers had been sidelined to a less-visited place in our lives – even as, ironically, we were beginning to occupy a more significant place in theirs. In the eternal way of things between all teen-bands and their fans, our need for them had at last receded. In our case, it had just taken a little longer.

We sat at our table, tanked up on Tab, which we still drank in preference to adult drinks, and watched the former boys of our dreams, themselves no longer boys but harassed men in their late twenties. As they launched into their signature tune,

'Bye Bye Baby', they looked like they had a lot on their minds. 'They've got a great future behind them,' someone cracked wise. I felt terribly sorry for them.

Sue P was telling a fascinated Emma about the studio apartment she and her husband had taken in Newport News, Virginia. I caught the words 'green paisley wallpaper'. Barbarino was shouting over the music, advising David about Louisville restaurants. Sue J was saying to no one in particular, 'Jeez, I can't believe I'm here. I have to get up at six.'

The writing was on the wall, and all of us could read it. The Rollers might well trundle down rock's lost highway for years to come, but right now they had pulled on to the hard shoulder, and the Tacky Tartan Tarts were getting out.

38

1994

First UK #1 of the year: 'Mr Blobby'/Mr Blobby
Biggest Roller hits of the year UK/US: None

DIARY, November first, 1994: 'I interviewed a couple of people for this forthcoming Radio 1 magazine show, "Soundbite". The theme of my piece is "Can Teen Idols Grow Up?" and today's subjects were a guy from East 17 and – yes! – Les McKeown. I rang him a couple of days ago and asked if he'd do it, and today he turned up at the production company studio in black boots, black biker jacket (passé!) and dyed (I'm sure of it) black hair. It was the first time I'd been face-to-face with him in 17 years. He didn't look bad – he's pushing 39 and is no spring chicken, but he's aged well. He depressed me a bit, though, cos he was saying he really wants to get his career going, but promoters only want him to sing Roller songs, whereas he wants to do his own music. "I just want to show them what I can do," he said. Poor guy.'

Needless to say, the eighties and early nineties had been unkind to both McKeown and the other Bay City Rollers. The album they made in New Jersey practically died at birth – I never even saw it in a shop – and the Rollers never again recorded for a major label. They didn't split up, however. They saw out the eighties touring universities and small clubs in the UK and US, Eric taking over as vocalist when Duncan Faure left. Eric made an abortive attempt to start another band, The Eric Faulkner Initiative, which failed when promoters kept billing him as 'formerly of the Bay City Rollers'.

Meanwhile, Leslie made various attempts to reclaim the spotlight, even releasing a techno version of 'Bye Bye Baby' under the name LRM. After a spell as a van driver in Germany, he came to a sort of *rapprochement* with his musical past and began singing Roller songs with a backing band. His attempt to use the Roller name was initially blocked by his former colleagues, who finally agreed that they would keep the name Bay City Rollers, while McKeown was allowed to tour as the unwieldy Les McKeown's Legendary Bay City Rollers.

Their former manager, Tam, served time on a gross indecency charge in the early eighties and Woody and Duncan allegedly got into trouble in South Africa over debts.

It was a pretty impressive catalogue of misfortunes by any band's standards. Which was probably why McKeown so readily agreed to be interviewed by me on Radio 1.

Yep, I'd got into the music business at last. I'd moved to London in 1982, and in 1985 started writing for *Melody Maker*, which led, meanderingly, to the job of rock critic at the *Guardian*. I was suddenly and amazingly in a position of some power, and got hate mail and a few fan letters. I even found a boyfriend. English. With an accent and everything. Basically, I wasn't doing badly for a girl from Millburn.

I took some care with my dress the morning of the Radio 1 interview, prodded by a faint echo of what Leslie had once meant to me. I wore a black pantsuit that did a surprisingly thorough job of hiding my thirtysomething ass, and my hair, grown out of its severe Rollers-era style, was flowing tressily. I looked pretty good, if I said so myself. Remembering the Betty Boop T-shirt and corduroy flares I'd worn the last time we'd met, I reflected that my dress sense had improved since I was a teenager.

Just before leaving the house, I played a bit of the Rollers' first album, *Rollin'*. My original copy was back in New York, but I had a Japanese-import CD, given to me by a friend as a joke. I'd never unwrapped it, but it didn't seem like there'd ever be a better time. I found it filed, for some reason, next to Oasis's recent debut, *Definitely Maybe*, and briefly pictured the expression on the Gallagher brothers' faces if they'd known who they were sharing shelf-space with.

As they were shakin' it to the shang-a-lang sound, I hummed along, the music, resistant to the improved audio quality of compact disc, rattling thinly through the speakers.

So I was pretty confident as I waited for him an hour later. I'd never before been confident, or anything approaching it, where the Rollers were concerned. Always, my encounters with them had been informed by the tension of wanting to impress and to mean something to them. I'd been constantly on my guard during the Roller years, so self-conscious about what I'd believed to be my flawed looks and unlovable personality I was never able to relax. I never felt I measured up to what they expected of a girl – even if I never knew quite what they did expect. I just figured I couldn't possibly be it, and even the three encounters with my Roller didn't ease the sense of inferiority.

But now, many years hence, I remembered it all with indulgent affection. I'd got a life, and the Rollers were no longer part of it. I was simply curious to see what Leslie would be like. I don't know what I expected to feel when he arrived. Love? Lust? The embers of painful teenage adoration stirred again into flames?

None of those things, as it turned out. When he walked in, touchingly punctual, his stride a shadow of his cocky boychild strut, I was just . . . interested. Interested and intrigued to know how the tables had been turned so completely, how I'd come to hold the balance of power in this little encounter. For it was plain that I did. Even as we shook hands, he looked to me for instruction about where to sit, when to speak, what to say.

'Go on in there,' I directed him, marveling at how unaffected I was by his presence. When he was seated in front of the microphone, he was keen to help. He didn't complain when we had to re-do a few takes, answering the same questions as enthusiastically the third time as the first. His desire to please made me want to cry.

'Should we get a level?' he asked, referring to the sound-balance but really meaning, 'I used to do this all the time, you know.' After the interview, which centered on whether it was possible to cross over from teen-idoldom to adult stardom (his answer was that it was incredibly difficult, and that he felt sorry for East 17, the young boy-band who also featured in my piece), he hung around for a cup of coffee. He sighed that it was proving harder than he'd expected to rejuvenate his career. He was at that point doing some behind-the-scenes work on German television, which he didn't especially enjoy, 'but it helps to fund my songwriting habit'. He'd joined the Rollers at eighteen, left at twenty-two and was about to turn thirty-nine (November 12 – I still remembered). His fame had lasted a scant four years, his subsequent obscurity four times longer.

He looked exactly like himself, but older. I'd expected baldness or infirmity, but he'd weathered pretty well. I guess I didn't look much like myself, as he didn't seem to re-member me. I was deeply grateful. He told me he was married to a Japanese former fan – he'd married a fan! I felt a vestigial prickling of jealousy – and had a ten-year-old son called Jube.

'Joo-bee?' I said rudely. 'I'll bet that was your wife's idea.'

He smiled, uncertain how rude to be back. At length he rose and said he had to get home. 'Thanks very much,' he told me. He smiled the thin-lipped smile that used to make my insides quiver. We shook hands and I saw him out. Poor guy, I thought, I must call Emma and tell her about this. But I never got round to it, and when I finally remembered, a couple of days later, the moment was gone.

39

1999

First UK #1 of the year: 'Heartbeat/Tragedy'/Steps
Biggest Roller hits of the year (UK/US): None

THE INTERNET produces 839 search results for 'Bay City Rollers'. Among them are Kjunkutie's Bay City Rollers Ring Page and Gerd Büskin's Home Page, the latter featuring a picture of a bespectacled fellow I take to be Gerd next to the old Roller logo. He claims his site has had over 60,000 visits, and the guestbook is full of warm reminiscences from women my age. Many of them say that their own children are going through the teen-idol stage, the consensus being that the Backstreet Boys are the top faves.

So people still care. The Rollers and their era still evoke enough emotion that some American devotees even stage a Rollerfest every August – this year's was in Philadelphia. Apparently, it always sells out well in advance. It's got nothing to do with me (honestly), but if I was ever in the neighborhood, I'd go. The chance to be seventeen again would be too lovely to resist.

The Tacky Tartan Tarts are in their late thirties now, and some of us are no longer in touch. No one knows what happened to Sue P after she moved to Virginia, and Lauren is rumored to be living in Canada – she developed a thing for ice hockey players after she got over the Rollers – but nobody is certain.

Cathy works in a Los Angeles recording studio, Emma is still in New York, where she's a record company executive, and Sue J, the stablest Tart, still lives in the same house in New Jersey. Kim is a Queens housewife, and Barbarino stunned us all by landing a job managing a reasonably successful singer. Funnily enough, none of us has kids. At least we'll never go through what we put our parents through.

The Rollers have had their ups and downs in the late nineties. Until recently the seventies revival that brought renewed popularity to groups like Abba and Hot Chocolate had failed to revive their career, but they continued to make a living on the oldies circuit. Alan, who turned fifty-one in 1999, had a heart attack a few years ago and then, horribly, a stroke which left him paralysed on one side, though he has recovered enough to resume touring. His brother, Derek, was arrested in Edinburgh in September 1998 on suspicion of 'indecency involving a youth under the age of 18'. After a spell in Germany, Leslie is back in Britain and – Rollerflash! – has resolved his differences with the rest of the group who are recording together and planning a comeback.

I only heard from McKeown once after the Radio 1 interview – during one of his legal battles with the other Rollers, he called to ask if I'd be willing to sign an affidavit that he was 'generally regarded as the group's most important member'. It had sunk to that level. Thankfully, they resolved the squabble without me. I wasn't unaware of the irony – imagine if I could have known all those years ago that one day my honey-dripping love-monkey would be asking *me* to attest to his popularity.

Pat McGlynn and Ian Mitchell last surfaced as special guests at the 1997 Rollerfest in Las Vegas, and Duncan Faure is based in South Africa and has a group called The Bluebottles.

Tam Paton is now a property developer in Edinburgh and appeared shockingly haggard on a recent documentary on the Rollers, which might give some vengeful Tarts cause to smirk.

Relations between Paton and his former charges are strained – the Rollers claim they never saw the royalties from an estimated 120 million record sales. Paton insists he's not to blame. He has scoffed at their comeback attempt: to Eric's description of Rollers '99 as a 'man band, not a boy band' he ripostes, 'An old-man band . . . you've got to grow up. I think The Bay City Rollers have gone. And they've gone for good.'

I feel sufficiently distanced to laugh at them now. Or so I tell myself. But one night not long ago I was in the kitchen, half-listening to the radio as I made dinner, and suddenly recognised a tinny guitar chord, followed by a feather-light voice piping the words, 'If you hate me after what I say . . . ah-ahhhh . . . can't put it off any more . . . just gotta tell her anyway . . .'

'Oh, my God, it's "Bye Bye Baby"!' I gasped. 'They *never* play this on the radio!' My boyfriend came into the kitchen and tolerantly put an arm around me. I squirmed free to turn up the volume, and shooed him away, flapping my arms to the music.

'Can't I share this with you?' he asked, trying to humor the lunatic. 'No,' I said with the painful wisdom of two decades of Rollerluv everlasting. 'You just wouldn't understand.'

EPILOGUE

IF YOU'RE WONDERING whether I ever saw my personal Roller again after they left Maplewood in 1981 . . . I did.

Melody Maker's news editor was friendly with a couple of members of the band, and invited them for a drink one afternoon sometime in the late eighties. 'Why don't you come meet them?' she invited me. 'You used to like them, didn't you?'

Overcome with curiosity – it was now at least seven years since I'd seen any of them – I did. We got to the pub and my Roller was already there, sipping a beer with Ian Mitchell. I sat on the other side of the table to get a good look, and what I saw at first evoked faint, sweet sadness, then mild wonder that I had ever been so hung up. He was astonishingly ordinary – a skinny, anonymous guy of about thirty, thinning a bit on top. I don't think I'd have recognised him in the street.

There was no spark of recognition on his part, either, for the first few minutes. But after a while he looked at me searchingly, finally asking, 'Haven't we met somewhere?'

'No,' I replied.

'Are you sure?' he persisted.

'Absolutely sure,' I said.

A NOTE ON THE AUTHOR

CAROLINE SULLIVAN grew up in Millburn, New Jersey. Since moving to London in 1982 she has written for *The Times*, the *Independent on Sunday*, the *Observer*, *Cosmopolitan*, *New Woman* and *Melody Maker*. She became rock critic of the *Guardian* in 1993.

A NOTE ON THE TYPE

The text of this book is set in Linotype Sabon, named after the type founder, Jacques Sabon. It was designed by Jan Tschichold and jointly developed by Linotype, Monotype and Stempel, in response to a need for a typeface to be available in identical form for mechanical hot metal composition and hand composition using foundry type.

Tschichold based his design for Sabon roman on a fount engraved by Garamond, and Sabon italic on a fount by Granjon. It was first used in 1966 and has proved an enduring modern classic.